Unless Recalled Earlier
Date Due

MAR 29 1988			

Pretoria's Praetorians

Pretoria's Praetorians

Civil–military relations in
South Africa

PHILIP H. FRANKEL

Senior Lecturer, Department of Political Studies
University of the Witwatersrand

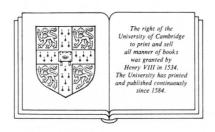

The right of the
University of Cambridge
to print and sell
all manner of books
was granted by
Henry VIII in 1534.
The University has printed
and published continuously
since 1584.

CAMBRIDGE UNIVERSITY PRESS

Cambridge
London   New York   New Rochelle
Melbourne   Sydney

Published by the Press Syndicate of the University of Cambridge
The Pitt Building, Trumpington Street, Cambridge CB2 1RP
32 East 57th Street, New York, NY 10022, USA
296 Beaconsfield Parade, Middle Park, Melbourne 3206, Australia.

© Cambridge University Press 1984

First published 1984

Printed in Great Britain at the University Press, Cambridge

Library of Congress catalogue card number: 84-5040

British Library Cataloguing in Publication Data

Frankel, Philip
Pretoria's Praetorians.
1. Civil supremacy over the military –
South Africa
I. Title
322'.5'0968   JQ1920.C58

ISBN 0 521 26440 5

For Angela and Andrea

Contents

	List of figures and tables	*page*	viii
	Acknowledgements		ix
	List of abbreviations		x
	Introduction. Analysing the South African military		xi
1	The South African Defence Force: the institutional and historical framework		1
2	The rise of the garrison state and the development of total strategy		29
3	Exterior manoeuvre: the dynamics of militarization		71
4	Militarization and conflict in the siege culture		124
5	*Quo vadis?* Praetorianism and political change		161
	Notes		184
	Select bibliography on the South African armed forces		204
	Index		209

Figures

1 Citizen Force career path   *page* 2
2 Organizational structure of the South African Defence Force   3

Tables

1 Career point and service distribution   37
2 Defence expenditure, 1958–83   72
3 Incidence of courts martial and convictions   135

Acknowledgements

Social enquiry, it has been said, forces us out of ourselves and into the lives of others. In moving into the lives of the South African military I have received assistance from numerous sources – from the local and British academic community whose South Africanists and military sociologists have provided intellectual stimulation for a difficult project; from the University of the Witwatersrand and the British Council whose financial generosity allowed me to take advantage of the various research opportunities in South Africa and beyond its borders; from elements associated with the Defence Force inclined to see the project as useful rather than subversive; and last, but by no means least, from members of my immediate family without whose emotional support the whole enterprise might never have reached conclusion. Needless to say, none of these sources bears responsibility for the way I have interpreted the social and political life of the Defence Force in its own right or within the broader context of the South African system.

Notes on terminology

The use of the term 'non-white' is considered by many to be derogatory and redundant in the modern South African setting. Hence the use of quotation marks. At the same time 'black' is a misnomer when applied indiscriminately to all of the subject race groups – Indian, Coloured and 'African' – although it is both convenient and fashionable to do so. For the purposes of this work, we intend to use the term 'non-white' as an equally convenient catch-all phrase referring to the collective of subject race groups (without due prejudice) and the term 'black' to refer to its 'African' component. The Coloured and Indian communities will of course be referred to as such.

For the purposes of this work, the term 'South African Defence Force' will be used interchangeably with the acronym SADF, or simply the term 'Defence Force'.

Abbreviations

AMI	Afdeling Militere Inligting (Military Information Service)
ANC	African National Congress
Armscor	Armaments Corporation
CDO	Civil Defence Organization
COIN	Counter Insurgency Unit
COSAWAR	Committee of South African War Resisters
CP	Conservative Party
DAC	Defence Advisory Council
DCC	Defence Command Council
DFAI	Department of Foreign Affairs and Information
DMI	Directorate of Military Intelligence
DPC	Defence Planning Committee
DSC	Defence Staff Council
DTA	Democratic Turnhalle Alliance
DTI	Direkteur Teen-Inligting (Directorate, Counter-Intelligence)
HNP	Herstigte Nasionale Party
LTU	Leisure Time Utilization Unit
MNR	Mozambique National Resistance
MPO	Munitions Production Office
NIS	National Intelligence Service
NRP	New Republic Party
PFP	Progressive Federal Party
SAAF	South African Air Force
SADF	South African Defence Force
SAMRAF	South African Military Refugees Fund
SAP	South African Police
SSC	State Security Council
SSCS	State Security Council Secretariat
SWAPO	South West Africa People's Organization
SWATF	South West African Territorial Force
TDF	Transkei Defence Force
UDF	Union Defence Force
ZAR	Zuid-Afrikaanse Republiek
ZARP	Zuid-Afrikaanse Republikeinse Polisie

Introduction. Analysing the South African military

The role of the military in South African politics is essentially unexplored when seen against the backdrop of the enormous output of literature on civil–military relations of recent years. Studies of South Africa have appropriated a good deal of scholarly energies as historians, sociologists and political scientists have applied their diverse skills to sewing together the past, present and future into some sort of reasonable understanding of the origins and consequences of apartheid society. Yet, despite the proliferation of knowledge on these two different planes, virtually nothing coherent and systematic has been said about the relationship between South African soldiers and the state as it has developed with the progressive institutionalization of apartheid, or, in a less abstract sense, about the role of the South African military establishment in the public and informal decision-making context of South African society. This scholarly oversight is an anomaly at variance with some of the major developments of past and contemporary South African history. South Africa has of course never enjoyed the dubious distinction of military rule along the lines of so many post-World War II Third World states. The structural features of modern-day South Africa may not even fall into the Third World category. Yet military leaders have played a direct or ancillary role in shaping the South African society we know today, in forging and subsequently developing the Union through the first three prime ministers, Generals Botha, Smuts and Hertzog, all of whom were military men, albeit in a non-career capacity.[1] In current terms, as one commentator puts it, 'knowledge of the armed forces of South Africa and how they relate to the rest of society and the power elite is indispensable' if we are to understand political and social movements within South Africa since the creation of the Republic, the mechanics of state control, adaption and change, and even foreign policy conducted on a global or regional basis.[2] Yet, as another source lamentably notes, the actual 'link between politics and the military appears to have been relatively neglected in the literature of South

Africa to date'.[3] In the last analysis, despite the odd self-justifying piece trotted out by the state or its irreconcilable antagonists, there is virtually nothing in book-length or journal form which represents a consistent and relatively analytical attempt to look at the South African military in its own social and political right, or, more broadly, which attempts to link the South African civil–military experience to the universal literature on military sociology and politics with its emphasis on how and why soldiers are drawn into the political process, the way they act on this involvement and the consequences for various types of society.[4]

There are, of course, innumerable societies where civil–military relations remain an unexplored area. One of the major problems confronting civil–military research continues to be that of disaggregating general findings to meet the peculiar historical and structural features of individual societies. Yet in some societies the neglected link between the military and politics is especially acute, particularly in conflict-ridden societies such as South Africa where so much of politics is reducible to sheer brute force and the application of state coercion. All social structures are dependent to some degree on the use of force, but there is a difference between putative and applied force, and the distinction is eroded in those societies such as South Africa where the state faces a crisis of legitimacy – indeed, an ongoing crisis of legitimacy – brought about by deep cleavage between ruling elites and masses, reinforced by an explosive mixture of interpenetrating class and cultural divisions. In these circumstances, which are acute within but not necessarily unique to South Africa, the individuals and institutions with access to the instruments and technologies of violence – among whom the military is in the forefront – can be absolutely decisive in the process by which power is allocated. As Alfred Stepan notes in his study of the Brazilian military, the response of soldiers to conflict in divided civil societies provides 'a large part of the answer to the question of who wins and who loses, who has power and who does not'. He adds:

When the armed forces prevent the winner of a presidential election from taking office, when they remove a government whose economic policies favor one class at the expense of another, or where they stage a coup to preserve the dominance of a racial, religious, tribal or linguistic group in a communally divided society, their actions clearly help determine which societal groups will gain or lose some of their most important values. Even those coups that are unrelated to group conflicts, primarily involving the defence of corporate military interests, are likely to affect political and economic outcomes.[5]

A conflict perspective on South African politics – one which focusses on the 'hard' institutions and processes at work to shape society, the police, the military and the bureaucracy within the network of state control – may indeed be the only realistic framework within which to see local developments, the more so as racial polarization takes hold and as power and public policy-making is centralized in state structures to which security organizations have preferential access. This is particularly important in the light of South Africa's new constitution whose design facilitates penetration by the Defence Force into the highly centralized organs of state security while excluding the overwhelming majority of South Africa's 'non-whites' from wielding the main levers of national political power. Whether or not the new constitution will feed rather than diffuse revolutionary pressures along lines suggested by both right- and left-wing opponents of the National Party, it is also important to recognize that military institutions are always vital to the balance of power in conditions of radical social transformation.[6] While theorists disagree as to *how* vital soldiers are in determining the occurrence and outcome of revolutions, most writers on South Africa have simply skirted the issue through their wholesale failure to link the military to the forces of counter-revolution in the local context. This is a gross oversight in the light of Barrington Moore's assertion that 'it is the state of the army, of competing armies, not of the working class, that has determined the fate of twentieth-century revolutions'.[7] This is not to deny the role of the working class in South Africa as sketched out in a sophisticated and accumulating literature on black proletarian resistance to apartheid. Work of this nature is indeed an important antidote to the tendency of political writing on South Africa to focus upon the formal mechanics of power worked through political parties, constitutions and more readily evident civil procedures. The political role of the South African military must nonetheless be seen against the historically validated backdrop that few revolutions succeed as long as the officer corps remains firm in its allegiance to the state. Alternatively, few fail in circumstances where military institutions respond to deep social tensions by defecting from the state or assuming a position of neutrality between the insurgents and the incumbents of state power.

There is, it must be emphasized, a growing recognition of the importance of the military in the South African political equation which corresponds to actual movements within civil–military boundaries leading to greater military participation in political and social affairs in recent years. Most students of contemporary South Africa would today concur with the statement that 'any analysis of South African politics will remain inadequate, incomplete and misleading without an understanding of the inextricable and inevitable role the military is playing in the formation and execution of policy'.[8] This reflects the material fact, in the words of another commentator, that 'the South African Defence Force [SADF] is no longer simply an instrument for policy implementation [but] an active participant in policy-making ... in military matters, in wider security issues, both domestic and external, and even in matters concerning the homelands and economic and foreign policy'.[9] The literature derived from these perceptions is, however, conceptually primitive for the most part, intellectually underdeveloped in many cases and questionable in its conceptual foundations in others. With a handful of notable exceptions – there is only one scholarly book-length study of the South African armed forces[10] – the extant literature on the South African military is overwhelmingly historical in focus, ranging from the esoteric to the trivial. This historical orientation is justifiable given the relatively recent appearance of the military in the South African political mainstream. Nevertheless, as the political profile of the Defence Force has risen and it has become increasingly institutionalized in public policy-making since the mid- to late sixties, the literature has consistently failed to keep pace with developments in the form of detailed sociological analysis. Today, while the potential student is confronted with a plethora of descriptive regimental histories of varying academic quality, he is hard put to find anything at all dealing with the origins and implications of growing military penetration into the formal and informal networks of South African society – apart from a number of highly speculative articles designed to flatter the ideological sensibilities of those who oppose the country's racial policies. Nor, with the odd exception, have there been any serious attempts to contrast or compare the South African civil–military experience with civil–military systems in other parts of the world, in either the developed or underdeveloped areas. The conventional approach is overwhelmingly configurative in spirit and basically ignorant of the growing range of writings on the topics of military sociology. Above all, however, the current literature is profoundly reductionist in one of two forms, neither of which do justice to the complex reality of civil–military politics in South Africa. On the one hand, largely under the influence of crude Marxist interpretations of the relations between society and its institutions, the military is portrayed as a pale reflection of the economic forces at work in the South African social substructure. In this idiom, where the soldiers seemingly follow the dictates of the white capitalist state, little or no attention is given to the universally accepted fact that militaries can conceivably be relatively independent subsystems in the overall social dynamic, with both the will and the means to shape as well as to respond to the dictates of public policy.[11] It is, I believe, grossly simplistic and reductionist to relegate the South African Defence Force to the role of a 'knee-jerk' agent of the white state, not only because the South African state is composed of a diversity of fragments each seeking to carve out its segmental and institutional interests within the transcending racial framework, but also because the military is one of the most powerful of these fragments by virtue of its dual responsibility for external and internal state control, with the real means to influence the conception, formation and implementation of public policy (either independently or through alignment with a variety of interests aggregated in forming the polity). Nor for that matter is the South African military the homogeneous, purposive and hierarchically controlled institution portrayed in much of the literature. As modern military sociology has progressively recognized, every military organization is to some extent a complex body differentiated along political lines, with the result that the cues provided by soldiers for civilian decision-makers are always a reflection of the type and measure of diversity present in any given military institution. This is not to deny the importance of race in giving coherence to the cognitions and behaviour of the South African military whose officer corps is overwhelmingly drawn from the ranks of the white elite whose values and interests it must then reflect. Yet is is fundamentally misguided to view the Defence Force as being in a state of what one author has dubbed 'frictionless co-existence', either internally or in its external relations with the social world.[12] In assessing the social and political dynamics endogenous and exogenous to the Defence Force establishment, due respect should also be given to service rivalries between South African officers, to differences in their social and cultural background, to their ambitions, age, rank, training, combat experience and their varied attachments to political parties, leaders and public policies which spill across the civil–military divide despite the levelling and inhibiting forces of organizational socialization. In the last analysis the South African military is composed of divergent human beings with values, feelings and perceptions of social and political affairs which cut across and complicate their common commitment both to maintain the corporate interests of the military and to perpetuate the existence of the white state apparatus. It is, I would assert, patently ridiculous to label a modern, complex and differentiated institution such as the South African military as a monolithic agent of a state power.

The South African military is, on the whole, a sociologically vital organization and it is precisely for this reason that claims to its non-political status are essentially specious. This means that South African civil–military relations cannot be realistically approached within the context of the formal and juridic notion that local military institutions are the non-political agents of state power concerned exclusively with the execution of public policy. The essence of this approach, with its intellectual origins in the lofty realms of British constitutional law, is enshrined in a variety of South African statutes, from the inspiring Defence Act of 1912 and through its subsequent amendments. Hence members of the

Defence Force are barred from the membership of any political party; they may not, according to the SADF Order of September 1970, participate in any meeting, demonstration or procession on behalf of a party while in uniform or while performing duties in terms of the Defence Act; and they may not take part in any activity furthering the interests of a political party or of candidates for election to parliament, provincial councils or any other public body elected on a political-party basis. Yet, as most contemporary theorists recognize, the 'liberal' format for the conduct of civil–military relations is essentially over-heroic and idealistic in its understanding of what military institutions actually do – as opposed to what they should do – in society: it is sociologically naive and, at a deeper level of criticism, basically misconceived when measured against the developments of both past and current civil–military history. It may or may not be desirable that soldiers 'intervene' in the civil political process (most of the current generation of theorists believe they should not), yet the fact is that soldiers often do so, for a range of reasons from the instrumental to the ideological; and this intervention forms the foundation stone of many military coups and governments in contemporary Third World countries.[13] Gaetano Mosca's acute comment, while it precedes the development of modern professional armies, is perhaps still of considerable relevance today. As he astutely notes, 'whenever and whatever governments have built up standing armies in order to deal with ... unruliness, or for other reasons, they have almost always found themselves at the mercies of those armies'. Be it the rebelliousness of the Strelitzes under Peter the Great, the Turkish mercenaries of the Abbasids or the Janissaries of the Ottomans, he grimly concludes that 'history teaches us that the class that bears the lance or holds the musket regularly forces its rule upon the class that holds the spade or pushes the shuttle'.[14] Even in the developed world, of which South African leaders claim their state a part, the distinctions between the lines of civil and military authority are so amorphous for political purposes, so caught up at the junctures between what one commentator has described as the 'intermingled world of strategy and policy',[15] that it is virtually impossible to make any clearcut case for the so-called 'non-political soldier' envisaged under the neo-British liberal paradigm. Indeed, there are precious few cases in the civil–military experience of the modern Western world where it can be shown that on matters of national security (the very meaning of which fluctuates from case to case) the political will of the military has been imposed on the civilians or, as the liberal model demands, vice versa. In the hard material context of public policy-making today, Gibbon's dictum in his magisterial study of Rome still holds water. As he notes, in a manner which still essentially describes the interrelations between modern civil and military authority in even the most 'advanced' industrialized states, 'the firmest and best emperors were obliged to mix blandishments with commands, rewards with punishments, to flatter the pride of the Praetorians, indulge their pleasures, connive at their irregularities, and to purchase their precarious faith by a liberal donative which . . . was exacted as a legal claim on the accession of every new emperor'.[16]

It is, in fact, particularly difficult to accept the notion of the non-political soldier obedient to civil authority in the specific South African context. There is simply no reason to believe that the various forces working to disturb the delicate civil–military balance described by liberal theory in other contexts are not also present in the South African case, be they in the form of the professional immaturity of the military establishment, the insensitivity of civil leadership to the prerogatives of military institutions or, in the last analysis, the fact that military professionalism is, in the words of one analyst, 'Janus-faced' (i.e. that modern career soldiers may abjure politics as beyond their realm of expertise yet, in turn, intervene in politics in order to protect their corporate isolation).[17] Indeed, when looking carefully at South Africa, it seems that the very nature of its history, society and politics conspires to produce the very socio-political conditions fuelling the contemporary situation where persistent patterns of civilian supremacy are the deviant rather than the normal cases in much of the non-Western world.[18] Allowance must of course be made for the fact that South Africa is not a typically Third World state, nor for that matter, despite the rhetoric of government, a typical state of Africa. Her military institutions are, for one thing, founded on strong, if adapted, British military traditions which lend strength to the technical subordination of the military to civil political authority. Yet, as countless analyses have pointed out, the South African state rests on relatively narrow class and racial foundations; state coercion is a predominant component of the arsenal of political control in the hands of the dominant white minority; and, as a natural extension, the 'hard' institutions of society – the police, the military and other components of the state security network – enjoy considerable access to social status among the elite, to state resources and the levers of public policy. Not all power stems, in the light of the Maoist dictum, from 'the barrel of a gun', yet in the South African case those who legitimately control the barrels of guns in the process of executing the will of the state must be a critical factor in the equation whereby power is distributed throughout society. There are, in addition, few reasons to believe that the power of these social formations will fade away in the course of immediate history. On the contrary, as the South African state has progressively shifted in an authoritarian direction away from its original mildly liberal inheritance, as national security has been redefined to encompass a range of issues beyond the purely strategic, and as internal and international pressures in favour of the politically disincorporated have intensified, so civil–military boundaries have inevitably tilted in favour of local military institutions in the public policy-making process. Full-time members of the Defence Force may well remain exceptions to public service legislation extending the political rights of civil servants (e.g. under amendments to the Public Service Act of 1973), yet the accumulating challenges to state security, as seen from the perspective of the executive branch of government, are progressively eroding the notion of the non-political soldier contained in the Defence Act from an ideal prescription to a misplaced description of the actual nature of civil–military realities. The conscription policies of the state, it should be added, invigorate the penetration of political influence into the South African Defence Force by virtue of the fact that national service is confined to members of the ruling white minority who are increasingly recirculated between the civil and military realm – as an alternative to the absorption of questionably loyal 'non-whites' into the state security structure. Segmental conscription of this type is notoriously politicizing in its impact on military institutions, because it blunts organizational socialization in the military by bringing soldiers and civilians into frequent contact. In the last analysis, the liberal conception of civil–military relations founders on the acute race and class distinctions at the basis of all political development in South African society. The military in South Africa is, when all is said and done, a key institution supporting the values and interests of the white minority. This institution may have its own corporate interests and may have reached a level of professionalism in the sense of having developed into a relatively exclusive body with an autonomous status apart from the mainstream of society, yet it is still irrevocably tied to the defence of special sectional interests associated with the perpetuation of South Africa's racial state. The South African military establishment may display many of the features of any other modern military force. Nonetheless, because it is locked into the state structure by a mixture of biological and functional forces associated with military–state relations, its actions can never be entirely free from the social and political cues emanating from the white sector of South African society. In such circumstances, the classic *quid pro quo* where civilians and soldiers respectively determine the principles and execution of national security policy breaks down, or is at least under considerable political pressure, for day-to-day and long-range decision-making purposes. In practice, the confusion between race, state, soldier and civilian generates a fusion of roles and functions in relation to which the polite theoretical distinctions between civil and military have little practical meaning.

I believe that a full-scale exploration of civil–military relations in South Africa provides a key to many of the dominant issues in contemporary and future South African politics – a key largely unturned or misturned in recent analysis. At a higher level of abstraction, a case study of the SADF could conceivably contribute to the ongoing debate over civil–military relations – to defining the role of the military in society, to show how soldiers respond to socio-political pressures, the consequences of militarization and its impact on the politics of ruling elites – all set within the peculiar racial and political configuration of South African society. At the same time I recognize that many of the lacunae and failings in the present literature on the military in South African society are a result of problems of access to the necessary material required to pass judgment on civil–military relations in the South African context. I am not insensitive to these difficulties although my basic feeling is that many of the research problems have been overstated or exaggerated without due respect for the variety of tools available to modern social scientists confronted with the task of indirect investigation. The fact that there is no official history of the South African Defence Force, that there is hardly a developed body of literature exploring the relations between the Defence Force and wider society on any systematic basis, indeed, the simple fact that the SADF is still very much an unknown quantity in its internal dynamics and as a factor in the civil–military arena, all attests to the real issue, which is that it is indeed difficult at the best of times to conduct research on the South African military – an institution, like the military of any other state, which is relatively closed, tightly bureaucratic in organization, intimately involved with the security of the state and thereby hostile to even the milder forms of academic penetration. Even in societies more genuinely democratic than South Africa military bureaucrats are reluctant to open their activities to public scrutiny. The tendency is exaggerated in South Africa where the progressive institutionalization of authoritarianism over the last thirty-five years has fed a general breakdown in public control over what the institutions of state say and do. Today, when political leaders in the ruling National Party purposely or unwittingly confuse the maintenance of 'national' (white) morale with the need to eliminate many sources of information potentially critical of the state or its agents in the bureaucracy, the police and the military, the activities of these agents – the police and military in particular – have simply disappeared behind a virtually impenetrable wall of security legislation. If so little detailed work has been done on the South African military at least part of the reason lies in the ever-widening conception of what constitutes 'state security' and in the ever-increasing refusals of disclosure justified by reference to the 'national interest'. Add to these difficulties the risk of prosecution under the widely formulated Defence

Act, the Official Secrets Act and a daunting array of complementary security legislation, and the erstwhile researcher into South African military affairs has neither the psychological nor practical incentives to investigate beyond the few existing, available, disparate and readily known scraps of data and information.

Despite this situation I nevertheless believe that there is adequate and reasonably attainable information to support research of better quality than has heretofore emerged – provided scholarship is persistent and creative enough in its detection and use. The difficulties generated by research on militaries are always relative and even if the South African military is particularly reluctant to open its official files there is still a substantial amount of unprocessed and readily available information on local civil–military relations to which academics can gain access with minimal risk, and without the official sanction of the Defence Force authorities with their natural preference for classified in-house studies. For one thing, civil–military relations is a two-sided process in which the military only directly controls one decisive element. It may be possible for the military to deny researchers access to official archives or (to a lesser degree) to individual members of the officer corps, but it can only partially veil the civil dimension of the civil–military interaction which takes place beyond its own institutional boundaries. In present-day South Africa, the impact of the military on society is readily visible in a way which circumscribes the Defence Act and the network of security legislation designed to intimidate the academically and politically inquisitive. Military institutions openly interact with members of the business community, they play a direct and indirect role in the process of designing national education policies at the secondary level and they force themselves into the public eye through the wide-ranging system of national conscription. These fibres binding civil to military society are widely and relatively freely reported in the daily press, in South African parliamentary reports and in the increasingly lengthy and sophisticated White Papers issued by the Department of Defence when publicly rationalizing and explaining the role of the Defence Force to the South African white community. This means that there exists a veritable minefield of data for the analyst with the time and patience to sift through the verbiage of parliamentary debates and newspaper reports, with the discrimination and intelligence to read between the lines and statistics of official Defence Force statements. Nor, it should be added, is the South African military that impenetrable institution described by a multitude of contemporary scholars. As the social role of the Defence Force has been extended, some individual members of the military welcome communication with external experts, not only as a means of incorporating civilian skills and technologies into Defence Force operations, but also as a tool for explaining and clarifying the role of military institutions in the seemingly Byzantine, complex and unfamiliar realms of civil society and politics. Even where it is impossible to forge individual channels of communication into the Defence Force there exists a large and relatively neglected historical literature on the South African military in the form of regimental histories and personal memoirs which provide insights into the culture, spirit and philosophy of South African military institutions.[19] When these are read with discernment and in conjunction with the official journals and magazines produced by the SADF (*Militaria, Paratus* and *Uniform*) it is possible to glean substantial and valuable material.

I do not wish to generate unfounded optimism. A considerable proportion of the empirical data at the foundations of research into the sociology of militaries which is present in other contexts is absent in the South African case, and much of this basic material cannot be compensated for by investigative manoeuvring or intellectual manipulation. Every study of the South African military at this point in time must inevitably be coloured with a deeper tone of speculation than might be considered analytically appropriate in other more open settings. Nonetheless, there exists a large body of unprocessed data which, if creatively used, reveals many if by no means all the major ingredients of contemporary South African civil–military interaction. Orchestrated against the background of the enormous and burgeoning literature on military soiciology from other developing and developed areas, this data can also be turned in a comparative direction – with due allowance for the particular structural and historical features within which South African civil–military relations are formulated. It is in this sense of an *interaction* between soldier and civilian with the backdrop of universal experience that the following study is conceived. I am not only concerned with the political behaviour of South African soldiers *per se*, but with the way in which this behaviour both reflects social tendencies and forces ingrained in the South African system and how it in turn feeds back into the civil mainstream to affect political institutions and processes – all against the theoretical background posed by civil–military interaction in other areas of the world. The state, of course, plays a crucial role in this process of inward and outward political movement. Since the state in itself is an outgrowth of an accumulation of historical and cultural forces shaping both the military and civil sectors of society, the first chapter is immediately concerned with the essential features of the South African military, with the organizational mechanics providing the filters for institutional behaviour and with the broad social and historical terrain from which these instruments have sprung. Hence, following an essentially descriptive subsection in which the basic institutional features of the SADF are presented as a means to portray the complex, differentiated and essentially modern qualities of the South African military establishment, we move to the historical crucible out of which the Defence Force has emerged – dominated as it is by the interaction between imported British imperial and indigenous Afrikaner military traditions. This dynamic, described as a dialectic between 'liberal' and 'kommando' conceptions of civil–military authority, sets the tone for one of the central pillars of this study; that is, that the current militarization of South African society, the growth of the garrison state with its accompanying siege culture and the emergence of so-called 'total strategy' represent a basic reinvigoration of the kommando ethic in the traditional heartland of Afrikaner political culture. Fuelled by a variety of political and economic changes in South Africa's internal and external relationships, this had led to a basic boundary shift in civil–military roles and the distribution of social power – neither of which are readily reconcilable with the 'liberal' model of civil–military interaction associated with the British, Commonwealth and (until recently) South African civil–military experience. The main body of this work, chapters 2, 3 and 4, is concerned with enunciating the relative breakdown of the British civil–military heritage in the circumstances of contemporary South Africa. Chapter 2 identifies the mixture of domestic and international forces which have fed the garrison psychologies and institutions characterizing modern-day South Africa; it considers in somewhat greater detail the changes in the officer corps of the SADF which have fuelled the politicization of the military establishment and it seeks to identify the mechanics of total strategy on the basis of the view that total strategy represents the ideological umbrella under which the Defence Force has begun to make a variety of intrusive movements into the civilian political realm. Chapter 3 is a straightforward exposition of the dynamics of militarization: it analyses, *inter alia*, the South African defence budget, the growth of the local armaments industry, the disappearing distinctions between the civil and military sectors of society as the military extends its web into national education, the scientific and business communities and, finally, the appearance of military influences in the highest of public decision-making bodies and state councils. Chapter 4 is concerned with the responses of South African society to growing military claims on the levers of political power and to social resources. The final chapter – an excursion into the political future backed by the civil–military experience in societies other than South Africa – attempts to assess the intermediate and long-range implications of militarization for South African society.

I

The South African Defence Force: the institutional and historical framework

The social and political behaviour of every military is always to some extent ascribable to statute – to the hard and readily identifiable prescriptions of laws, conventions, administrative codes and constitutions. Hence it is always possible to infer some first-order understanding of the nature of particular civil–military systems from juridic statements, bearing in mind that the ability of law to shape society varies from case to case, according to historical and cultural experience. In this regard, the role of the South African Defence Force in the South African system is directly, if imperfectly, defined by the tasks assigned to it under the Defence Act of 1912 as subsequently amended on a variety of occasions. According to the 1957 version of the original 1912 Act, the tasks of the Defence Force (or any part thereof) are basically fourfold. They involve defending the Republic from foreign attack, preventing and suppressing terrorism and other forms of internal disorder, acting to preserve life, health, property and the maintenance of essential services in general and, in the last analysis, undertaking 'such police duties as may be prescribed' at any time by the civil authorities. At the same time the behaviour of any military institution (or set of institutions) is also a reflection of its organizational characteristics, of the particular structures and forms of the military as a functioning social entity and the fashion in which these have developed. This means that it is simply not enough to look at the Defence Act in order to understand the link between the military and civil sectors of South African society, the less so as the SADF has developed into a highly complex and internally differentiated bureaucratic organization with the intrinsic capacity to act beyond the tasks and formal roles as described by statute. The Defence Act may well have been a reasonably perfect instrument for analysing the South African military at an earlier stage in its development – possibly in 1912 when the decision was taken to forge the regiments, militias and volunteer units of the Cape, Transvaal and Natal into a single unified military force. But today, seventy years later, when the SADF is a highly professional and internally diversified institution not comparable with the five regiments of the South African Mounted Rifles originally constituting the first Union Defence Force, the Defence Act is grossly inadequate in providing cues as to what the Defence Force does, within itself, and in wider South African society.

Any analysis of the SADF must begin with a description of its basic institutional characteristics or, more specifically, with the recognition that we are dealing with a highly developed set of social institutions subdivided into many specialized components as a result of the process of modernization and environmental adaption. At the beginning of the seventies the SADF consisted of roughly 133 Permanent Force organizations, 225 Citizen Force and 218 Commando organizations, interlocked with one another through formal affiliations and surrounded by an uncountable array of support organizations at the boundaries of civil–military society. The manpower feeding the formal network is of two basic types: professional career-oriented soldiers constituting the relatively small Permanent Force core of the South African military establishment, and, concentrically surrounding the essential core in ever-wider circles, part-time manpower in the form of national service conscripts, members of the Citizen Force (national servicemen who have completed their initial military training but who are obliged to render periodic service to the Defence Force for a number of subsequent years), Active Citizen Force Reserve members, Commando members and, in the outermost ring, white males between the ages of 55 and 65 included in the ranks of the National Reserve (see Fig. 1). Both permanent and part-time manpower is channelled into the Defence Force through the four major service arms – the Army, Air Force, Navy and Medical Service – each of which is a distinct

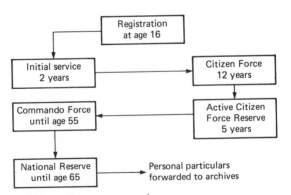

1 Citizen Force career path
   Source:'Your Guide to National Service' (Pretoria: South African Defence Force, 1 Military Printing Unit, 1982) p. 11

component of the local military establishment headed by its own Chief (the Surgeon-General in the case of the Medical Service), who is in turn responsible to the civilian Minister of Defence acting through the supreme military authority of the Chief of the Defence Force, previously known as the Commandant-General. The Chief of the South African Defence Force (currently General Constand Viljoen) is the chief military executive officer responsible for the implementation of ministerial policy regarding the command, control, organization, discipline and efficiency of the SADF, and in this capacity he is Chairman of the Defence Command Council (DCC), the highest command body and apex of the 'Defence Family' composed of the combat forces and their support services, the staff divisions at Defence Force Headquarters in Pretoria and the Armaments Corporation (Armscor) (see Fig. 2). The DCC, designated the Supreme Command until 1972, also includes the commanders of the combat forces (the respective Chiefs of the Army, Air Force and Navy), the Surgeon-General (since the recent elevation of the Medical Service to the status of a fourth full service arm), the Quartermaster-General (head of the Logistics Staff Division), and the Chief-of-Staff, Operations, formerly known as the Chief of Defence Staff, charged with issuing operational directives to the Chief of Defence Force Staff Divisions, coordinating strategy and

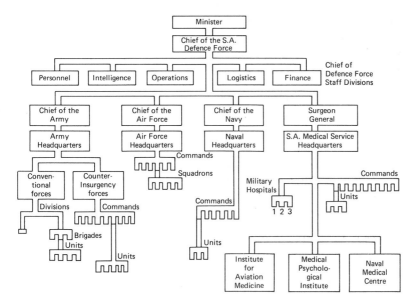

2 Organizational structure of the South African Defence Force
Source: 'Your Guide to National Service' (Pretoria: South African Defence Force, 1 Military Printing Unit, 1982) p. 4

mobilization-planning. Decision-making within this supreme military body is based on the principle of corporate leadership subject to ministerial approval, and is supported and assisted by three subsidiary bodies who provide the informational input for DCC deliberations. These are the Defence Staff Council (DSC), chaired by the Chief of the Defence Force and including his five Chiefs-of-Staff, the Chaplain-General and the Director-General of Resources; the Defence Planning Committee (DPC), chaired by the Chief of the Defence Force and including the Chiefs of the Army, Air Force and Navy, the Chiefs-of-Staff for Operations, Logistics and Finance, the Chairman and Senior General Manager of Armscor; and, thirdly, the Defence Advisory Council (DAC) consisting of the Chief of the Defence Force, the Minister of Defence, the President of the Armaments Board and a number of civilians invited to participate in the workings of the body on the basis of ministerial approval. Each of these three subsidiary organizations are assigned specific tasks. The DSC, as its title suggests, is concerned with the internal management of the Defence Force and the coordination of its staff activities. The DPC, established in 1976 to 'ensure the full participation of all members of the Defence Force in the planning process',[1] oversees the procurement of armaments, the annual defence budget and the planning activity of the SADF in accord with military policy formulated in the Defence Command Council. In this sense, both the DPC and DSC are important mechanisms for the implementation and translation of DCC decisions into applied and operational defence force programmes. The DAC, created in 1973 as a three-way system of communication between the military, the civilian government and the private sector is, in its turn, an important contact point between civil and military society. Consisting of influential industrialists and financiers, top technocrats and members of the local scientific community who are either consulted or coopted into the workings of the Council by means of ministerial invitation, the DAC has emerged as the primary institution for the exchange of opinions between the elites of government, the state security apparatus and the representatives of capital.

Despite periodic shortages in public funds for defence purposes, much of the organizational history of the SADF is a history of reorganization.[2] During various periods in South African history, particularly prior to World War II during the Depression years, military development was seriously restricted by competing non-military claims on the national economy. Many of these tensions are still echoed today, most notably in the competition between the military establishment and the private sector for the body and soul of skilled white manpower. Yet the Union Defence Force was formed with a number of organizational lacunae which subsequently needed to be remedied if the military was to be welded into a relevant and effective fighting force. The Defence Act of 1912, for example, gave rise to a very primitive staff organization composed of a handful of officers with widely allotted tasks. Thus, until 1917 when the rigours of World War I exposed its insufficiencies as a system of command and control, the Union Defence Force was effectively headed at any one time by no less than three loosely related officers (a Commandant-General of the Active Citizen Force, the Inspector-General of the Permanent Force and the Commandant of Cadets) responsible to the Minister of Defence, advised by a Defence Council consisting of four experienced ex-military officials. In the period since World War II internal reorganization has taken on a new momentum as South Africa's internal and international security situation has declined, as the nature of warfare has changed in the nuclear era and as the SADF has come to employ increasingly more sophisticated military technologies in its function of upholding the state. These combined pressures have fuelled an unprecedented era of reconstruction and development in the annals of the South African military. Some of the resulting organizational changes have represented attempts to improve, clarify and consolidate the statutory foundations of the Defence Force in substantive operational terms: hence the frequent amendments to the original Defence Act of 1912. Some of the numerous changes are essentially formal and technical, for example the rapid and often confusing turnover of officer designations, others – the decision in 1957 to change the term 'Union Defence Force' to 'South African Defence Force', the subsequent elimination of 'foreign' decorations, medals and regimental titles – are more directly linked to the consolidation of Afrikaner national power. Yet many of the series of institutional adaptions, particularly those initiated since the beginning of the sixties, are clearly concerned with the more weighty task of transforming the SADF from a historically loose and creaky organization into a highly rationalized device for the preservation of white state power.

The tenure of P.W. Botha as Minister of Defence was perhaps the most significant and energetic among the various efforts to convert Defence Force structures into a tightly programmed specialist organization with clear lines of command, specified procedures for the delegation of internal authority, and articulated distinctions between administrative and executive functions. In 1966, for example, many of the routine administrative and logistical tasks of the Chief of the Defence Force (then still known as the Commandant-General) were transferred to a new system of offices composed of the Directorates-General for Personnel, Administration, Management Systems and the Quartermaster-General acting under the coordinating authority of a so-called Chief of Defence Force Administration (previously the Adjutant-General). By delegating his daily responsibility for general administration, efficiency studies, quartermaster matters and the like to this new institutional creation, the Chief of the Defence Force was subsequently freed to concentrate exclusively on his command and combat functions. In 1975 the Directorates-General for Administration and Management Systems were disbanded and most of their functions transferred to the Comptroller of the South African Military Finance Service. During 1974 the tendency towards rationalization and the separation of executive and administrative roles was extended a step further with the establishment of a fully articulated Chief-of-Staff system based on five specialist divisions, each headed by a Chief-of-Staff with the rank of lieutenant-general, directly responsible to the Chief of the Defence Force in the case of Headquarters staff sections and to the respective Chiefs of the combat services in the case of Army, Navy and Air Force staff sections. Three of these five staff divisions are today partially concerned with activities previously performed by the defunct Secretariat of Defence, one of the first victims of the rationalizing movement of the mid-sixties. Since 1966 most of the Secretariat's administrative work has been vested in the Operations Staff Division whose head, the Chief-of-Staff, Operations (once the Inspector-General), is responsible for executing the daily top-level administration of the Defence Force, for top-level operational, strategic and logistical planning, and for coordinating the work of the five specialist staff divisions.[3] With the militarization of the civilian Secretariat its role in the realm of materials management has been appropriated by the second of the new specialist staff divisions, the Logistics Staff Division, headed by the Quartermaster-General, formerly the Chief of Logistics Services.[4] Since the introduction of a system of logistics management in the SADF during 1974 this particular division is concerned with a variety of tasks including the acquisition, storage, movement, maintenance, distribution, recovery and disposal of military equipment and supplies; with the movement and quartering of personnel; with the regulation of works services; the disposal of fixed property; and the codification of procedures for the treatment of material in accord with the requirements and priorities initiated in the Operations Staff Division. Finance, one of the main tasks of the redundant Secretariat, is now handled by the Finance Staff Section (once the Military Finance Service) headed by the Comptroller.[5] In 1978 the nine directorates of this division, the accounting office of the Defence Force, also provided a variety of management, computational, language and documentation facilities and services for military use. The present staff system of the Defence Force contains two final important elements, the Personnel Staff Division headed by a Chief-of-Staff previously designated the Chief of Defence Force Administration, and the Intelligence Staff

Division. The latter has a relatively short history as a specific and independent division of the Defence Force: it was only after South Africa's withdrawal from the Commonwealth that the military terminated its reliance on British intelligence sources to establish a Directorate of Military Intelligence (DMI) in 1961.[6] Throughout the sixties, however, the functioning of the new body was constantly confused as a result of competition from civil security organizations, particularly the Bureau for State Security, and as its lines of authority were shifted between the Chief of the Defence Force and his supporting staff. Greater clarity in the role of military intelligence emerged with the implementation of the proposals of the Potgieter Commission (established to investigate state security organization) in 1972. Today it is the task of the Intelligence Staff Division to collect, collate, evaluate, compare and interpret information in support of the formation of force-level, strategic and operational policies. DMI operations, as well as those of its ancillaries in the Division (DTI, counterintelligence, and AMI, the Military Information Service established in 1972), have doubtless been assisted by the recent demise of their civilian competitors in the ranks of the intelligence community. The Personnel Staff Division, as its title suggests, is concerned, *inter alia*, with the recruitment and selection of uniformed and civilian military personnel; with administering conditions of service; seeing to the physical and spiritual welfare of Defence Force members; allocating and controlling manpower resources; promulgating Defence Force orders; compiling, amending and drafting regulations; and operating archives and military museums.[7] In addition to their multiple internal tasks, some of the various directorates and subsections of this division are involved in activities beyond Defence Force boundaries, most notably in liaising between the SADF and public bodies and private organizations in the civil sector. As such, the Personnel Division is an important contact point between the Chief of Defence Force Staff system and a number of military-oriented elements in wider civil society. This includes not only organizations and groups which perform supportive functions for the military establishment – state school cadet corps and welfare institutions along the lines of the Southern Cross Fund (see below p. 98) – but organizations whose activities complement the functional subdivisions in the military's personnel section. Hence the manpower directorate of the Personnel Staff Division becomes a focal point for interaction between the military and the private sector on human resources issues. The seemingly mundane Personnel Division is also important as an instrument of military socialization. Since it is concerned with paramilitary training (through its cadet directorate) and for the 'spiritual welfare' of recruits, it is a vital link in the process of disseminating the organizational values of the Defence Force within its own institutional realm and beyond that to a wider civil audience.

Each of the four service arms of the Defence Force is headed by its own Chief (the Surgeon-General in the case of the Medical Service), each with the rank of lieutenant–general. The Chief of the Army, who, in the past, has variously been designated the Army Chief-of-Staff, the Director-General of Land Forces and the Chief of General Staff, heads the largest of the service arms.[8] His functions include commanding, training and administering the Army in accord with power delegated by the Chief of the Defence Force; planning and executing internal security schemes within the framework of DCC policy; seeing to the combat-readiness of the Army and to its provisioning, storage and control of specialized equipment. Since 1978 the South African Army is itself divided into two divisions of seven brigades, cross-cut by the standard functional division between infantry, artillery, engineers, signals, technical services and armour. Each of these corps is in turn subdivided into specialized components: thus the Infantry consists of Mechanized Infantry, Motorized Infantry, Paratroops, Mounted Infantry (on horses or motorcycles), Dog-Handlers and Trainers, and the elite Reconnaissance Commandos. While rationalization policies have tended to concentrate institutional power in bodies directly attached to Defence Force Headquarters in Pretoria – since 1977 even the Navy Headquarters has been based in the land-locked city – Defence Force strategy regarding internal organization has also been dominated by the traditional belief that primary threats to state security emanate as much from internal as external sources beyond South Africa's boundaries. Defence Force planners are actually very sensitive to the security risk posed by the local black majority population. This marks a continuation of many of the feelings and perceptions surrounding the initial creation of the Defence Force shortly after the establishment of the Union. In 1912 the concern with internal control was expressed by provisions in the Defence Act making for the creation of a citizen army or popular militia whose white members would be divided into fifteen military districts covering the total surface area of the country. With the deterioration of South Africa's internal security situation since the early sixties this initial emphasis on counter-insurgency waged by rapidly deployed white manpower on a nationwide basis has been invigorated, with the result that today the Army is as much an internally-oriented counter-insurgency force as it is an outward-oriented instrument for conducting conventional warfare in support of the territorial sovereignty of the state. The organizational mechanism for the internal role is the age-old system of military districts, known as commands since 1933, and now reduced from fifteen to nine. Today all Permanent and Citizen Force units as well as Commandos fall under the head of each command for training, housing, administrative and disciplinary purposes. This officer, normally a brigadier, is specifically responsible for preventing insurgency in his designated area and initiating counter-insurgency operations under the ultimate authority of Army Headquarters in Pretoria. As the supreme local representative of the Chief of the Army, the head of each command is additionally charged with managing Commando matters in his decentralized area of control, organizing civil defence and rendering aid to the police and local authorities short of formal mobilization during periods of civil disaster.

The conventional and unconventional capacities of the Army in protecting the state against its external and internal enemies are augmented by the South African Air Force – one of the most professional and effective air forces on the African continent – by the Navy, whose work it is to protect South Africa's 1,500 mile coastline and 300,000 square mile zone of economic exploitation, and, to a lesser extent, by the South African Medical Service, the fourth and last of the service arms recently elevated to comparable status with the Army, Air Force and Navy. Very little needs to be said about these military subunits in the light of the fairly extensive literature surrounding their activities.[9] The Air Force, as is well known, is important as an element in landward defence, supporting the combat mobility of the Army and providing air support for its operations, as well as being of importance in its own right. Much of the success enjoyed by the Army in recent Angolan operations – in Sceptic, Protea, Daisy and Super – is directly attributable to the mobility of deployment afforded South African ground-based troops by Air Force helicopters involved in cross-border operations. The Navy, while small in size, is again one of the most powerful forces of its type on the continent. Armed with a lethal mixture of locally manufactured and imported modernized equipment, including eight fast patrol craft armed with French Exocet and Israeli Gabriel missiles, it monitors the entire South Atlantic and Indian coastlines directly adjacent to South Africa and is responsible – as numerous South African politicians frequently point out – for the basic defence of the Cape sea route. As the nature of the threat to the South African state has shifted landward the Navy has also given birth to its own Marine Corps, presently active in the border areas of Namibia.

As befits a highly complex network of specialized organizations, the manpower needs of the military are served by a highly differentiated collection of feeder organizations involved in the production of skilled manpower. General training in Army staff duties, intelligence work, field security and techniques of warfare is provided by the South African Army College at Voortrekkerhoogte.[10] The work of this institution, established originally as the South African Military School at Bloemfontein in 1912, is supplemented by the special corps schools – the Artillery School at Potchefstroom, the Artillery Air Defence School at Youngsfield, the Infantry School at Oudschoorn, the Armoured Corps School at Bloemfontein and the Corps of Engineers and Signals Schools respectively. Since its establishment in 1949 the Army Gymnasium at Heidelberg (originally at Pretoria) is concerned with the training of junior commissioned and non-commissioned officers in the Citizen Force, while the relatively new Army Battle School offers advanced training in conventional warfare to Permanent Force personnel. The work of this latter institution is complemented by that of the Danie Theron Combat School in Kimberley with its emphasis on Commando-conducted counter-insurgency operations. The Air Force College and Air Force Gymnasium at Voortrekkerhoogte are the main channels for skilled personnel entering the Permanent or Citizen Force Air Force, with both offering officer training in staff duties and administration as well as instruction in hard warfare. Since the establishment of the first Air Force Flying School at Swartkop in 1932, the activities of the College and Gymnasium have been supplemented by a number of regional flying schools including those at Dunnottar and Langebaan (both of which offer instructor training on various types of aircraft) and the Flying School at Pietersburg (responsible for advanced jet flying training and pilot attack instructor training). There is also an Air Navigation School at Ysterplaat and an Air Defence School at Waterkloof concerned with the basic training of controllers and radio operators. Skilled naval personnel are in turn the products of either the South African Naval College at Gordons Bay, the Naval School at Saldanha Bay, the more specialized Gunnery, Anti-Submarine, Communications and Diving Schools (all at Simonstown), or the Radar School in Durban. Commissioned and non-commissioned officers in the Medical Service are normally graduates of the South African Medical Service Training Centre established in the old Army Gymnasium headquarters in Pretoria.

The entire intricate system is topped by two elite institutions offering inter-service training, namely the Military Academy at Saldanha Bay and the South African Defence College established in 1973 in Pretoria. Since its creation as a branch of the Military College in 1950, the Academy has been concerned with joint officer formative training for all future Permanent Force officers by way of a Bachelor of Military Science degree offered under the auspices of the University of Stellenbosch (prior to the establishment of the Academy at Saldanha in 1956, the University of Pretoria). Many, but by no means all, of the current generation of South African military leaders – including General Magnus Malan, ex-Chief of the Defence Force and now Minister of Defence, General Viljoen, the current supreme head, and General Geldenhuys, Chief of the Army – are Military Science graduates of the Academy, mainly from the student body of the early fifties. This common educational experience, as we will note in more detail below, is a crucial element in the perceptions of politics and society held by the contemporary military hierarchy and, in particular, in the meanings they assign to the concept of total strategy. The South African Defence College, on the other hand is generally regarded as the inner intellectual core of current military strategic and social thinking. Established with the purpose of providing joint staff courses to Army, Air Force and Navy officers selected for senior staff and command appointments, the Defence College, now known as the Joint Defence College, has become an important forum within which the military elite discusses strategic and social policy in the light of both imported and indigenous civil–military conceptions. Since the College periodically offers a National Defence Course open to senior government officials and influential members of the private sector concerned with state security, it is also an important mechanism for orchestrating and linking the interests and policies of South Africa's entrepreneurial, military and governmental elites.

It is, in fact, absolutely crucial to look behind the formal structure of the SADF in order to identify a number of shaping institutional factors without which it is virtually impossible to understand the spirit and workings of the South African military and the precise nature of civil–military relations in South African society. In the first place and above all, the South African military fits into the local pattern of dominant institutions in its racially exclusive composition and internal distribution of authority. The South African military has not entirely escaped the incorporative pressures inducing various local institutions to dilute their racial foundations as the modernization of South Africa demands a wider pool of skilled manpower. Yet, although the various subject groups – blacks, Indians and Coloureds – have been brought into the military in a fashion which has led various commentators to label the Defence Force as a unique vehicle for black mobility, the military remains an essentially white institution in ethos, manpower and command structure. Within these racial parameters the South African military is dominated by the Afrikaner segment of the white elite in a society where, despite the role of race in building elite cohesion, communal politics waged between English and Afrikaner are still significant. With increasing domestic and foreign threats to minority rule, ethnic divisions among whites have tended to give way to racial solidarity in support of the state. Nonetheless, Afrikaners enjoy greater access and mobility within the bureaucratic organizations of state – including the military – in a way which feeds English suspicions concerning the consolidation of Afrikaner state power. This is important for the way the English-speaking community views the social role of the Defence Force and its relationship to the Defence Force through the medium of national service. It should be noted, in addition, that less than one-third of South Africa's military manpower consists of permanent, full-time, career soldiers. Because of the racial nature of its recruitment policies and its inability to compete for manpower with the private sector, the SADF is essentially a citizen military whose professional core, the Permanent Force, constitutes a mere 28 per cent of total manpower. Surrounding this core are assorted civilian workers, auxiliaries, and two major concentric circles – the Citizen Force fed by a national service system providing 46 per cent of SADF members, and, on the outskirts of the defence network, the Commando Force, composed of national service-men (some with specialized counter-insurgency training received at the Danie Theron Combat School in Kimberley) organized into regional groups with a view to guarding key installations and facilities in various areas of the country.

This extensive reliance on conscripted manpower has two important implications. First, the perennial infusion of civilian influence into military institutions and the subsequent circulation of personnel between the civil and military sectors of society reduces the capacity of the military to socialize its members into strong corporate affiliations. Corporatism and professionalism are two distinct qualities in modern military organiz-ations, and while the South African military may be a professional body in the sense of possessing a common set of techniques and operating pro-cedures, it does not necessarily follow that beyond a hard core of per-manent members it enjoys a strong and distinctive sense of institutional identity. Secondly, while the extensive national service system provides channels through which military influences can be projected into civil society, the network functions reciprocally to erode the insulating barriers between military and civil society. The net effect is a situation where it is relatively difficult to immunize civil society from military intrusion on the one hand, and, on the other, to isolate the Defence Force from civilian intrusion into military affairs.

Any detailed interpretation of the social and political role of the South African Defence Force also requires that it be viewed as a military institution against the background of the various civil–military prototypes developed by theorists in recent years. In this way some coherence may be imparted to the study of the interaction between soldiers and different types of past and contemporary society. I do not intend to launch into a detailed discussion of the so-called 'aristocratic', 'liberal', 'professional' and 'penetration' models – the four major models currently dominant in civil–military theory – except to emphasize two points which are of particular importance in linking the South African civil–military experience with the wider theoretical literature.[11] In the first place, South Africa's present civil–military system falls squarely, but by no means perfectly, into the 'liberal' category characterized by the predominance of civil over military authority, and by professional (but technically non-political) military institutions acting as executive agents of the state in the implementation of public policy. The imperfect nature of the 'fit' is however of critical importance, not only because every working civil–military system is no more than an approximation of the ideal prototypes developed by theorists,[12] but also because the South African military tradition is an outgrowth of historical circumstances which have mediated the complete transplantation of British liberal-type civil–military norms into the local environment. This means, secondly and above all, that if we are fully to appreciate civil–military relations in South Africa, in their own right and as part of a more universal phenomenon, it is essential that we (a) indicate the role of British imperialism in shaping South African perceptions of military and social relations during the course of the last two centuries, and (b) show how the British heritage has been bent, in the process of transplantation, under the shaping force of indigenous cultural and political influences.

It is not our intention to document fully the British military experience in South Africa: there are numerous regimental histories and analyses of British imperial policy which do so. British imperialism in Southern Africa, it needs to be said nonetheless, was a mechanism for cultural projection as well as a system of power, with the result that many of the organising values and institutions found in the South African Defence Force today are a direct result of the exposure of local military forces to the century-long influence of British military tradition.[13] The impact of British militarism, it should be emphasized, did not effectively cease with the establishment of the Union. Technically, the creation of the Union Defence Force in 1912 indicated that South Africa was branching out on a new and independent military path of its own. Yet British military withdrawal from South Africa was a phased rather than an instantaneous process in which British values, standards and conventions were artificially maintained for a number of years, in a manner befitting a situation where independence was granted a mere eight years after a violent armed struggle between the forces of the colonizer and those of the colonized. In effect, the creation of the Union of South Africa was accompanied by a special arrangement in terms of which elements of the Imperial garrison were to remain in South Africa for an undefined period in order to protect British strategic maritime interests.[14] It was not until the outbreak of World War I when Britain gratefully accepted General Louis Botha's offer that the UDF take over the defence of

South Africa, that the majority of the British garrison was withdrawn from the coastal ports of the Cape and Natal and assigned elsewhere.[15] A small force of mainly artillerymen and engineers was still left at the Cape; the Union did not acquire rights to Imperial installations until after the conclusion of the war and it was not until 1921, with the abolition of the South African Military Command (the War Office designation for the Imperial Military Command in South Africa) that the last residues of British troops finally departed from South African shores.[16]

Even after 1921 the young Union Defence Force remained closely tied to its British military heritage, both in sentiment and in the material process of developing its own institutions to meet the defence needs of the new South Africa. Indeed, for the full forty years between the creation of the Union and South Africa's eventual withdrawal from the Commonwealth in 1961, Britain remained the focal point for the Union Defence Force in the process of articulating its internal structures and devising pathways for institutional growth. Lacking any definite and alternative military model to that introduced by British colonialism, it was only natural that the leaders of the nascent South African military would gravitate towards British experiences and norms in the task of shaping the Union Force from an extended police organization into a fully fledged and highly professional corporate body of soldiers. Hence, both the South African Air Force and Navy were created as virtual replicas of their British counterparts. When the very earliest of South African naval units (the Cape and Natal Naval Volunteers) were amalgamated into a single division in 1913, the new unit was immediately incorporated into the Royal Navy under the mustering of the South African division of the Royal Naval Volunteer Reserve.[17] The disciplinary codes of the embryo navy were those currently in force in the Royal Navy and much of the early history of the South African Navy is that of an adjunct to its larger and older British counterpart.[18] The organizational values imparted during the process of military training are crucial components of officer attitudes, and British institutions and procedures played a pivotal role in forging the UDF into an effective fighting unit in its earlier years.[19] The initial operation of the UDF was set in motion by a curious mixture of professional British soldiers, ex-Boer officers and members of the Cape Mounted Rifles, and the British element was to play an important role in officer education thereafter. British officers were active in establishing South Africa's first military college,[20] and as late as 1930 the Commander of the South African Navy was a British officer on loan from the Royal Naval forces.[21] The fledgeling South African Air Force was an active participant in the Commonwealth Joint Air Training Scheme established in August 1940 with a view to training Royal Air Force, South African Air Force and other Allied air and ground crews for wartime operations at South African bases.[22] It is estimated that over 30,000 South African pilots, bomb-aimers, navigators and other personnel were trained under the auspices of this programme with its multiple opportunities for communication between South African and other Commonwealth military personnel.[23] Detailed statistical research remains to be done on the overseas assignments, travel, posting and training of UDF officers, particularly on South African enrolment at Sandhurst.[24] On the basis of available research it seems that few junior UDF officers attended Sandhurst courses, certainly far fewer than their counterparts from the Rhodesian Army.[25] Nevertheless some of the more senior officers doubtless attended courses at such British institutions as the Imperial Defence College, the Joint Services Staff College or the Army Staff College prior to the exclusion of South African candidates following the withdrawal of the Republic from the Commonwealth. Six of the ten original pilots of the South African Aviation Corps (the embryo of the South African Air Force) received their practical and theoretical aviation training at the Royal Flying School at Upavon and South Africans subsequently appear as pupils in the standardized course offered to Commonwealth pilots at Britain's Royal Air Force Staff College.[26]

The technologies employed throughout most of South Africa's military history as well as the defence responsibilities of South Africa as a member of the Commonwealth contribute to the long-enduring pattern of communication and cultural interchange between British and South African soldiers. Technology is a notorious carrier of social information and for most of the twentieth century South Africa has been heavily dependent upon British military equipment standardized to meet the uniform defence needs of Commonwealth members. While this dependence has now been broken, partially as a result of diversification in the Republic's arms procurement policy, partially as a consequence of shifts in South Africa's industrial base allowing for the development of an indigenous arms industry, it is doubtful whether the South African military would have existed in any real operational sense were it not for the British provision of armaments. The South African Air Force, for example, was launched with an 'Imperial Gift' of 100 aircraft, and this mixture of British De Havillands, Avros and scout planes was to form the basis of SAAF operations for many years after 1920.[27] The equipment of the South African Army during World War II was exclusively British in origin and the only major purchases by the Army in the period 1945–60 were British Centurion tanks (subsequently modified into the locally produced Olifant). The first three ships of the South African Naval Service (the survey ship HMSAS *Protea* and the minesweepers *Immortelle* and *Sonnebloem*) were all British donations as were the first three major warships acquired by the South

African Naval Force towards the end of World War II.[28] Following the Simonstown Agreement the British complement in the South African Navy was increased by a further six frigates, ten minesweepers and six seaward patrol boats purchased by South Africa at a cost of £18 million by the terms of the agreement.[29] Indeed, as official SADF sources note unashamedly: the South African Navy 'is moulded in practically all respects on the pattern of the British Royal Navy. Every warship of the Navy, every individual major equipment item including all gunnery and communication equipment is [or was until recently] of British origin.'[30]

The use of common technology, it is widely recognized, brings men together. Military technology can in turn function as a medium of political communication as soldiers educate each other in the use of equipment or through the provision of specialized service and back-up skills designed to offset technical obsolescence. The so-called 'special connexion' linking the South African and British military establishments is, however, also the result of the more tangible principle of 'joint defence' historically enshrined in the Commonwealth arrangement. The element of standardization in equipment, training and organization in the South African and British defence forces from the creation of the Union to 1961 is a direct extension of the notion that Britain is obliged to come to the defence of its Commonwealth partners in times of war and that her partners are in turn responsible for the defence of Britain and Empire in times of emergency. This concept was built into the Act of Union,[31] it was subsequently put into operation four years later with the outbreak of World War I, and later confirmed at the Imperial Conference of 1921 subject to the rider that 'it is for the Parliaments of the several parts of the Empire upon the recommendations of their respective governments to decide the nature and extent of any action which should be taken'.[32] From the point of view of the flow of social information along the Anglo-South African channel, 'joint defence' has had two discernible implications. First, it has supported high-level institutionalized contact between the leaderships of the South African and British militaries for much of the fifty-year period between 1910 and 1961 in times of peace and, in particular, in times of war. The Imperial War Cabinet (of which Smuts was a leading member) is obviously the leading institution in this communications network, yet given the tendency of most Commonwealth countries (including South Africa) to abrogate their independence in military planning, strategic policy, armaments provision and military intelligence to joint committees under British supervision, such mundane organizations as the Commonwealth Advisory Committee on Defence Science and the Commonwealth Committee on Clothing and Defence Stores must be regarded as integral elements in the institutional grid coordinating Commonwealth military matters and facilitating the flow of information between its various members.[33] Secondly, and perhaps more significantly, joint defence meant a high degree of personnel interchange between Britain and the Commonwealth countries, once again intensified in times of warfare. Tylden has made the point that, with the exception of the Indian Army, South African troops 'have stood side by side with Britain in more campaigns than troops of any other country'.[34] Whether or not this is absolutely true, the fact remains that the South African military has been highly active as an ally of Britain on the two major occasions during the twentieth century when the Empire has gone to war. Despite the fact that South African entry into both world wars was accompanied by considerable domestic turmoil threatening to disrupt the delicate ethnic balance of white society, eventual combat participation by the South Africans was an important component in the calculus of Allied victory – both in 1918 and twenty-seven years later. During World War I the South African Army served with distinction in Flanders and France as well as in German East Africa and South West Africa, where British assistance was limited to a few armoured cars of the Royal Navy.[35] South Africans formed two of the first four Royal Flying Corps squadrons mobilized for the French front and subsequently some 3,000 members of the South African Aviation Corps were mustered as Number 26 Squadron of the Royal Flying Corps, including Captain Beauchamp Proctor (winner of the Victoria Cross) and Sir Pierre van Ryneveld ('father' of the South African Air force).[36] South Africa's Royal Naval Volunteer Reserve was mobilized in August 1914, served in South West Africa, and then formed four contingents of 400 officers and men who left for England to serve with the Royal Navy.[37] This pattern was repeated in 1939–45 with the Army active in North African and Italian theatres, with South African naval officers and seamen being seconded to the Royal Navy and the Royal Marines,[38] and with South Africans figuring highly in the ranks of airmen engaged in the Battle of Britain.[39] There can be no doubt that the South African Navy played an important role in safeguarding the Cape sea route and South Atlantic and Indian sea lanes during these difficult years, nor can there be any understating of the work of the Army and Air Force in defeating the Axis powers in the Horn of Africa and assisting the westward advance of the 8th Army in North Africa. Given the exceptional importance of joint combat experience in facilitating the exchange of social values between soldiers, the crucible of both world wars is also an important element in the pattern of communication and interconnexion between the South African and British militaries.

The combined effects of this long and intense intercourse between the British and South African military establishments is readily evident today – in the medals and uniforms worn by South African officers, in the ranking system of the SADF, its promotional norms, regimental conventions, disciplinary codes, training procedures and, above all, in the general adherence of its officer class to the cardinal principles at the foundations of the British civil–military model. These principles are embodied in the notion that military authority be subordinate to the political authority of the civil state. At the same time, the contemporary South African Defence Force is not simply a neo-British 'liberal' clone transplanted into the African continent and entirely dictated to in its methods by imported models. To accept this premise is to ignore the fact that while British imperial power has carried British military norms to the African subcontinent, these norms and institutions have, in their turn, been forced to adapt to the peculiar and different demands and stresses of the South African environment. There are, it should be added, distinct intellectual, spiritual and cultural differences in the various combat arms of the contemporary South African Defence Force which, as numerous commentators note, reflect the different 'take' of British military values in the various service arms. Hence, the Navy (and to a lesser extent the Air Force) is considerably more Anglophile in its institutional codes and conventions than is the current Army, whose standards and patterns of behaviour differ quite significantly from those found in the British defence establishment. This reflects in part, the relatively greater ability of the Navy and Air Force to attract English-speaking recruits; and, in part, the technological requirements of naval and air forces which, relative to armies, are universally more cosmopolitan and outward-looking in their institutional orientations. Most fundamentally, however, the Afrikaner quality of the Army mirrors the fact that landward military forces are always most intimately tied to the exercise of state power. The social formations which predominate in armies, which shape their internal values and external relations with civil society, are almost always involved, by default or conspiracy, in the crystallization of their own state power.

British social and political values, including British notions of civil–military interaction, have never really rested easily in Afrikaner society. Hence, shaping the military to accord with Afrikaner values and purging it of its imported styles and traditions has been an important component in the process by which Afrikaner nationalism has sought historically to capture the institutions of the South African state and bend them into compliant instruments of apartheid ideology. The 'time of trial and tribulation' referred to by one military historian in describing the political experiences of the Union Defence Force in the aftermath of the Nationalists' accession to power is not readily comparable with a purge of military ranks and institutions. Nevertheless many British-oriented officers now in retirement are inclined to describe the lot of the Defence Force hard upon

1948 in these dramatic terms, when 'nationalizing' the military was an important priority for the Malan government. The subsequent replacement of British designations, decorations and ranks by indigenous insignia, the renaming of regiments to deprive them of their traditional identities, and the introduction of bilingualism as a requirement for officer status, were all part of creating disincentives for English-speakers to pursue a military career as a means to reinvigorate Afrikaner civil–military traditions. What is important moreover is that there *is* an Afrikaner civil–military tradition, or, to put it another way, the implantation of British civil–military norms into South Africa did not take place *tabula rasa*. On the contrary, the origins of South African military history actually precede the advent of British colonialism by 150 years, and, during this period, a variety of civil–military concepts were developed within the local context of white settler defence to form a foundation of ideas and practices upon which British militarism was to build, in inter-action and, more commonly, in conflict. Foremost among these early concepts was the so-called 'kommando', derived from the tradition of Cincinnatus with its emphasis on irregular military action conducted by the citizen-soldier. The kommando was in its turn an outgrowth of the principle, established at the Cape in 1659, that all white citizens (or free burghers) would bear arms to assist regular soldiers in its defence and, indeed, would bear the brunt of warfare on the border areas of the interior.[40] Subsequently a Burgher Militia was established, modelled on the Dutch militia in Holland, with musketeers and (later) cavalry units to be deployed against marauding Hottentots and Bushmen. In 1686, by which time annual militia drills at the Castle constructed by van Riebeeck had 'assumed large and interesting proportions',[41] a Burgher Watch of six companies of citizens (each 30 strong under a sergeant and corporal) was created by governor Simon van der Stel as a metropolitan equivalent of the Militia working in the outer districts and linked to the Castle by an elaborate system of flag signals. The new unit was originally concerned with night patrol and preserving order in Cape Town but its functions were subsequently broadened to include the prevention of arson, theft and other offences committed by renegade members of the local slave community. Both the Burgher Watch and Militia were linked by the Burgher Council which was responsible for the annual appointment of officers subject to the Council of Policy of the Dutch East India Company, while official registers of all free burghers between the ages of 16 and 60 were maintained by the authorities in Cape Town and the landrosts (senior judicial officers) in the rural areas. With the passing of the years the new kommando organization grew in size and military experience. In 1708 it consisted of two full companies of infantry and a mounted company at

Drakenstein and Stellenbosch: by 1795 these had increased to seven infantry companies and eight-and-a-half companies of 'Draghoenders' (Dragoons) or 'Burgher Cavallerie' stretched as far afield as Swellendam and involving the services of some 3,000 men. Technically the first full kommando operation was that against Bushmen marauders in the Drakenstein area in 1715.[42] Theoretically, all kommando operations required governmental approval, following which the burghers were issued with company ammunition. In actuality the kommandos were fully operative in short but sharp punitive operations without Castle clearance well before 1715. Since the conduct of kommando operations was left entirely at the discretion of their members, a tactically adept system of military defence ideally suited to the needs of a small and isolated colonial minority responsible for its own protection in an hostile and alien environment soon developed. While kommandos were by no means unanimously efficient in rounding up stock thieves or exacting retribution on the indigenous inhabitants, by the mid-eighteenth century they had succeeded in pushing the Bushmen far into the interior, advanced onto the Karoo plains and developed the first practical experience of what was later to be known as irregular guerrilla warfare.

The kommando as a form of military organization cannot be reduced to a single type across the broad sweep of South African history. Kommando units have varied in size from a handful of individuals to formations in excess of a thousand members, they have fought under Dutch, British colonial and Boer Republican auspices; some have been fed, paid and equipped by government acting through appointed officers; others have recruited leaders on an elective basis and functioned as distinctively independent citizen forces. British colonialism also fluctuated in its attitudes towards the kommando system, from employing it as a military tool as circumstances demanded, to actively seeking its eradication for a mixture of strategic and political reasons in favour of regular, standing military formations. In neither nineteenth-century Natal nor the Cape Colony – in the areas where British authority was most intense – did kommando-type notions take hold of the civil–military system with the same impact as in the two Boer Republics beyond the purview of British governance in the northern interior. It was in these northern regions however, in the Transvaal and Free State Republics established in defiance of British imperialism, that the kommando was brought to its apogee as a form of civil–military organization. Nurtured in the Great Trek, the hunting expeditions of the Boers, innumerable conflicts with black tribes and in two major wars against British imperialism in the course of the century, the kommando was in fact to emerge as one of the corner-stones of Afrikaner society with intellectual and organizational implications extending into the furthermost realms of politics and culture. This reflected, in the first instance, the military value of the kommando, its crucial role as a mechanism for community defence against external threats, most notably that posed by the proximate British presence. While many analyses of the Boer War attribute the Boer defeat to the cumbrous and seemingly antiquated kommando military system – to its inability to defend captured territory or to instil the military style and procedures associated with regular warfare of the type waged at Ladysmith, Mafeking, Kimberley or along the Tugela[43] – the defence of the two Boer Republics was a distinctively kommando effort. The war machines of both had undoubtedly made concessions to the organizational and technological exigencies of modern warfare in the period leading up to the outbreak of hostilities in 1899. In the Free State, President Boshoff first departed from kommando reliance on horse and rifle by establishing a State Artillery in 1857, armed with 12 cannon; in 1864 President Brand spent a further £1,000 on refurbishing the unit, placing it under the command of an ex-Royal Artillery officer.[44] A comparable if larger State Artillery was established in the Transvaal in 1874 and subsequently expanded following the end of British annexation in 1881.[45] Both the Boer Republics also made use of voluntary personnel – particularly the Free State during the Basuto Wars[46] – although volunteer units were ultimately subsumed in the standard kommando forces at the outbreak of war. In addition both Republics entered the war with conventional police forces, the highly disciplined South African Republican Police (the mounted ZARPS) in the case of the Transvaal,[47] the Free State Police, formed partially from the 'Rijdende Dienstmacht' (a patrol organization existing between 1889 and 1896) in the case of its sister republic.[48] Yet the regular component of the Boer forces mobilized during the two-and-a-half year war was very small in relation to the 69,000 burghers, 2,100 international volunteers and 13,300 colonial rebels, most of whom were mustered as kommandos during this period.[49] At the outbreak of the war the State Artillery of the Free State numbered roughly 400 men operating fourteen 17.5 cm Krupp fieldguns under the command of Major Albrecht of the German Army,[50] while the Transvaal Artillery consisted of roughly 350 men backed by an assortment of ox-drawn Creusot cannon, Maxims and howitzers.[51] The bulk of the war effort was overwhelmingly borne by kommando horsemen lightly armed with Martini-Henri rifles and forged into highly mobile and irregular guerrilla units. In the purely military realm, it should be added, the kommando was also a vital element in the consolidation of Afrikaner power in the South African heartland, crucial to pacifying black resistance in the face of Afrikaner expansion. In its original form the kommando system was conceived as an instrument of defence designed to protect the Cape against both its seaward and landward enemies. Thus the kommandos at the Cape saw service against the British invasions of both 1795 (where at the Battle of Muizenberg they were betrayed by their officers, most of whom identified with the House of Orange) and 1806 (when they composed most of General Janssens' forces against a numerically superior British army). The regular forces of the Boer Republics also played an important part in quelling black opposition to Afrikaner rule – the Free State Artillery during the Basuto Wars of 1858 and 1865–68, the Transvaal State Artillery during the course of five tribal wars from 1882 to 1894.[52] Nonetheless, the very ethos of the kommando was shaped by the exigencies of so-called 'native policy', by expeditions against Obiquas (Bushman bandits who stole cattle, occasionally killed owners and made travel unsafe in the earliest days of the Cape), and could easily be converted to an offensive instrument for suppressing tribal uprisings and compelling black chiefs to recognize the authority of the Afrikaner states. This does not of course mean that the kommando was always effective as a tool of Afrikaner imperialism, particularly in long campaigns such as the Sekhukhune War of 1876 when it was difficult to hold the irregulars together, where blacks were armed with firearms or in mountainous terrain, near Barberton, Lydenburg or in the Zoutpansberg. The decision to create state artilleries was not originally motivated by the presence of the British enemy; rather it was an attempt to supplement the forces of the kommando with high explosives and full-time soldiers in dealing with the belligerent 'Bantu'. For the most part these dealings were settled by the strength of the kommando. 'If the kommando was successful', as one historical treatment points out, 'the result was commonly the expulsion of the tribe or the settlement of the whites over the heads of the tribesmen, who were in this wise reduced to what was to be the fate of the great mass of ... Natives – rightless squatters or labour-tenants on European-owned properties'.[53]

The kommando systems in the two Boer Republics were not entirely similar: in the Transvaal the kommandant-general was directly elected by the burghers for a ten-year period of office, whereas in the Free State the process was more indirectly democratic, all enfranchised burghers electing assistant field cornets, field cornets and kommandants who then in turn elected their own kommandant-general.[54] In both Republics however the kommando was more than a mere military system to be mobilized to maintain internal order, quell rebellion and defend the state against its external enemies. On the contrary, the kommando stood at the centre of a mesh of social relations extending from the military to the deepest realms of Afrikaner politics and culture. In the first place and most tangibly, the kommando hierarchy was from its very inception uniquely adaptable for purposes of administration in an environment where carefully articulated bureaucratic structures were either underdeveloped or simply lacking. From the earliest days of the Cape Colony, officers of the kommando were given a mixture of military and civil administrative tasks. The notion of the kommando district as a basic administrative division was subsequently transported north to the Boer Republics, particularly to the Free State, where no provision was made for a department of war or kommandant-generalship during peacetime circumstances, and where, in effect, the kommando only basically functioned as a military tool in times of war. While this was not the case in the Transvaal, where the kommando was regarded as a more distinctively permanent military device, kommandants and field cornets were effectively assigned civil functions outside the sphere of war in the famous 33 Articles of Potchefstroom (approved at Derdepoort in 1849) in terms of which a defence structure for the ZAR was created. The kommando was also a powerful socio-cultural institution with a formative impact upon multiple aspects of Afrikaner political culture. Common language, adherence to the Calvinist faith, and political and military arrangements embodied in the popular assembly of burghers and the kommando were undoubtedly the main integrating forces in the Afrikaner community prior to the Trek and particularly thereafter.[55] While the kommando ethic certainly assisted the militarization of Afrikanerdom in the hostile conditions of the South African interior, the actual organization and operation of the kommando also assisted the growth and dissemination of democratic and individualistic ideals within the ethnic boundaries of the Afrikaner community. The Boer War years distinctly eroded the original participatory thrust of the kommando with the popular election of officers and mass involvement in Councils of War being curbed in favour of a more centralized system of leadership recruitment and decision-making.[56] The exigencies of large-scale combat against regular British forces also prompted considerable differentiation in the command structure of the kommando, the initial hierarchy of kommandant-general, kommandant, field cornet and assistant field cornet giving way to a far more complex pattern of authority embodying various types of *hoofofficieren*, *Stafofficieren*, *kommando-officieren* and *onderofficieren*.[57] Yet for most of its history the kommando tradition of a directly or indirectly elective officer corps encouraged a sense of democratic participation and political efficacy among kommando members which was to be an important component of the 'volkdemokrasie' of the Afrikaner people. This was further reinforced by the general absence of formal military discipline in kommando ranks, either because elected officers were naturally reluctant to exercise their authority, or because of familial ties between kommando members which cut across distinctions of military rank. All members of the kommando were, of course, technically equal and entitled to proffer advice in Councils of War: the result was that each burgher-soldier was theoretically a general who obeyed orders voluntarily and often acted entirely in accord with his own initiative on the battlefield. Since the mobility of the kommando demanded the self-sufficiency of each horse and rider, there developed a deep affinity between the burgher and his African environment as well as a rough, frontier individualism whose mark remains indelibly imprinted on Afrikaner culture today. The kommando was also important as an instrument of early socialization and as a mechanism for assigning and recognizing status in the Afrikaner community. Much of the schooling which the young rural Afrikaner received in hunting, *veldcraft* and the handling of weapons was a mere preliminary to his participation in kommando ranks at a later stage. The manner in which he subsequently acquitted himself in the kommando would determine the prestige with which he was regarded by his family and the wider community: this prestige in civil society would in turn determine rank and authority in the kommando system. The kommando was naturally antithetical to the development of the Boer into a distinctively professional and regular soldier. Kommando members were basically farmers acting in defence of their property (or extending their property) at their own cost, with their own weapons and often accompanied by their families on supply wagons parked in the rear of the action in the highly symbolic yet strategically effective *laager*. Herein lay perhaps the greatest weakness of the kommando as a military system. At the same time it engendered in the Afrikaner spirit the notion of the nation-in-arms, of the sometime-citizen-sometime-soldier engaged in the Afrikaner version of the 'people's war' in defence of community and homeland. Under such psychological conditions the dividing line between political and military authority could never be as sharply articulated as that demanded by the 'liberal' model of civil–military society. In practice the question of civil–military relations was a burning political issue in the context of Afrikaner frontier nationalism both during the Trek and for many years thereafter. Initially the position of chief executive and kommandant-general was fused together in a single office. In the Transvaal, for example, the kommandant-general was also the political leader prior to the formal establishment of the ZAR in 1852, and in effect he remained chief executive for a further six years thereafter. It was not until 1858, with the creation of a separate presidency as head of state, that the chief of the Republican military forces was formally demoted to the position of servant of the civil executive along the lines dictated by the liberal civil–military model. Even then the kommandant-general remained head of the Executive Council for the life of the Republic, technically the second to the President but frequently able to command extensive popular and personal support.

The whole kommando tradition is absolutely crucial in understanding civil–military relations in South Africa, much of whose history represents a dialectic between the imported British 'liberal' understanding of the relationship between the military and society and the indigenously derived kommando notion which is so intrinsically central to the culture of Afrikaner politics. Two points are essential for interpreting this interplay in correlation with the current state of civil–military relations. Firstly, while there are intellectual and practical points of contact between the liberal and kommando traditions of civil–military relations, the two are essentially different in a way which reflects their different origins. The British model, arising as it does from relatively developed social conditions, emphasizes warfare of the type involving the deployment of disciplined, heavy fire-power, military formations. The kommando by contrast, emphasizes the use of small, lightly armed and highly mobile units geared to irregular and individual action appropriate to the conditions of frontier society. More importantly, the kommando differs from its competitor in its conception of soldiering and the dividing lines between civil and military society: whereas the liberal model stresses soldiering as a discrete, permanent and professional activity of autonomous status in functionally differentiated society, the kommando emphasizes the free flow of influences across the civil–military boundary personified in the citizen-soldier. Each model in turn identifies different criteria for social status in the military and civil sectors. From the point of view of the liberal type, military status is authentic, clearly distinguishable from political action and a reflection of the corporate identities of advanced military institutions. Under kommando-type frontier conditions, however, obfuscation of civil–military boundaries leads to a strong coincidence in the personnel occupying elite civil and military positions. Ultimately those with civil status have military prominence and those with military status, civil prominence. Finally, the two traditions differ in their understanding of the role of the military in social development. The liberal model, honed in relatively stable democratic conditions with a plenitude of specialized manpower, reserves the task of building the community to the civil sector under the protective umbrella of military institutions concerned exclusively with the strategic task of protecting the state. In the kommando, on the other hand, low levels of socio-economic development and the general hostility of the environment conspire to extend the Clausewitzian notion of 'Volksbewaffnung' (the arming of the group with the ostensible purpose of waging 'peoples war') to integrate the military into the social mainstream across a wide range of tasks. Hence the soldier is not a soldier *qua* soldier in his responsibilities : he is the nation-in-arms responsible for the dissemination of soldier ideologies, for building the economy and protecting its cultural and moral interests apart from its purely strategic foundations.

None of this would be of more than heuristic importance except that the role of the military under the kommando tradition echoes many of the features, roles and attitudes of the military in the contemporary political network. This in its turn reflects the fact that despite technological developments and the more mundane attempts of Britain to break the hold of the kommando on Afrikaner values and ideas of social organization, the very social and political values ingrained in the kommando concept remain relevant and central to the spiritual repertoire of the Afrikaner people. This is partly due to the historical pedigree of the kommando in Afrikaner political culture and its proven effectiveness as a means of structuring society. The resilience of the kommando with its connotations of the nations-in-arms also reflects its perfect fit into an environment where a racially beleaguered minority is faced with problems of defence and extension, of ensuring its own military and political perpetuation against an arithmetically superior indigenous population. Either way the establishment of the Union and the Union Defence Force is not contiguous with the triumph of British civil–military conceptions and the disappearance of the kommando from the realms of South African history. In reality the system emerging with the creation of the Union represents a careful adaptation of British policy in line with white South African sensibilities in the light of continuing imperial strategic and economic interests on the subcontinent. In the political realm this meant a constitution modelled along Westminster lines yet deviating from the pure type in its failure to recognize universal franchise and in its creation of a provincial administrative grid aimed at decentralizing power. In the civil–military realm, imperial pragmatism meant a diluted version of the British 'liberal' prototype with important concessions to indigenous Afrikaner kommando tradition.[58] The Union Defence Act of June 1912 did not, in effect, create a South African military solely with an eye to protecting the territorial sovereignty of the new state against external powers. As one commentator notes:

[In] 1910 the idea of great world wars to be waged in the near future had no place in the minds of South Africans, with the result that the main objects in the training of the new [Union Defence Force] were more with a view to possible trouble with the natives than to the organization of contingents for service overseas.[59]

In these circumstances, with the creators of the Defence Force looking 'inward' to the racial power constellation in the new state, the incorporation of traditional and indigenous notions of civil–military organization would easily come into play. The outcome is reflected in the basic provisions of the Defence Act which 'succeeded both in encompassing the military traditions of the past and in establishing an efficient defence system'.[60] In accord with these 'traditions', non-whites were immediately debarred from service in the new Defence Force (subject to the pragmatic rider that parliament could, if necessary, resolve to eliminate this provision in the future).[61] In addition, following extended correspondence between Smuts and Merriman over the merits of a professional as opposed to a conscript army,[62] it was decided to establish a defence structure giving expression to both the British notion of a standing regular force *and* the Afrikaner kommando tradition of the nation-in-arms. Hence the UDF was to consist of two components: on the one hand a small Permanent Force of approximately 2,500 men organized along British lines and armed with its own battalions of field artillery, and, on the other, a Citizen Force and Citizen Reserve, the former to be recruited from volunteers and ballotees drawn from all European citizens between the ages of 17 and 60, the latter to consist of all other Europeans organized into Rifle Associations on the basis of their obligation to render service to the state during times of both peace and war.[63] While the Citizen Reserve (the so-called Skiet Vereniginge) was perhaps the more perfect inheritor of the kommando legacy – it was in fact 'virtually the kommandos traditional to the countryside, making their own rules and, subject to ministerial approval, choosing their own officers'[64] – both of the citizen elements represent a perpetuation of the nation-in-arms concept, the kommando reinstitutionalized and given statutory weight by a dominant and exclusive racial minority determined on its own self-reliant survival and protection. As if to add weight to the internal functions of the new white force a peculiar (and subsequently controversial) provision was added requiring the written consent of every soldier should he be called upon to render service 'outside South Africa'.

Echoes of the kommando appear sporadically throughout twentieth-century South African history – in the decision of South Africa to enter the two world wars, in the rhetoric and actions of the Afrikaner paramilitary movements of the thirties and, more recently, as South Africa moves into garrison statehood in the face of internal and international efforts to alter its racial order. Much of the history of the South Africa Defence Force since 1910 is actually concerned with the various themes and tensions present in the Defence Act at its inception. While the primary function of the military remains true to the tradition of providing force in support of the white state, many developments within its institutions, and their relationship to wider South African society, reflect the unresolved questions raised by civil and military leaders on defence and military questions at the time of the Union. The balance of ethnic power within the elite continues to dog the political relations between civilians and soldiers even though the edge has been taken off Afrikaner–English conflict by the common and transcending interest of both segments of the white community in maintaining a monopoly of racial power. The role of the subject races in the state security network so casually dismissed with the promulgation of the original Defence Act of 1912 has been highlighted with the passing of the years, with black participation in the South African armed forces during World War II, with the tightening of the geo-strategic noose around the Republic since the early sixties, and with the general incapacity of the small white population to service both the military and the economic manpower needs of the system. As the internal and international pressures on apartheid have increased since 1945 many of the intrinsic contradictions in the South African civil–military system have risen to the surface: the old debates over whether the requirements of the state are better served by a professional or citizen army, by regulars, kommandos, traditional or innovative forms of organization have been reinvigorated to take on a new relevance and urgency in the conditions of the present era. It is to the contemporary that we now turn in order to evaluate the legacy of the past.

2

<>-<>-<>-<>-<>-<>-<>-<>-<>-<>-<>-<>-<>-<>-<>-<>-<>-<>-<>-<>-<>-<>-<>-<>-<>-<>-<>-<>-<>-<>-<>-<>

The rise of the garrison state and the development of total strategy

Militarization in South Africa is unintelligible when considered apart from the enormous changes in the country's internal and international situation since the accession of the National Party to power in the late forties. In the last thirty-five years South Africa has taken on many of the institutional and psychological features of the so-called 'garrison state'. At the material level the long period of National Party rule has witnessed the transformation of apartheid from a crude and loosely articulated doctrine of racial repression to a highly sophisticated programme for the design and development of authoritarian state structures. The result is a social network which, if not entirely authoritarian, is still sufficient, in its centralised power structures and denial of popular aspirations, to support systems of military influence and political organisation with their characteristic disregard for values of tolerance, justice and democracy. The psychological costs of three-and-a-half decades of apartheid are equally conducive to militarization, even if they are sometimes less tangible than the visible inroads into the institutional fabric of local democracy. As members of the dominant elite have, with rare exceptions, accepted the principle of politically disincorporating the majority as the only workable political norm, and as deference to constituted political authority has in turn displaced critical awareness as the context for the making of public policy – as indeed the elite has built allegiance into an essentially illiberal climate – so the forces of illiberalism have capitalized upon their advantage in the process of institutionalizing a basically repressive society.

The reactions of white South Africa to its post-war political environment are at least in part the result of international hostility. The concrete expressions of world antipathy to South Africa's racist system are directly expressed in the changes of status experienced by the Republic since the conclusion of World War II – by the contrast between the late forties, when South Africa was an esteemed member of the international community, a prime mover behind the Charter of the United Nations, and the current situation, where she is a pariah state, barred from participation in an array of inter- and non-governmental organizations, frequently sanctioned by the United Nations and virtually friendless in political circles where she has historically enjoyed good standing. Despite South African claims to represent Western interests on the African continent and in its southern region in particular, by the mid-sixties even her staunchest supporters in the Western alliance were forced to distance themselves from the Republic in order to conform to international reaction over South Africa's illegal occupation of Namibia, its support of Rhodesian independence and its internal racial policies. These developments, muted after the war but intensifying with the passing of the years, are salient to the evolution of South Africa's civil–military system in a number of distinctive ways. Firstly, the international arms boycott – one of the clearest manifestations of global repugnance at apartheid – has raised the domestic prominence of the military as Defence Force leaders have been forced to come together with the elites of government and business in the process of devising strategies to re-root apartheid in military soil. International embargoes on South Africa have generally had the effect of shifting power balances within the local elite constellation: just as previously obscure sporting, business and cultural bodies have been catapulted into the political mainstream by virtue of the vacuum created through policies of international withdrawal, so the defence establishment has been brought into political decision-making circles in accord with Huntington's classic proposition that national security threats induce a fusion of military and political decision-making, with soldiers a dominant element in the shaping of national security policy.[1] Today, as the range of national security issues extends to include such diverse topics as the international arms embargo on South Africa, Namibia and internal subversion, so the degree of executive liaison between civil and military authority has developed into an unprecedentedly intimate pattern of contacts between the leaders of government and its military. In the process by which both seek jointly to design means for the protection of the state, the political capital of the SADF inevitably rises, as does its ability to set the agenda for government. In the second place, the isolation of South Africa over the years has naturally ruptured many long-standing links with the outside world, particularly links with Britain. South Africa's withdrawal from the Commonwealth in 1961 was undoubtedly the most important in this series of amputations for both political and military reasons. Politically, withdrawal paved the way for Afrikanerdom to realize its ideal of re-creating a South African Republic adjusted to the dictates of modern apartheid. Militarily, the breaking of ties with the Empire meant cutting the transmission belt between the South African Defence Force and the British military institutions long responsible for the penetration of British civil–military norms into the local military establishment. The fact that the British military regarded maintenance of this connexion as neither possible nor desirable outside the Commonwealth framework assisted the rapid dismantling of the network of treaties, arrangements for personnel exchange and joint participation through which the two forces had communicated since the creation of the Union. Thirdly, and perhaps most importantly, the growing international isolation of South Africa combined with the political disturbances wrought by African nationalism in the southern African region has fed a distinctive garrison state psychology in the Republic – which inevitably works in favour of the visibility, status, political influence and, one might add, material claims on society by the military establishment. Since 1960 when, for the first time since World War II, a massive programme aimed at the modernization of the defence force was initiated, the military has increasingly pressured civil society for greater resources to be employed in its national security role. Today, in an atmosphere where the majority of whites are deeply insecure in their belief in an imminent and massive 'total onslaught' on South Africa by communist powers, it is difficult for any white politician intent on survival to denigrate the value of military service, to deny military expenditure, things martial, or, to a lesser degree, to prevent the military accumulating political power. In addition, as the majority of the elite has absorbed official propaganda to the effect that South Africa is today indeed in a garrison situation, so the use of physical force as a means of problem-solving has been popularized to the detriment of more persuasive and non-coercive techniques for managing social conflict. In such a situation institutions associated with the use of force, the 'managers of violence' to use Lasswell's famous phrase, the military and police experience a unique elevation in status relative to the 'soft' organizations of society, the parliamentary bodies, the judiciary and the media, whose operating ethics are altogether more complex, subtle and civil. In South Africa the visibility and prestige of the military today characteristically increases with each turn of the domestic or international screw. One noted commentator on military sociology has also observed that 'in normal times of peace, promotion opportunities for the military are really very limited. The military man is not so dull that he cannot see where's the rub: in times of peace. The great thing about war is that it makes vacancies and warrants the violation of that law of seniority which is the sole privilege natural to democracy'.[2] Militaries, no less the South African military, thrive on wars or on war-like situations. 'Hard' organizations of this type tend, in addition, to develop institutional stakes in perpetuating the climate of fear feeding their popular status. Thus the credibility with which the South African military exerts claims to political influence and social resources is directly dependent on the psychology of 'total onslaught' being maintained as a general credo of the white elite.

These developments originating in the international system must be seen against the background of two important developments in the domestic arena in order to appreciate fully the precise boundary shifts between the civil and military sectors. Firstly, the growth of the garrison syndrome in the minds of white South Africans has generated an intellectual climate increasingly hostile to the liberal concepts of society which are at the heart of the British civil–military model of the SADF. In general, elements in the Afrikaner segment of the white elite have begun to move ideologically outwards, if not necessarily to liberalize in the strict sense of the word, as the sociological naivety of fundamentalist notions of apartheid has been exposed by economic modernization with its characteristic capacity to stimulate urbanization, transethnic political identities and functional integration independent of culturally determined patterns of social trans-action. The recent recognition of urban blacks as a permanent social formation in 'white' South African cities, the creation of non-ethnic institutions to manage some of their social and administrative needs in these cities, and national development plans envisaging decentralization which cross-cuts homeland boundaries are important indications of this trend. Moreover, as Afrikanerdom has moved outwards in the face of ideologically unanticipated structural changes, so South African liberal-ism has moved inwards to stake its claims to mainstream elite membership as its notions of politics elicit decreasing sympathy among blacks moving into more radical forms of political consciousness. The result is the emergence of an ideological grey area in white South African politics where, on a common field dominated by concepts such as 'pluralism', 'consociation', 'federalism' and 'decentralization', white liberals and Afrikaner nationalists of various hues come together. This is not to ignore important points of principle continuing to divide the National Party from the Progressive Federal Party, nor is it meant to portray each as a homogeneous organization. Nevertheless, the growing dilution of liberal attachments to majoritarian democratic ethics has encouraged Afrikaner-dom to intensify its attack on the entire institutional milieu within which residual forms of liberalism thrive and upon which they ultimately depend. In the field of civil rights this has meant further diminution of the realm of individual and group freedom to which a retreating liberalism – in the media, the judiciary and the universities – has raised increasingly token protest since the accession of the National Party to power in 1948. In the constitutional field the National Party has, since the mid-seventies, capi-talized on the growing detachment of local liberalism from its British sources to abolish the bi-cameral parliamentary system, convert the legislature from an elective to a partially appointed body, and redesign the executive to concentrate power beyond legislative recall. Following the 1983 referendum these fundamental violations of the Westminster spirit and constitutional type will be taken further under South Africa's new constitution based upon an attenuated consociational arrangement with virtually unrestricted executive authority.[3]

These developments inevitably feed the erosion of liberal-type civil–military norms: as the last intellectual foundations and institutional supports of local liberalism are dismantled or consigned to the realms of the irrelevant by an increasingly authoritarian climate, it is inevitable that members of government, the military and the general public will waver in their convictions regarding the traditional pattern of civil–military arrangements, display token resistance in their defence and thereby clear the field for reorganization and change on the part of civil and military elements riding the crest of a reordered system. Civil–military boundary shifts are not only, however, a reflection of burgeoning illiberalism in the South African context. They also have much to do with important recent changes in Afrikaner class structure. One important consequence of these changes is the emergence of new leadership types within the National Party whose perceptions and action styles are readily compatible with military norms related to rationalisation, instrumental decision-making and the centralisation of power in clearly articulated hierarchies. This does not necessarily mean that Afrikanerdom is de-ideologizing in the sense of discarding apartheid baggage. The recent rise of the right in a manner reminiscent of previous movements to 'purify' the *volk* in the face of forces seeking the erosion of group identities attests to the resilience of tradition in constraining the modernization of Afrikanerdom under the impact of industrialism and urbanization. Yet these same forces of modernity have undoubtedly thrown up leadership strata among both Afrikaner governmental and military elites whose doctrinal commitments are flavoured with unprecedented pragmatism and whose ethnic attachments are contaminated by essentially middle-class, urban, technocratic values. The result, the basic source of crucial division between *verligtes* (moderates) and *verkramptes* (arch-conservatives) in modern Afrikaner politics, is a coming together of like-minded civilian and soldier in relation to the problems, challenges and strategies of South African politics. As the so-called 'managerial revolution' has enlisted support on the part of specific segments of Afrikanerdom – politicians fascinated by the techniques of organization, military men with their natural bias towards rational cost-effective action, and, in addition, the Afrikaner business community intent upon maximizing penetration into the traditionally English-dominated world of capital – so the basis for a fully fledged political coalition, with values distinct from and, in many cases, heretical to the traditional ideological mainstream of Afrikanerdom has been created.

Structural changes in Afrikanerdom are projected into the political elevation of the South African military through the idiosyncratic relationship forged between P.W. Botha and the leadership echelons of the Defence Force. Indeed, as numerous commentators note, the rise to prominence of the Defence Force has much to do with the personal relationships forged between the prime minister and his defence chiefs – within the broader context that both originate from the growing technocratic and managerial climate in the urban sectors of Afrikaner society. In many ways the rise of the military in South Africa is a matter of executive invitation – not necessarily in the sense that the military is called in to 'save' the government, as occurs in many other areas of the world, but in the more subtle sense that there are certain basic and common characteristics in the operating styles, interests and historical experiences of many of the personnel forming the South African executive and military elites which create the foundations for a workable political alliance. The well known forcefulness with which Botha approaches public policy-making, his emphasis on planning and rationalized forms of action are, for example, highly congenial to the more professionalized elements of the South African officer corps impatient with the more random and low profile approach to decision-making embodied in the previous Vorster government. The current prime minister values expert advice, the Defence Force is an important source of specialized manpower and both Botha and the leading elements in the military are essentially aggressive management-types with the tendency to reduce social problems to their bare essentials, infer strategic responses, and follow through with action dictated by strict technocratic criteria. This common orientation towards South African society and its problems reflects the personal history of Botha, his outstanding flair for organization and administration transferred from the National Party to the Defence Ministry and subsequently to the office of prime minister. It also reflects a variety of organizational developments within the officer ranks of the Defence Force to which we will turn in more detail in a later part of this chapter. At the same time the link between Botha and the military is not simply a matter of similar perception and style. While it cannot be demonstrated that the present executive–military alliance is a result of any calculated plan forged between 1966 and 1980 with the specific intent to raise the political status of both Botha and the Defence Force, there can be no doubt that the intimate ties between the current executive and the military establishment (arguably the most intimate in South African civil–military history) are the direct result of a symbiotic patron–client system forged consciously or inadvertently during Botha's fourteen-year tenure as Defence Minister. From the point of view of Botha, this long period was a valuable opportunity to cultivate political contacts outside the realms of the National Party in an environment whose hierarchical ethos and emphasis on planning and management blended perfectly with his own operating style and personality. From the point of view of the current generation of military leaders, many of whom owe their influence within the Defence Force to Botha's interest in identifying and promoting officers of apparent intellectual and administrative talent, the prime minister's demonstrated concern with the institutional interests of the SADF, his willingness to open channels for it to project these interests into the highest realms of public policy, and his unprecedented attempts to modernize and develop the military establishment are a sharp contrast to previous experiences with lack-lustre civil leadership. The Botha years in the Defence Ministry were undoubtedly a period of positive change in South African military history. The material conditions of military service were vastly improved, numerous organizational adaptions were made in order to rationalize the workings of military institutions, the Defence Force was flattered with the most sophisticated and modern technologies and equipment and given new access to the levers of the national budget. In the emerging climate of mutual confidence and trust, close personal associations were forged between Botha and a number of strategically placed senior officers, most notably General Magnus Malan, appointed the youngest-ever Chief-of-Staff of the Army by Botha, Chief of the Army, Chief of the Defence Force and subsequently Minister of Defence upon Botha's accession to power. While the political infighting surrounding the collapse of the Vorster government in the wake of the so-called 'Information Scandal' is still a matter for speculation there can be little doubt that the Defence Force was an important chip in the bargaining surrounding the eventual emergence of Botha as prime minister.

In these terms the rise of the military must be seen as the result of a combination of international, domestic, structural and idiosyncratic forces: the isolation of South Africa from world society in a fashion conducive to the growth of siege psychologies; the intensified institutionalization of authoritarian ideologies and social forms; movements in class internal to Afrikanerdom; and the political *quid pro quos* developed between the present incumbents of high military and executive office are all ingredients of the complicated configuration behind current shifts in civil–military boundaries.

There is, it should be emphasized, no direct trade-off between the social and political influence wielded by the civil and military sectors of society, and soldiers do not automatically move into political vacuums in the civil realm – least of all soldiers of the type of the South African Defence Force devoid of the experience and tradition of political involvement. In reality, the hermetic sealing of South Africa against the outside world, the severance of ties with the British defence establishment, the death gasps of local liberalism and the emergence of close associations between executive and military elites provides the setting and the incentives for the military to accumulate political capital. The actual response of the Defence Force to these incentives is an entirely different (and, one might add, normally ignored) issue which is intimately tied to the structural characteristics of the South African military, their organizational experiences, their level of professionalization, their corporate interests as defined by the officer corps, the class background of officers, their communal identities, self-images and political attitudes. In the last analysis, militarization in South Africa is not only a matter of movements in the civil sector beyond the institutional boundaries of the military: it is the intersection of these particular movements with internal ones within the Defence Force as a heterogeneous and dynamic institution composed of officers with different personalities, backgrounds, career experiences and generational attach-ments which are absolutely crucial.

During the course of this study considerable difficulty was encountered in collecting raw data on the social composition of the present and past South African officer corps, with the result that many of the fascinating hypotheses linking social background to military behaviour engendered by the extant literature could not be tested in any systematic manner. Nonetheless, the career trajectories of 86 senior SADF commanders were traced on the basis of data drawn from various sources, from biographies, autobiographies, military histories and publicly available Defence Force publications including the 50th anniversary edition of *Militaria* whose *Leiers Deur Die Jare, 1912–82* (compiled by Kommandant Nothling and Lieutenant E.M. Meyers of the Military Information Bureau) provided a useful index of the personnel considered by the military to be their most important leaders and, in so doing, furnished an initial foundation for this study. The 86 officers subsequently examined (46 from the Army, 21 from the Air Force, 9 from the Navy and 10 from the Medical Service) include the heads of the Defence Force since its establishment in 1912, the heads of the four (previously three) service arms, senior staff officers attached to Defence Force Headquarters over a fifty-year period, as well as important divisional commanders active mainly during World War II. For each individual officer a 'career point' was calculated according to the middle year of tenure in his highest office: this enabled us to disaggregate the entire group into eight categories corresponding to the entire period in which the Defence Force has been in existence. These eight categories are of officers whose career point was fixed between 1912–20 (these were mainly officers embarking on a military career well before the end of the nineteenth century); a second group corresponding to the decade 1920–30 (whose military intake is set in the mid and late 1890s); the group 1930–40 (entry point into military service generally between the beginning of the twentieth century and the outbreak of the World War I); 1940–50 (entry point World War I and the early twenties); 1950–60 (entry point mid-twenties); 1960–70 (entry point early thirties); 1970–80 (entry point late thirties, particularly the outbreak of World War II, and the forties); and lastly, a category of officers whose career points occur in the first two years of the eighties (the current batch of senior commanders most of whom embarked on a professional military career in the first half of the nineteen-fifties.[4] The correlation between career points and the four services of the SADF is indicated in Table 1.

1 *Career point and service distribution*

Category	Army	Air Force	Navy	Medical Service
1912–20	5	—	—	1
1920–30	4	—	—	—
1930–40	2	—	—	1
1940–50	6	6	3	2
1950–60	4	3	1	3
1960–70	7	5	—	1
1970–80	11	5	4	1
1980–	7	2	1	1
	46	21	9	10

Scanning the data reveals the South African military elite to be a highly heterogeneous body composed of an extraordinarily interesting collection of individuals: these include two Springbok rugby players and a fairly distinguished boxer (Lieutenant-General H.J. Martin, Major-General J.N. Bierman and Kommandant-General S.A. Melville respectively), a number of knights of the realm (Colonel Sir R.H. Price, Brigadier Sir E.N. Thornton, Major-General Sir H.T. Lukin and General Sir H.A. Van Ryneveld), a professor of physiology and a chemistry lecturer (Colonel E.H. Cluver and Lieutenant-General W.J. Bergh, present Chief-of Staff, Finances), the brother of a dissident clergyman (General C.L. Viljoen, present Chief of the SADF), the son of Nationalist member of parliament and scientist (the past Chief of the SADF and now Minister of Defence, General M.A. Malan), and, almost inevitably, the leader of an attempted coup d'état, Brigadier-General C.F. Beyers, leading light in the famous 1914 Rebellion. More fundamentally, however, the data points to a number of trends and developments at the highest levels of the SADF over the last fifty years which are of considerable importance to the current pattern of civil–military relations when viewed against the theoretical background of the extant military-politics literature.

First, the data tends to confirm that the military elite is becoming increasingly Afrikaner in character with the Defence Force increasingly tied to the consolidation of Afrikaner state power. Whether the SADF has ever been an ethnically indiscriminate institution in its top command structure, even within the limited racial parameters of the white elite, is seriously questioned by our data. In the 1912–20 category, 5 of the 6 officers whose career points are fixed in this period were of English extraction and as late as the 1940–50 grouping this ethnic imbalance was maintained, if somewhat diluted – a mere 6 of the sample of 16 senior officers originating in the Afrikaner section of the white community. The accession to power of the National Party in 1948 initiates a radical reversal of the established pattern, although, as we have already emphasized, the process of 'indigenizing' the military as part of the consolidation of Afrikaner power cannot be seen as a 'purge' in the formal sense, being limited by the ratio of black to white manpower. To a considerable extent, still manifest today, the military leans heavily on English manpower in maintaining the security of the state in the face of black majority pressure and it was this consideration, possibly above all others, which inhibited the Nationalists from pursuing a consistently radical policy of loading the officer corps with Afrikaners in the years immediately after they took the reins of power. Nonetheless, for reasons we have already indicated, many English officers were induced to surrender prematurely their commissions in the late forties and early fifties in a way that was to turn sharply the balance between the ethnic groups in the upper reaches of the Defence Force command structure. This is clearly reflected in our data, in the 1950–60 category, where only 3 out of the sample of 11 senior officers were of English extraction, one of whom (Brigadier P.C.C. Blair-Hook) was assigned to the relatively minor position of Surgeon-General. Although the last two years of this decade saw the appointment of the multi-talented General A.S. Melville as Kommandant-General, Afrikaner predominance in the hierarchy of the military elite continued unabated and progressively: in the 1970–80 category only 6 out of a total of 21 officers with career points in the decade were of English extraction, in the 1980+ category, that is, the contemporary crop of selected top commanders, a mere 2 out of 11.

Career-entry points into the military have also altered, although this is to be expected given the development of the SADF into an authentically modern and national force and the gradual severance of political ties from Britain and, subsequently, the Commonwealth. The shifts that have occurred are periodic. In the case of the first three of our categories, covering the period 1912–40, entry into the South African military on the part of the officers who were subsequently to reach the most senior of positions basically stemmed from three diverse sources: in the earlier part of the period Afrikaners who had been members of the Boer forces (e.g. General Beyers, the first Kommandant-General of the Citizen Force of the UDF), Englishmen who had been attached to crypto-British South African units – the Cape Mounted Rifles (Brigadier-General J.J. Collyer), the Kaffrarian Rifles (Colonel Sir. R.H. Price) or the Natal Carbineers (Brigadier W.E.C. Tanner) – or, in the last instance, soldiers with regular British military experience along the lines of Colonel M.C. Roeland, first Quartermaster General of the UDF and previously of the Royal Munster Fusiliers. In the second period, covering the two decades 1940–60, UDF careerists naturally begin to make an appearance in the highest ranks but there is still a strong British contingent in the form of officers initially schooled in the Royal Air Force (Brigadiers H.G. Willmott and P.C.C. Blair-Hook), the Royal Navy (Rear-Admiral G.W. Hallifax and Commodores S.J. Dalgleish and F.J. Dean), and the British Army (General C.A. Fraser). While there is a correspondent between ethnic background and entry point – top Afrikaner officers tend to have made their way to the higher ranks through the UDF, English officers through 'outside' military institutions – there are occasional divergencies from the overall pattern, for example Brigadier W.H. Du Plessis who began his career in the Duke of Edinburgh's Own Rifles. In the third and final period however, 1960 onwards, the Defence Force is almost completely indigenized as far as entry point and career are concerned. With the exception of a smattering of top naval commanders with British Merchant or Royal Navy experience, virtually every officer, English or Afrikaner, has moved up through the local Defence Force following an initial point of entry. Many of the Afrikaner officers whose careers peak during these two decades, particularly during 1960–70, originally came to the Defence Force as a result of Special Services Battalion experiences.

The net effect of these developments has been to re-orient channels of political communication into the military, to transform the military from an institution motivated by a British and imperial ethos into an organization whose leadership, despite its intrinsic professionalism, is particularly receptive to ethnically coded social messages. This is not to ignore the fact that the SADF, allied as it is to the white state, is in a broader sense susceptible to racially based communications, particularly when the security of the state is threatened. The basic responses of the Defence Force are still distinctively shaped by values, interests and developments embedded in the experiences of the white elite, despite recent changes in recruitment policy which open its ranks to Indians, Coloureds and blacks and rhetorical commitment to a policy of non-racialism. Yet as the old Anglophile officer class, with its imperial socialization, fundamental commitment to the liberal civil–military prototype, and political leanings towards the defunct United Party, has given way to a new breed of member with cultural connexions to attitudes, movements and political cues emanating from the Afrikaner segment of civil society, so the SADF has become increasingly alert to the thinking and behaviour of political decision-makers. In previous periods the flow of political information between governmental and military elites was far less perfect in its cultural foundations. While the Anglicized Afrikaner (or Afrikanerized Englishman) in the higher reaches of the government or military establishments may have served as a bridge between the two, the element of cultural compatibility was never as marked as at present where both have fallen under Afrikaner ethnic dominance. Today the military is peculiarly penetrable by Afrikaner interests, particularly the Army, the most thoroughly Afrikanerized of the services. Inasmuch as this ethnic connexion is supplemented in its political workings by personal and familial ties between Afrikaners transcending the civil–military divide, and by a system of national conscription responsible for constant recirculation of personnel between civil and military society, a complex network exists for communication between Defence Force leadership, the upper hierarchy of government and the Nationalist Party, and the collection of entrepreneurial, religious and cultural institutions of modern Afrikanerdom.

Our data also reveals that the combat experience of the military elite is becoming increasingly regionalized and unconventional in flavour. If each combat experience in a single theatre of operations is assigned one point for each of the 86 officers in our survey, and if each of our eight career-point categories is then correlated with the four major conflicts involving South Africa this century (i.e. the Boer War, World War I and II, and the war along the Namibia–Angola border), a distinct three-phase pattern emerges reflecting military events of the broad 1912–82 period. In the first of these phases (1912–40) the combat exposure of the senior officers whose career points fall within this period is dominated, as can be anticipated, by either the Boer or First World Wars. Equally expected are the results for the 1940–80 categories: the majority of officers whose careers peaked during these four decades cluster in their combat experience in World War I, with secondary exposure for Air Force personnel in Korea. The most intrinsically interesting group is the third category, the

1980+ grouping composed of the current batch of top officers, the great majority of whom, entering upon a military career in the early or mid-fifties, were simply too late to see overseas service. What little field experience these officers have is limited to the low-intensity warfare of the Namibian–Angolan border: of their number (eleven) only two have any real experience of conventional operations outside the southern African subcontinent, Vice-Admiral R. A. Edwards, Chief of the Navy (1980–82) and Lieutenant-General A. M. Muller, previously Chief of the Air Force. In both cases this combat experience is at considerable historical distance – the former served in artillery and technical services during World War II, the latter in No. 2 Squadron of the SAAF in Korea. As for the rest of the contemporary generation, in contrast to their predecessors, many have no combat experience whatsoever.

Combat experience may or may not have a politicizing effect on the soldier: the extent of his professionalism, his social background and the conditions he confronts after exposure to warfare are all intervening factors. On the other hand, the type and duration of combat experience can be absolutely crucial in shaping the political attitudes of soldiers, particularly in conditions of inter-generation tension. This is particularly important in the light of the fact that the combat exposure of the current generation of senior officers (and doubtless that of their inferiors) is limited to counter-insurgency in Angola or Namibia. This particular type of warfare, as countless theorists point out, is distinctly more political than its conventional counterpart where the fundamental deciding factor is, in essence, mobilized coercive power. As the SADF has come to appreciate during its fifteen years in Namibia, the outcome of counter-insurgency operations, however, is determined by a combination of military and political action the purpose of which is less to defeat the enemy in decisive battle than it is to strangle his supply of human and material resources by denying him the allegiance of the civilian population. Mobile soldiers are generally more receptive to political communications than their counter-parts in fixed bases,[5] and, as in other theatres from Malaya to Algeria and Vietnam, the logic of counter-insurgency in Namibia has had the effect of drawing the military out of their pure and isolated fighting role to develop patterns of connexion, interaction and participation in the daily social activities of indigenous civil society. In this sense, the various SADF-initiated civic action and socio-economic development programmes in Caprivi, Ovambo and the Kaokoveld, which are today an integral part of the South African war effort in Namibia, are not only important in the contest between SWAPO and the South African military for the goodwill and cooperation of the Namibian peoples, that is, as a variable in the strategic balance, but also in their role of exposing and sensitizing South

African soldiers to the various influences, features and demands of black civil society. While the physicians, teachers, agricultural experts, planners and administrative personnel are actually deployed by the SADF to counter what it loosely described as 'the variety of onslaughts' on the people of Namibia,[6] the personnel in the civic action programmes inevitably, if inadvertently, become channels for the transmission of political messages into military ranks. The long war in Namibia has also naturally expended military influence in the public policy-making process, directly in Namibia, and indirectly in South Africa itself. For understandable reasons, virtually no major current decision on Namibia is taken without reference to military and strategic considerations either fed into various civilian public-policy bodies in the form of information or physically represented by the presence and participation of top officers in the affairs of civilian councils. The extent of this military influence is so great that some commentators have been led to conclude that in the policy-making realm Namibia is, to all intents and purposes, a military fiefdom. In South Africa itself this is obviously not the case; yet the fact that the country is at war, albeit engaged in a limited low-intensity operation, has distinctly enhanced the access enjoyed by military leaders to the top civil decision-making institutions and increased their authority and weight in influencing deliberations. The net result is that while the political insulation of the middle officer ranks is being eroded by involvement in grassroots community activity in Namibia, their seniors are accumulating experience, confidence and expertise in the delicate tasks of civilian political dealing. The proximity of Namibia to South Africa and its apparent surface similarities to socio-political conditions in the Republic is also salient to the political reactions of the present generation of officers. This is particularly the case because the exigencies of waging war have forced the military authorities in Namibia to adopt a variety of policies not readily reconcilable with the principles of apartheid enforced at home. Recognizing the importance of winning popular allegiance, the military has emerged as an important force for deracialization in the territory. While it is difficult to identify military pressure on the Turnhalle government, the military have certainly welcomed the removal of racial barriers to social intercourse between black and white in Namibia, and the extension of political rights to all segments of the population. The majority of the officer corps in Namibia has also been impressed by the reliability of black troops in the operational zone, and by the ability of black, white and Coloured soldiers to interact on a non-racial basis. While this is not to suggest that Namibia is resocializing the officer corps in a liberal direction – the reforms initiated in Namibia are basically functional adaptions – there are doubtless individual officers whose perceptions of South Africa have been coloured by the non-racial experience of Namibia, and who reason from one context to the other.

Whatever the content of the internal debate over Namibia there can be little doubt that it is being conducted by a generation of officers profoundly more proficient, sophisticated and professional than any of their predecessors. Our data clearly shows that prior to the group of officers with career points in the period 1950–60, few SADF senior personnel had any record of extensive attendance at civil or military institutions of higher learning. With the exception of high-ranking officers in the medical corps the characteristic career path was one of rough and ready advancement through the ranks with little to no exposure to what one leading theorist has broadly described as the 'background of general culture for the mastery of military expertise'.[7] In a certain sense this acted as a political safety valve: as Nordlinger notes, 'there is a positive rather than inverse relationship between the level of (military) expertise and the likelihood of (military) intervention'. And he adds:

Officers who have graduated from the military academy, who have taken advanced training courses and have attended war colleges, who have specialized intelligence-gathering, managerial and logistical skills ... are most likely to harbor disrespect and disdain for civilians who cannot govern competently. [They] are also most likely to believe that their military skills can be transferred to the civilian sphere where they will decidedly improve governmental performance.[8]

The politicization occurring with advanced training is not of course concomitant with intervention: a 'trigger' in the form, for example, of civilian interference in corporate military affairs is normally necessary to transform the disposition into action.[9] Yet the fact remains that over the years, particularly since the end of World War II, the training of South Africa's officer class has progressively shifted away from purely vocational duties, with the organizational skills to which Nordlinger refers being added to the battlefield ideas of combativeness and heroism as dimensions of the military experience. This is partially reflected in the 1960–70 and 1970–80 categories of our sample, but the thrust to professionalism is above all in evidence in the contemporary crop of top officers, the 1980+ grouping. With an erstwhile chief military instructor in the Military Academy (Lieutenant-General P.W. van der Westhuizen, present Chief-of-Staff, Intelligence), a past lecturer in the same institution (Lieutenant-General W.J. Berghe, Chief-of-Staff, Finances), and two baccalaureates in military science (notably Chief of the Defence Force and of the Army, General Viljoen and Lieutenant-General J.J. Geldenhuys respectively), this group is arguably the most professionally advanced in local military history. Since the international isolation of South Africa has also produced a whole new generation of officers bred in local military institutions of higher learning where they are exposed to a diversity of indigenous and imported civil–military values other than the traditional British model, it is realistic to expect that the new aggregate of military professionals will approach society and politics with a mixture of military idioms neither fully 'liberal' nor purely 'kommando'.

The technocratization of the current officer corps is, of course, not synonymous with liberalization: indeed, as numerous military sociologists have noted, in the standard military technocracy 'the entire notion of "inputs" into the political system – the human supports, demands and mobilization stemming from authentic political parties, interest groups, ideologies and even myths – is virtually ignored in an exclusive concentration on "correct" policies, "rational" decisions, and a "good image" abroad'.[10] Nevertheless there is considerable concordance between the present perceptual and operating style of the South African military and the executive arm of government which stems directly from a common technocratic-managerial approach to decision-making and social problem-solving. While primordial considerations may still inform the attitudes and behaviour of both the military and executive elites, the presence in each of men with common interests in rationality, efficiency and streamlined administration makes for highly effective and mutual communication. Prime Minister Botha's emphasis on high-power management techniques and administrative controls in the process of resolving social and institutional tensions strikes a very responsive chord among the new breed of top soldiers. The top soldiers in their turn are increasingly becoming a sociological mirror of the new type of civil Afrikaner – increasingly urban, pragmatic and free of the tenuous bonds of ethnic affiliation. It is out of these ingredients that political bonds are formed between the military and the executive in a fashion which reflects deeper movements in Afrikaner political culture.

Today the South African military is at that delicate and confounding point in its political development where its officer corps is torn between tradition and the political impulses generated by contemporary events. On the one hand changes in leadership composition against the background of Namibia are propelling the military towards a more active and participant role in politics and the formation of state policy; on the other, the military has no real tradition or experience of political involvement with the understandable result that it approaches the world of civil politics with considerable circumspection and due caution. In every society the military is to some extent wary of the Byzantine world of civilian politics so sharply distinguishable from the world of the soldier with its clearly articulated structures and hierarchically determined systems of authority. This is no less the case in South Africa where the officer corps views the political realm as hostile and unfamiliar, where there is considerable awareness of the incipient ability of political involvement to disrupt the unity of purpose and identity in military institutions, and where the political experience gleaned from Namibia is still considered by many top military officials as insufficient to support a more distinct political commitment by the Defence Force in the domestic South African environment. The top officers are also deeply sensitive to the 'moral barrier' between civil and military society arising from the fact that the historical experience of South Africa is basically hostile to the accumulation of political power by the military. South Africa is not readily comparable with the variety of Iberian states where frequent military intervention in the political process has been elevated to the status of an accepted and institutionalized means for the transfer of power. The South African officer corps continues to tread relatively lightly in the political realm for fear of having its actions labelled illegitimate.

In these circumstances it is misplaced to see the Defence Force as eagerly waiting in the wings of the political process, straining at the bit in anticipation of political power. The level of political self-confidence in the Defence Force simply does not support this conclusion. In addition, the tentative movements of the military into the social and political process have generated considerable resistance on the part of various segments of the white elite with institutional stakes in limiting the accumulation of political power by the military. This process, with its tendency to create both moral and material disincentives to militarization, adds to the ambiguity with which the soldiers approach politics. Yet the South African military is not entirely firm in its resistance to political pressures – were this the case the militarization of South African society would not be proceeding apace. Indeed, in a manner analogous to other politically pressured militaries in various parts of the world, a good proportion of its time and energy is devoted to the task of justifying its growing, if reluctant, political involvement – to an elite public unfamiliar with the concept of soldiers-as-politicians, and, no less importantly, to its own internal elements who have difficulty in reconciling political with professional commitments. Many professionalized militaries are uncomfortable with distinct political status: many (South Africa, for example) seek to rationalize their new roles and identities by developing social theories or proto-ideologies the basic purpose of which is to convey the image that the behaviour of the military is both professionally correct and motivated by the best interests of society. Indeed, as Alfred Stepan has pointed out, the growth of national development ideologies, the weaving together of military behaviour with social and political abstractions in the process of legitimating military movement into the civilian realm, is the crucial indicator of militaries on the road to accumulating political influence and capital.[11]

Total strategy – the 'national' development ideology of the South African Defence Force – draws inspiration from a wide variety of historical and cultural sources. In tracing the intellectual origins of total strategy it is readily apparent that South African military leaders have imbibed deeply of the counter-revolutionary experiences of the United States in Vietnam, of the British in Malaya and of the French in both Algeria and Indo-China. At the same time, the ideological and strategic spirit of the South African military is particularly and peculiarly Francophile in character and if there is any single figure whose writings have had a formative influence in how the current generation of Defence Force leaders interpret the world in relation to counter-insurgency, it is above all the French general, André Beaufre, whose various works are at the basis of virtually every lecture at the Joint Defence College – the primary institution for socializing South Africa's military elite, one of the main contact points for communication between government, the private sector and the state security apparatus, and, since the early seventies, the think-tank for the formation and development of South Africa's total strategy. The term 'total strategy' is taken directly from Beaufre's *An Introduction to Strategy* described by the distinguished military historian Liddell Hart as 'the most comprehensive and carefully formulated treatise on strategy ... that has appeared in this generation'.[12] Indeed, when one looks at total strategy in depth and in relation to Beaufre's writings, it appears to have very little intellectual content independent of these writings, very little authenticity of its own. Total strategy, we would contend, is essentially Beaufre writ large in the particular counter-revolutionary context of contemporary South Africa.

In these circumstances, the political behaviour of the South African military in relation to total strategy requires an extended excursion into Beaufre's writings, an in-depth analysis of the basic conceptions behind his cardinal statement that strategy is always 'the art of applying force so that it makes the most effective contribution towards achieving the ends set by political policy'.[13] These conceptions, which are fed into the minds of South African officers in the course of their exposure to the Joint Defence College and other institutions of military learning, are essentially three in number. In the first place, Beaufre's understanding of strategy is basically idealistic within the framework of the original definition stated above: while it accords due significance to the role of material factors in the 'art of applying force', it ultimately reduces all forms of strategy, warfare and social conflict to what Beaufre describes as a 'dialectic of wills [where] a decision is achieved when a certain psychological effect has been produced on the enemy: when he becomes convinced that it is useless to start or alternatively to continue the struggle'.[14] Tactics, traditionally the art of utilizing weapons to maximize impact, and logistics, the science of supply and *matériel* movement, are integral to all strategic outcomes, but in the last analysis the interplay of material factors, the use of technique and equipment, is ancillary to the fundamental clash of wills, the 'art of the dialectic of two opposing wills using force to resolve their dispute'.[15] The emphasis placed on the psychological surrender of the enemy as a precondition to his material defeat is complemented by the second pillar in Beaufre's conceptual model, namely his emphasis on war as an inevitably total and all-embracing phenomenon under the technological and structural circumstances of the contemporary age. The nature of warfare, as noted by numerous theorists, has undergone basic transformation during the course of the twentieth century: its time-scale has lengthened with the broadening of theatres of operations and extensions in the lead time required for the production of supporting material resources; the qualitative aspects of resources have largely displaced the available quantity of resources as decisive strategic criteria; and the concept of manoeuvre has become progressively more abstract as warfare has become a grand contest between opposing industrial and scientific potentials rather than a matter of movement involving military formations. At the same time the major implications for the strategic calculus of each of these changes in the modern age is superseded above all by the fact that warfare has become a total form of social interaction, breaking free of its essential military boundaries as modern societies move to higher and more intense levels of internal and external interdependence. This totalization of warfare is not of course absolutely exclusive to the current age: warfare has never been entirely monopolized by military action, every past war contains economic, diplomatic, ideological and political components and traditional strategy accepts this as an unavoidable fact in its various recipes for different military situations. Today, however, interdependence between the military and non-military components of warfare is at a premium in an intrinsically interdependent world where it is impossible to separate the political, economic, ideological and military realms under the universally destructive purview of the nuclear umbrella. The nation which continues to view warfare through a purely or basically military prism, according to Beaufre, is strategically defective and disadvantaged in the face of an opponent who appreciates the coherency of effective strategic action and who is able to weld his military and non-military capabilities into an integrated programme. Total onslaughts of this type demand total counter-strategies, not in the traditional sense of coordinated military action on land, sea and in the air, but coordinated in the sense of aligning military policy with political policy, with foreign policy, financial policy, economic policy and production. Inasmuch as total strategy represents a form of search behaviour, its purpose is to identify actions outside the military field which render assistance to military action. Military action is, in turn, only a single component of strategic action in the total mode of operations where 'action is total and ... must prepare ... and exploit the results expected from military operations by suitable operations in the psychological, political, economic and diplomatic fields. Total strategy in the "direct mode" consists of the planning and conduct of this whole range of actions'.[16] This emphasis on the so-called 'direct mode' of strategic action raises the third and final component at the centre of Beaufre's formulation, namely that, under prevailing conditions of interdependence, the lines which traditionally distinguish war and peace are no longer absolute. Warfare 'in the old style', that is, 'by military forces with drums beating and colours flying' is, according to Beaufre, 'a curiosity'.[17] Indeed, contemporary warfare is of two distinct types, involving either direct confrontation between conventional military forces in a specific geographic area of operations (what Beaufre terms 'total strategy in the direct mode') or 'total strategy in the indirect mode' where contestants manoeuvre for advantage on a broad social plane and where the brute actualities of military combat are only one more direct dimension of the competitive process. To use Beaufre's descriptive terminology, war today can be waged in two 'keys', the major, the direct mode, where the enemy is confronted head-on by force, the minor or indirect mode of total strategy, where confrontation is basically random and insidious and the medium of force more mediated. Yet while both idioms of conflict can be identified at various points in history and continue to exist side by side in a complementary manner, today there is a distinct tendency towards warfare waged in the minor key – through indirect strategy. Warfare, to use another of Beaufre's metaphors, is currently more a matter of infection than surgery: 'old style warfare with its battles was a sort of bloody surgical operation. The new style war with its nuances is more analogous to the creeping infection of an illness.'[18] Indeed, as cold war supplants hot war, as mankind recoils from the full use of his destructive potential to explore the more devious channels for conflict 'total strategy in the indirect mode is probably the strategy of the future'.[19]

Much of Beaufre's effort is geared to exploring this 'strategy of the future' particularly towards bringing its various manifestations (guerrilla warfare, insurgency, revolutionary warfare and wars of liberation) into line with contemporary developments in warfare and international relations. Drawing on his own personal experiences with the French army in Algeria and Indo-China, Beaufre devotes considerable attention to the variety of military and non-military techniques used in the indirect mode of total strategy and to the various major forms of interaction conceivably taken in this 'minor' form of strategic interaction. Thus he makes the point that effective indirect strategy required a mixture of subtle and brutal technical ingredients ranging from the construction of moral coalitions to blunt counter-terror, while distinguishing between the 'erosion manoeuvre' in indirect action (where the enemy is progressively worn down through a long process of attrition involving the minimal application of scarce resources), and the so-called 'piecemeal' or 'salami manoeuvre' where his material and psychological resources are chipped or gnawed away in small successive stages. He also persistently distinguishes between indirect and direct total strategy in the process of stating his case in favour of each as specific action types. While both have the common objective of seeking to enlarge freedom of action to the material and psychological detriment of the enemy, the means that each utilize are quite different. In the direct mode outcomes are determined through military confrontation: in the indirect mode outcomes are realized through manoeuvre and methods not necessarily determined by the immediate demands of military victory. In practice indirect strategy amounts to a 'tough form of negotiation' whose aim is less to force the actual capitulation of the enemy than it is 'to suggest to him that he should consider as a possible compromise a solution which accords with our political objectives'.[20] In addition, while direct total strategy takes place through 'interior manoeuvre' (by actions taken or not taken in the local crucible or zone of military interaction in accord with the precepts of guerrilla warfare developed by Mao, Lenin or Guevara) it is in the 'exterior manoeuvre' (in the policy realm beyond the boundaries of immediate military interaction) that the decisive actions and decisions are formulated and applied. Thus while conventional warfare is determined within a specific geographic field of battle, the real game of indirect warfare is played on the 'external' front, in the way that antagonists exploit the hearts and minds of whole peoples, in their relative moral fibre, on the broad terrain of society and economy where each seeks to exploit the structural vulnerabilities of the other. Lastly, and perhaps most importantly, indirect and direct strategy differ in their appreciation of the relationship between force and intellect in the context of warfare. All strategic modes, according to Beaufre, can be classified by virtue of the preponderant value assigned to force. In the direct mode it is force which is decisive: in indirect strategy however 'grey matter takes over from brute force'.[21] In the latter idiom, force is not eliminated: it plays a role in setting the touchlines of the battlefield and exploiting situations of manoeuvre. In the last analysis, however, it is the relative and reciprocal intelligence of the adversaries which is critical in determining the dialectic of wills, the way that each creatively and efficiently deploys his material and non-material resources rather than their respective net quantities.

The importance attributed to 'grey matter' in indirect strategy is one of the hallmarks of Beaufre's writings with their emphasis on strategy as an intrinsically non-material dialectic of wills. 'War', as the distinguished French general understands it, is 'little more than a mathematical check on the efficiency of preparations made':[22] because indirect warfare is an 'infection' or 'disease [which] must be taken early' under conditions characterized by the 'galloping advance of science', victory accrues to the contestant in the more advanced state of preparation.[23] In contrast to earlier times where strategy was a question of 'putting into practice' in accord with the evolving nature of military equipment, 'preparation is now of more consequence than execution':[24] no longer is the strategic calculus a matter of tactics and the possession of resources – rather it depends on the preventative deployment of resources, on dynamic action initiated prior to the outbreak of hostilities, based on careful research and constantly reviewed in the light of changing situations and organizational priorities. The strategist in the indirect mode 'is like a surgeon called upon to operate on a sick person who is growing continuously and with extreme rapidity and of whose detailed anatomy he is not sure: his operating table is in a state of perpetual motion and he must have ordered the instruments he is to use five years beforehand'.[25] Effective strategic action in the indirect mode also demands careful coordination between national strategy and national policy. While Beaufre does not explicitly argue for the subordination of the political and civil task of policy-making to the military task of devising strategy, he nevertheless sees the traditional pattern of civil–military functional distinctions as increasingly redundant under the conditions of modern total warfare. In replacing 'the intuitions and approximations which have so far been the rule in the traditional conduct of that which has served as strategy' by scientific exactitude it is important to recognize the artificiality of this division for most practical purposes.[26] The business of determining policy objectives and allocating resources may continue to be the prerogative of civil authority but if total strategy is to succeed, in either of its two manifestations, there must be 'continuous osmosis between policy and strategy' with a greater degree of interchangeability in the roles of soldiers and politicians.[27] If strategy is to be 'a fund of learning growing continuously with each generation'[28] it can no longer be the pure preserve of the military, and policy the preserve of the politician. Planning finally includes tactical selection geared to the 'interior manoeuvre' and dictated by the variable factors of time, material and moral force. At this juncture Beaufre proceeds to a discussion of conventional counter-insurgency techniques through which indirect strategy may be put into operation in the actual zone of military confrontation.

It is important to any understanding of the political consequences of Beaufre's doctrines for military behaviour that he does not see preventative planning, the coordination of strategy and policy, or the selection of counter-insurgency tactics as sufficient in themselves to set the course of strategic interaction. Each is a necessary component of the eventual strategic outcome, but the ultimate determinant lies in the 'exterior manoeuvre', in the *mélange* of military and non-military actions taken in the broad social arena surrounding the limited setting of military conflict. Reasoning from his idealist conception of strategy Beaufre additionally argues that the touchstone to strategy lies in the minds of men, in their conceptions of material progress and social justice, in the collection of religious, national and cultural ideals which have motivated non-rational behaviour since the sixteenth century. In the contemporary ideological age, Beaufre argues, it is not material military force which fuels the strategy of warfare, but psychological action which paves the way for military action as a means to resolve the process of strategic contestation. In these circumstances it is not only 'total' action in the 'exterior manoeuvre' which is decisive, but, more specifically, action on the wider plane, nationally or internationally, which twists the psychological balance between the contesting forces. To the extent that the enemy can be psychologically weakened he is deprived of the moral and material resources necessary to continue waging conflict. Ultimately it is the 'moral disintegration of the enemy [which] causes him to accept the conditions it is desired to impose upon him'.[29] In the indirect mode of total strategy, where force is a factor held to the minimum, 'all depends upon correct appraisal of the psychological keyboard and correct exploitation of the great emotional currents which can cause one side to act and the other to capitulate'.[30] The effective implementation of total strategy in these circumstances requires that national opinion be politically and psychologically prepared well before the actual initiation of hostilities, that the morale of the population and those fighting be raised and kept constant at all times, and that nation and army be physically and psychologically knit together in order to withstand enemy attempts to build psychological counter-pressure. It follows in this situation where the 'only true success is psychological success'[31] that the instruments of psychological warfare exceed simple firepower in strategic status.

One critical if final point needs to be made before proceeding to apply Beaufre's strategic formulation to the specific behaviour of the South African military. Beaufre constantly reiterates the importance of rooting psychological action in the exterior manoeuvre in a 'political line' or 'theme' whose internal images, symbols and metaphors can be manipulated to create that 'irrisistible avalanche-like advance ... discouraging resistance and amassing goodwill' at both the national and international levels of conflict.[32] If total strategy is to succeed in simultaneously developing the crucial moral fibre of the state and eroding the moral fibre of its opponents, it must therefore be packaged in a well-reasoned ideology consonant with the dominant emotions of the population it desires to spur to action and capable of publicly exploiting the vulnerabilities and contradictions of the enemy programme in a way which saps his popular support, his political motivation and his willpower. Since 'restriction of the use of force must be balanced by the magnitude of the psychological repercussions',[33] in the indirect mode of strategy in particular, 'choice of the political line to be followed is therefore a decision fundamental to the success of the entire operation.'[34] It follows that total strategy requires those whose task it is to formulate strategy, that is, the soldiers, to become, at least in part, political analysts – if not to set policy goals then at least to identify the junctures where popular beliefs and sentiments are translatable into operation strategy. This is the essence of Beaufre's vitally important statement that:

[The] strategy of action must be considered in its political and social context. Action takes place in the midst of events and sets out to cause some event to occur. We can do nothing, therefore, unless we understand the events in which we propose to intervene and the forces which will act or react to the furtherance or hindrance of the action envisaged. *The concept of strategic action, therefore, necessarily stems from political analysis.*[35] [my emphasis]

Indeed, he continues in his injunctions to his military readership:

[The object of the political line] must be to deprive the enemy of his trump cards. There are two facets to this: we must first maintain and increase our prestige, not merely by showing that we have adequate force available but also by showing that the future we hold out has possibilities (progress of our civilization, international aid, etc.); secondly, *by thoroughgoing reforms we must cut the ground from under the feet of the malcontents.*[36] [my emphasis]

Whether these precepts are absorbed literally, uncritically and *in toto* by South African officers brought into contact with Beaufre's writings during the course of their organizational socialization cannot be proved in any absolute empirical fashion. Nor do Beaufre's theories on counter-revolutionary warfare constitute the intellectual sum total of South Africa's own 'total strategy' which is in many ways a distillation of various contemporary ideas governing counter-insurgency drawn from both European and American sources.[37] These are in turn fed through the prism of South African conditions where they are informed by the thinking of a variety of individuals and organizations outside the military framework. The resulting 'total strategy' is, as we have already noted, a syncretistic formulation blending peculiarly South African conceptions of the social and political world with a variety drawn from imported foreign sources, and put together by soldiers, civilian technocrats, government officials, academics and virtually anyone else in the general public with knowledge to contribute to the strategic issues of the day. It would also be wrong to attribute to the South African military the degree of intellectual endeavour brought by some militaries to the development of institutional ideologies or programmes for national security, either in their strategic role or as a precursor to legitimating the seizure of political power. Stepan, for example, notes that, prior to its coup of 1964, the Brazilian military 'went about the study of all phases of Brazilian political, economic and social life'. In the top institutions of military learning 'the colonels and the low-ranking generals studied inflation, agrarian reform, banking reform, voting systems, transportation and education as well as guerrilla warfare and conventional warfare. In many of their studies some of the funda-mental aspects of Brazilian social and economic organizations were severely challenged as needing change if Brazil was to grow economically and maintain national security'.[38] This is not paralleled in the South African case where the higher strata in the military hierarchy have not as yet applied themselves with comparable intensity to a full-blown, sys-tematic and detailed analysis of the multivariate aspects of the South African political system, the culture and the economy. The importance attributed by Beaufre's total strategy to political diagnosis has undoubtedly prompted the staff and individual participants in Joint Defence College activity to undertake some preliminary investigations of the local social and political framework with an eye to devising plans to secure the future safety of the state. However, it would be wrong to conclude that these germinal efforts constitute a tightly integrated design for South Africa along the lines suggested by the most vehement critics of the Republic's brand of total strategy. The total strategy of the South African military is actually far less coherent, less internally integrated and considerably less conspiratorial than at first appears to be the case. If many of the top officers experience difficulty in precisely identifying the features of their own total strategy apart from some loose and often caricatured concepts of the workings of domestic and international society, it is exactly because South Africa's total strategy is still basically viscerotonic, more of a mood composed of imperfectly linked semi-developed ideas than a sophisticated and carefully articulated formula for the direction of society.

In analysing the content of the rhetoric, statements and official pronouncements of the South African military it is nonetheless clear that there is *a* total strategy, however amorphous its features, and that *the* total strategy enunciated by Beaufre has found a very receptive audience in local military circles. There can be no doubt that the intellectual element of the SADF as well as their civilian counterparts working within the logic of total strategy have absorbed the totalist and embracing spirit of counter-revolutionary action at the centre of Beaufre's programme. In these circles the ostensible onslaught against South Africa is total and 'instigated by monolithic organizations ... in absolute control of all the means available to their states'.[39] The appropriate response of all South Africans concerned with the safety of the state should therefore be total ('total onslaught'), to use the conventional terminology of the SADF, demands 'total involvement') and it logically follows that the means to defend the state must be similarly all-encompassing in strategic nature. While it is difficult to sustain objectively the notion of a 'total onslaught' on South Africa,[40] the triumvirate of 'totalities' ('total strategy', 'total onslaught' and, more recently, 'total involvement') appear with persistent and monotonous regularity in virtually every significant public speech by contemporary military, and to a lesser extent, governmental leaders. Countering the internal and external enemies of South Africa, according to representative official Department of Defence documents, demands 'the involvement of the entire nation in the maintenance of law and order and in the defence of the Republic of South Africa.'[41] Defence, in its turn, 'is not a matter for the Defence Force only, but also for each department and citizen: it demands dedication, vigilance and sacrifice – not only from the Defence Force, but from all who are privileged to find a home in this country'.[42] In a fashion distinctly reminiscent of Beaufre's interpretation of change in post-World War II warfare and international relations, SADF official papers note that the 'maintenance of the sovereignty of a state's authority has, through the evolution of warfare, shifted from a purely military to an integrated national action'. Hence, the resolution of conflict 'in the times in which we live demands interdependent and coordinated action in all fields – military, psychological, economic, political, sociological, technological, diplomatic, ideological, cultural etc'.[43] In the last analysis the total strategy formulated through South Africa's State Security Council means 'the comprehensive plan to utilize all the means available to the state according to an integrated pattern in order to achieve the national aims within the framework of specific policies'.[44] Total strategy is therefore 'not confined to a particular sphere, but is applicable to all levels and all functions of the state structure'.[45] Strategy à la Beaufre is also a matter of revision and advanced planning: it is 'not something constant [but] must be adapted to changing situations in respect of, for example, the threat, manpower potential, the financial climate, domestic or foreign policy'.[46]

The nature of the threat confronting the state in South Africa is analogous to the indirect challenge to state authority discussed by Beaufre and, in local military (and civil) opinion intimately tied up with the global ideological struggle. While growing Eastern bloc involvement in the southern African region has raised the spectre of direct military confrontation between South African forces and local or foreign surrogates of the communist world in the minds of military planners, the SADF's views on revolution and conflict are still predominantly informed by the belief that the internal and external enemies of South Africa do not in themselves possess the human and material resources to confront the state directly. The so-called 'total onslaught' is therefore seen as an essentially indirect and surrogate affair where Cubans or East Germans acting as auxiliaries for the African nationalist movements engage in the 'erosion' or 'salami' manoeuvres described by Beaufre, chipping away at the territory of the state or waging a war of attrition through which the ability of the state to defend itself in a psychologically or physically effective manner is eroded over a prolonged period. At the same time the South African military reflects the almost paranoid concern of white opinion with Marxism, communism or, of late, the activities of Soviet imperialism on the African continent. Virtually every public exposition of total strategy by the military and governmental authorities is replete with the crudest of imagery and symbols linking all forms of internal disorder and regional inter-state conflict to communist machinations or the presence of Marxist agitators in one devious form or another. In a redundant fashion reminiscent of the Cold War at its coldest, the United Nations arms embargo on South Africa is, from the point of view of total strategy, the result of a communist plot engineered directly from Moscow or orchestrated through anti-South African elements within the Republic, throughout the Third World – the so-called 'Afro-Asian bloc' – or black states on the African continent. The efforts of local African nationalists to promote political change, the expulsion of colonialism in the territories adjacent to South Africa, indeed, the entire international abomination of the apartheid system is in one way or another attributed to Soviet attempts to seize South Africa as the strategic jewel of Africa.[47] In such circumstances the aims, intentions and objectives of African nationalism, Soviet foreign policy and Pan-Africanism are indistinguishably and simplistically reduced to a virtually nonsensical and distorted hotch-potch. One might dismiss this as absurd were it not characteristic of the way in which the military and governmental leaders of one of Africa's most powerful states view the social and political environment of their continent. Thus the 'strategies, policies and aims of the Republic of South Africa's enemies' include 'the expansion of Marxism by fomenting revolution in Southern Africa', 'the overthrow of the white regimes in Southern Africa so that the militant African bloc can realize its aspirations with regard to the destruction of so-called colonialism and racialism and the establishment of Pan-Africanism' and action 'in order to unleash revolutionary warfare in Southern Africa and, by means of isolation, to force the Republic of South Africa to change its domestic policy in favor of Pan-Africanism'. The Arab bloc 'with certain exceptions' – most notably South Africa's oil suppliers – can also 'be regarded as the patrons of the African bloc in its hostile actions as far as these serve its own purposes'.[48]

Total strategy as it is understood in South Africa then proceeds from this peculiar diagnosis of the South African condition to a series of apparent prescriptions whose purpose is ostensibly to inoculate local society against the infection of internal revolutionary warfare as articulated by Beaufre. In the first place, as clearly evidenced in the official statements of the military, the SADF has absorbed one of the main pillars of Beaufre's theory, namely, that effective strategy in the indirect mode of action places a premium on the coordination of political and military authority. While the South African military does not necessarily see itself as a more effective instrument of social change than civil leadership (in the way that impelled the Peruvian officer corps under Velasco to seize political power),[49] it is similar in that total strategy arises from the pervasive if often unarticulated belief among the higher-ranking South African officers that the country is caught up in a long-term and quite fundamental crisis which threatens both the white state and the corporate interests of the military as an integral element of the racial state structure. The antidote to this situation is seen to lie as much, if not more, in the political as in the military realm. Hence the statement repeated *ad nauseum* by South African military leaders that the solution to the country's problems is '20 per cent military and 80 per cent political'. In practice, the preferences of the South African soldiers run in the direction of carefully coordinated action, much along the lines prescribed by Beaufre and characterized by Stepan as 'the single symphony' by which militaries integrate energies and resources against the threats that confront them.[50] Today the SADF advocates as an essential component of national defence and total strategy 'coordinated action between all government departments, governmental institutions and other authorities to counter the multi-dimensional onslaught against the Republic of South Africa in the ideological, military, economic, social, psychological, cultural, political and diplomatic fields'.[51] National security demands coordination on 'political action, military/para-military action, economic action, psychological action, scientific and technical action, religious–cultural action, manpower services, intelligence services, security services, national supplies, resources and production services, transport and distribution services, financial services, community services and telecommunications services'.[52]

This emphasis on a coordinated total effort has extremely important implications for the organization of the political system and the role of the military within it. The SADF is careful to emphasize the predominance of civil authority in instituting and operating total strategy: the function of the Defence Force in the grand design is explicitly 'directed by Parliament ... [and] defined by the Defence Act'.[53] At the same time it is quite apparent that the range of social activities falling within the realm of total strategy as defined by the military leaders leaves very little room for individuality or civil liberty as understood in democratically organized society. Militaries, on the whole, have scant respect for these values: as hierarchical-bureaucratic organizations with a Hobbesian view of man, military institutions are normally impatient with the articulation of individual or group interests and tend to favour centralized government and strong planning by the public sector over pluralism and mobilization politics.[54] If the tone and content of total strategy is any indication of military preferences, then the South African military seem no exception to the rule that soldiers are more comfortable with social administration than government, with the concentration of power within a framework of managerial activism rather than its dispersion on a negotiable democratic basis. Indeed, top officials in the SADF have gone so far as to concede publicly that there is a fundamental and irresolvable conflict between the requirements of total strategy and those of democratic government. However, the coordinative and all-embracing features of total strategy also provide the foundations for the military to rationalize and legitimize an expanded role for itself in the new integrated pattern of social and political development. While the emphasis is on joint action by the civil and military authorities, it is not insignificant nor a matter of slipshod terminology that the emerging national security plan is labelled 'total strategy' rather than 'total policy'. This highlights the predominance of the strategic dimension, that is, the functional area where the military enjoys a monopoly of expertise and experience. In these circumstances, much as in various Latin American countries where the military has manipulated its own national development plans to carve out a political constituency, it can be anticipated that the SADF will move into a variety of social roles beyond the conventional task of implementing national security policy.[55]

The SADF's conventional functions are also influenced, however, by Beaufre's precepts, particularly his emphasis on dynamic strategy in the 'interior manoeuvre' (in the zone of actual military confrontation). The help offered to the 'independent' homelands in developing their own security forces to act in conjunction with those of the Republic and, above all, increased SADF operations across South Africa's international boundaries (in Angola, Mozambique, Zimbabwe and, most recently, Lesotho) reflect the notion that if counter-revolutionary strategy in the indirect mode is to be effective it must not only deter but actually eliminate enemy resources situated in external sanctuaries. Since the Angolan invasion of 1976 the Defence Act has been amended so that the Defence Force is now not only 'capable of operating in any part of the Republic of South Africa' but also in 'neighboring states'.[56] As the geographical noose tightens around the Republic it can be anticipated that pre-emptive or retaliatory SADF strikes across regional boundaries will increase in both size and number. The intellectual progenitors and planners of total strategy are not however insensitive to the importance attributed by Beaufre to 'exterior manoeuvre' under conditions of indirect warfare – to the series of actions on the broad social plane distinct from the immediate scene of military confrontation. As we shall demonstrate in far greater detail in the following chapter, the basic shifts in civil–military boundaries over the last twenty years are a direct result of the military moving out of the barracks into society in order to put into operation the 'exterior' function as described in Beaufre's writings. The militarization of South African society is in fact the logical consequence of Beaufre's assertion that, in indirect total strategy, 'it is the exterior manoeuvre which is decisive and it is here that our priority effort must be made'.[57] The value placed by the SADF on the spiritual as opposed to material preparedness of the nation is less the outgrowth of lingering mystical-religious feelings associated with the idea of 'the nation' than it is a reflection of Beaufre's decidedly more modern belief that registered psychological gains are central to the exterior manoeuvre in the ideological circumstances of contemporary warfare. The attention lavished by South African officers on John Dunn's *Modern Revolutions*, with its focus on the relationship between revolution and ideology, indicates that the local total strategists have clearly absorbed Beaufre's admonition that the dialectic of wills and ideas is central to the process by which contesting strategists explore each other's vulnerabilities as a means to enlarging their freedom of action.[58] The appreciation by the SADF that the news media are 'an essential link in the total strategy',[59] its frequently reported attempts to manipulate the press in the interests of promoting the image of the Defence Force, its 'civic guidance' programme for internal and external consumption, and its concern with the paramilitary training of white youth through the cadet system are some of the multiple manifestations of the military's belief that ideas are as potent as weapons in the conduct of counter-revolutionary warfare.

Ideological manipulation, as Beaufre points out, depends on the pre-existence of a definite and consistent 'political line'. No indirect conflict can be successfully concluded unless military action is linked to a specific political cause whose visible exploitation is the means to mobilize the supporters and potential supporters of the state (both within and beyond its boundaries) and to discredit the actions of those presuming to seize state power. This dictum has important implications for the manner in which the SADF enters the political arena and for the way it operates, once having established itself there. Officially, military and government pro-nouncements take pride in the independence of South Africa, in its ability to maintain moral strength and authenticity in shaping its internal policies despite the intrusion of international opinion and in its capacity to develop the material resources to withstand anti-apartheid pressure conducted on a virtually global basis. Unofficially however both the SADF and Nation-alist leadership is aware of the importance of international support in upholding some variant of the present system. This importance is increased in the light of Beaufre's injunction that the outcome of indirect wars are almost always determined by the level and commitment of external assistance. The tendency of total strategy to raise the ceiling of coercion and to streamline apartheid along cooptive lines is at least partially attributable to the desire of the white elite to redefine the pattern of state control along more benevolent lines for international consump-tion. The military itself is inclined to break down the world community into three reasonably distinct categories separate from each other accord-ing to their respective relations with South Africa: the hostile powers (the Soviets, their international communist supporters and most members of the Afro-Asian 'bloc' concerned with the revolutionary transformation of the Republic); the potentially friendly states (mainly Western powers with a cultural and historical tradition similar to that of South Africa, but also including a number of Latin American and Asian countries of decidedly conservative persuasion); and a 'remainder' group, a motley collection of states whose feelings towards South Africa run neither in a markedly hostile nor in a markedly sympathetic direction. Inasmuch as total strategy is geared to foreign as well as domestic policy purposes, the latter two groups, particularly the Western states in the second category, are singled out as targets for a barrage of pro-South African propaganda which if not necessarily involving direct action by the Defence Force certainly enjoys its most enthusiastic backing. Part of this public relations exercise involves projecting the 'positive' features of South African society through official diplomatic channels and front organizations established among busi-nessmen, sportsmen and community leaders in Britain, Western Europe and the United States (who for a variety of motivations have a direct interest in maintaining links with South Africa). The result is that not only the local Department of Foreign Affairs and Information but also a variety of otherwise perfectly respectable if conservative-leaning overseas groups and individuals become wittingly or unwittingly incorporated into the embracing total strategy network. As exponents of the view that apartheid is redundant and South Africa is moving consistently in the direction of structural reform these elements become important pawns in the broader process of exterior manoeuvre. The thrust of total strategy in this direction is however basically ideological and emotive rather than cerebral, rational and persuasive. Indeed, as it has become increasingly difficult to market South Africa except in the most gullible of international circles, total strategy in its external propaganda role has become increasingly reliant on the manipulation of virulent ideological symbols and metaphors related to the anti-communist struggle. Today, in a manner which seems to indicate a growing predominance of the military over civil diplomats in setting the style if not the actual substance of South African communications directed abroad, the Republic's leaders seem less concerned with winning potential friends and influencing neutral people through educative persuasion than through attracting allies by exploiting the most elementary of their political instincts and anxieties. Thus it is no longer a question of supporting South Africa because its elite is sincerely pursuing reform or because its geographic location and mineral resources are strategically significant: rather it is that if the potential friends of South Africa do not proffer support they will be failing in their attempt to halt the world-wide spread of materialistic, atheistic repressive communism.

The military and civil formulators of total strategy are sufficiently acute to realize that effective ideological manipulation requires a material foundation which lends concrete support, immediacy and vitality to the images and symbols in the propaganda armoury. This is particularly important where the credibility of psychological tools is at issue, either on the part of the international community, most of whose constituent elements are not readily persuaded by the South African cause, or on the part of the domestic public – the Indians, Coloureds, blacks and some white fringe groups upon whom rabid anti-communism does not resonate productively or easily. Beaufre has also emphasized the unity and coherency of strategy, that is, the complementarity between interior and exterior action, between practical and psychological strategic objectives, all of which combine to influence the outcome of the competitive calculus. There is strong support in both military and governmental circles for the view that if total strategy is to succeed at all in mobilizing domestic and external resources behind the state it cannot confine itself to rarified ideological action. Since interior and exterior action must be consistent it is important that the psychological devices employed internationally be simultaneously projected inward in the task of consolidating domestic opinion in support of the state. The result is that the average South African living in the era of total strategy is subject to the same ideological barrage as his counterparts over the national borders – except for the critical difference that he is far less favourably placed to erect cognitive barriers to the superficially persuasive arguments, metaphors and symbols of total strategy than his counterparts beyond South Africa's borders. More importantly however, the success of total strategy depends on material policy actions which crystallize the links between people and state on the widest possible basis and which exploit the vulnerabilities of those seeking to overthrow the state before their local and international audience. It is the so-called 'national political policy' of the Defence Force to 'lead the homelands of the Republic of South Africa to self-determination and independence'.[60] This is compatible with stated government policy: yet it is also perfectly in line with the unstated and more insidious intention of total strategy to separate the political aspirations of urban and rural blacks, to elevate the former to reserve elite status on the farther fringes of a white-dominated coalition of racial minorities (white, Indian and Coloured), and to isolate the latter in a system of compliant authority dependent upon the charity and patience of central decision-makers in white Pretoria. The military is, on the whole, peculiarly fascinated with the notion of separation, not necessarily on the traditional basis of separation between the races, but rather between those individuals and groups constituting the 'democratic opposition' (elements unconcerned with the drastic reformulation of South African society irrespective of race) and those aiming their activities at revolutionary change, once again irrespective of their racial origins and affiliations. Since it is calculated that neither the Indian nor Coloured minorities is likely to throw in its lot with the preponderant black majority – at least in the long-term – the political and economic advancement of these two communities has become an integral part of the attempt of total strategy to wean the maximum number of adherents into the state coalition. Thus it is specific Defence Force policy to 'further Coloured and Indian interests by the creation of their own governmental bodies and, by the establishment of constitutional machinery, to serve matters and actions of communal interest'.[61] Whether the same cooptive logic applies to the urban black population, particularly its small but influential middle-class segment, remains one of the crucial aspects of South African politics which will be dealt with in more detail below.

The appearance of national development strategies in military ranks is, in general, an important indicator of their politicization, and soldiers, despite their inherent conservatism, are often among the first elements in society to recognize the need for structural reform.[62] Whether they act upon this recognition to press for public policies to alleviate the lot of the lower classes is, of course, another matter altogether. In general, proto-ideologies along total strategy lines tend in the direction of system maintenance and perpetuation of the status quo rather than system transformation.[63] This is particularly so in cases such as South Africa where – as we will consider in more detail below – the preservation of the corporate identity of the military is inextricably intertwined with the perpetuation of the established distribution of social power. There is, however, much in South African military history and in contemporary political experience perfectly congenial to the logic and spirit of total strategy as it has developed in local military and civil circles over the last fifteen years, which sets the framework for total strategy as we have described it and which, in the last analysis, generates the basic impulses behind the new strategic movement. Firstly, and above all, South Africa's total strategy is an instrument of counter-revolution designed by the political and security apparatus of a beleaguered racial elite confronted by a variety of structural pressures auguring a major transformation of its status should they in the fullness of time come to social fruition. Although the challenges to the white monopoly of power have assumed various different forms throughout the course of South African history, white resistance to any attempts by the majority to disturb this monopoly is a constant throughout the whole local historical experience. Much of South African history can be reduced to a series of strategies geared to the transcending objective of maintaining white minority power. The total strategy we see today has its spiritual and intellectual origins in the whole historical repertoire of state control, from the pass system instituted in the earliest days of white settlement, through the manipulation of black migrant labour in the process of industrialization, to the development of an intense and interpenetrating security apparatus in the last thirty-five years of Nationalist government. In many respects total strategy differs from previous exercises in white state control only by the sophistication of its means and the coherence with which they are woven together. It may be the most concerted counter-revolutionary package developed by the white elite in response to the current set of pressures, but its aims and objectives are far from historically unique in that they are consistent with the age-old determination of the minority to maintain predominant power.

Total strategy is also less perceptibly linked to the kommando theme in South African civil–military history even though, as we have already suggested, the contrasting 'liberal' model is more suitable as a device for describing contemporary civil–military relations. The technical thrust of total strategy is peculiarly a by-product of the modern age, of the inter-dependence between states, of the potency of ideas in an era of secularized politics and, in the last analysis, of the development of thermonuclear weapons of destruction to the point where direct confrontation between states becomes inconceivable. Yet the very 'totality' of total strategy echoes the age-old notion of the nation-in-arms attempting to protect its survival in accord with its cultural identity and ingrained historical ideals. This is particularly salient in the South African context where, as we have noted at some length, this very notion, expressed through the kommando, retains a certain vitality in Afrikaner circles even though it may no longer be possible to resurrect the idea of the 'citizen-soldier' in all its manifes-tations. Today, as one South African military authority notes in a study of the strategic potential of the kommando, it is absolutely unrealistic to view security as 'dependent ... on the horse and gun as our forefathers were in the open veld'.[64] 'Trained for conventional warfare through two world wars and with an older generation experienced in formalized soldiering on the European pattern' the military structure no longer lends itself, either practically or psychologically, to the loose and unconventional arrange-ments associated with kommando patterns of military action.[65] Yet the spiritual impulse of the kommando lies in circumstances of social isolation – of frontiersmen far from colonial authority, or Trekkers isolated in their fight for survival in the great interior reaches of South Africa – and the very same feelings of distance and threat have undoubtedly been regenerated as South Africa has been pushed to the margins of the global community. Many of the opponents of total strategy fail to appreciate this important historic and emotional dimension with its roots deep in the Afrikaner way of defining the social and political world. While they belabour total strategy for its incipient authoritarianism, for the threat it poses to civil liberty and for its emphasis on national coordination, they often fail to appreciate that the idea of the nation armed and in unity is entirely characteristic of the way the Afrikaner has traditionally confronted threats to his security through most of South African history.

The attractions of total strategy for the South African military and political elite also stem from more immediate and contemporary sources, many of which we have already identified in our preceding dissection of the underlying factors in civil–military boundary shifts occurring in recent years. As the experience of militaries other than the South African makes clear, search behaviour for proto-ideologies or national development programmes along total strategy lines are deeply influenced by military perceptions of regional and domestic political developments and by the need of soldiers to reduce to some sort of coherent formula their experi-ences in upholding the security of the state under dynamic conditions. In

Latin America, the success of the Cuban revolution and the subsequent appearance of a radical and mobilizing rhetoric in the political language of many states has been important in promoting the development of ideologies in the military institutions of many countries.[66] In South Africa, as the strategic noose has tightened and the military has been drawn into a more distinctly regional role, so the military (and the civil) authorities have become increasingly attentive to the ramifications and ideologies of contemporary global conflict. With subcontinental conflict defined as a partial expression of the wider conflict between East and West, military planners have been brought in touch with the currently fashionable doctrines of total, limited and internal war: inasmuch as operations in Namibia have thrown these various theories into bold and practical relief, SADF leaders have been stimulated in their search for concepts to weave the various strands of their regional experiences into some sort of integrated pattern or construct. Unlike many Latin American militaries, the South African Defence Force has not moved in the direction of articulating its own concepts of national development as a result of the belief that civil political groups are incompetent in their role as rulers and leaders of the country.[67] While the South African military may differ with the civil authorities on numerous technicalities of government, total strategy is not consonant with the appreciation of the civil sector, designating it as bankrupt in meeting political demands, internal security and the stresses of industrialization. Nor has the movement of the South African military towards total strategy been assisted by external forces with an eye to their own strategic interests. Thus one finds nothing in the South African case analogous to the Brazilian situation where, prior to 1964, United States military advisers actually established the national war college, designed its programme and assisted the officers in their thinking along counterinsurgency lines in a way which intensified their negative feelings towards civil authority.[68] On the contrary, as we have already noted, the increasing pariah status of South Africa since the end of World War II has resulted in a diminution in military links between the Republic and the outside world with a consequent reduction in the international exposure of her soldiers. The external world has nevertheless played an important role as a transmission belt for the total strategy concepts found in abundance in the network of local military institutions developed in the wake of South Africa's isolation, particularly since her departure from the Commonwealth. The SADF has long prided itself upon the use of 'available literature and the experience of others in irregular and highly mobile methods of warfare'[69] and since the severance of most of its practical and intellectual ties with the British military establishment in the early sixties it has become an active shopper on the international market, not only for arms and military technology, but also for strategic ideas and concepts adaptable to the indigenous military tradition and the escalating demands of the Namibian conflict.[70] Total strategy as understood by the contemporary South African military is, as already noted, a transplantation of French ideas on counter-insurgency drawn from the experiences of the French military in Indo-China and Algeria and filtered through Beaufre's conceptual spectacles. Since the French have also been active as arms suppliers to South Africa (the entire submarine fleet is French in origin), a fairly extensive pattern of direct contact has developed between the French and South African militaries despite the international arms embargo. The prime minister, P.W. Botha, visited France on one of his rare trips abroad, during 1975 in his capacity of Minister of Defence.[71] Similar trips have since been undertaken by numerous top members of the South African defence establishment. Since most have absorbed Beaufre's idealist view of strategy with its connotation of 'elan vital' some have undoubtedly come into contact with the idea of the military as 'la grande muette', an overarching arbitrator of developments in the social system.[72] While American literature on counter-insurgency abjures the totalist flavour of its French counterpart, the intellectual pedigree of total strategy also contains technical and programmatic elements drawn directly from United States experiences in combating communism in Latin America and Vietnam. It is perhaps not insignificant to the political role of the SADF that many of the Latin American coups of the sixties and seventies were initiated by officers trained at Fort Leavenworth or the Inter-American Defence College – both of which placed considerable emphasis on civic and political action by the military as a vital ingredient in the management of 'communist-inspired' internal warfare.[73] It is also perhaps not insignificant that the current Minister of Defence and previous Chief of the South African Defence Force, General Magnus Malan, is a Fort Leavenworth graduate – one of the few South African officers to have received American training. The South African military have also imbibed deeply, directly or indirectly, of the strategic experiences of both the Taiwanese and the Israelis in the course of their intentions to forge closer links between the internal community's pariah nations. The Taiwanese connection, in particular, is highly valued by South African officers by virtue of the small republic's unremitting struggle against communism since the first years of its formation. With the burgeoning of relations between Taiwan and South Africa under the P.W. Botha administration, numerous South African military personnel have visited the island adjacent to the Chinese mainland, including members of the SADF's military intelligence section – possibly the key internal institution for the dissemination of total strategy doctrines throughout the Defence

Force. Similar practical and intellectual ties exist between the South African and Israeli militaries: independent of exchanges in *matériel* and military technology, many South African officers take their cues from the Israelis in the process of putting total strategy into operation. Many wax enthusiastic over the organizational ability of the Israeli Defence Force in actively combating 'terrorism' and Israeli action against the PLO in her neighbouring territories is an important source of inspiration for the SADF pre-emptive strikes against ANC bases in Lesotho, Angola and Mozambique. The high regard in which the Israelis are held is doubtless reinforced by apparent links between the PLO and some of the black liberation movements active in Southern Africa.

The road to total strategy is also partially endogenous, the collection, collation and distribution of its internal components being the work of numerous institutions situated in the local context. In the first instance, the development of military ideologies and national development plans is always the result of communications across the civil–military divide, the effect of which is to sensitize the soldiers to patterns of social and political activity outside the realm of their normal role functions. Once again it is important to distinguish between the South African and other experiences: civilian business groups do not actively penetrate the military in an attempt to influence its officers as was the case in Brazil during the early sixties,[74] nor are civilians used as sources of specialized information with the same intensity as in United States institutions of higher military learning. The South African military is still very much a distinctive and encapsulated institution in its civil relations along the strict 'professional' lines described by Huntington.[75] At the same time as the liberal prototype of civil–military relations has come under pressure in recent years (and as civil–military boundaries have shifted), so the tendency towards involving civilian skills and information sources in the activities of such institutions as the Joint Defence College has proportionately accelerated. Today, the frequency with which 'outside' elements are invited to participate in seminars and lectures in the College is far more pronounced than in the recent past, partly because of organizational imperatives associated with the modernization of the Defence Force, partly because the current generation of officers is far more attuned to the value of specialized knowledge originating in non-military quarters than their predecessors. The result is a mutually reinforcing system for the communication of strategic and social information where top soldiers seek out civilian contacts in the logic of total strategy and are, in turn, confirmed in that logic by the 'total' conception of military action projected by civilian specialists. Growing threats to the state and public order have prompted an explosion of growth in the South African security industry and there are numerous private organizations which are today available to supply the Defence Force with practical advice on putting its total strategy into operation. The activities of these organizations are complemented by numerous institutions of higher learning and research who willingly or inadvertently assist the military in refining and developing its proto-ideology. The University of Stellenbosch is alone among South African universities in being formally linked to the SADF through its military science degree offered in conjunction with the Military Academy at Saldanha. (This was previously the function of the University of Pretoria prior to 1956 when the Academy moved from the Transvaal to the Cape Province.) Yet in virtually all of South Africa's universities there are political and strategic experts who are absorbed as sources of information and intellect into the military establishment through their research, their appearance before government commissions or, in some cases, in a contracted capacity for teaching or research purposes. This tendency to feed and articulate the mixture of myths and information upon which total strategy depends is particularly pronounced in the case of the Afrikaner universities and research organizations situated near Defence Force Head-quarters in the Pretoria–Johannesburg area. In this category would be included the Institute for Strategic Studies at the University of Pretoria, the Rand Afrikaans University, whose Department of Politics contains a former director of military intelligence, and the University of South Africa where a Citizen Force kommandant divides his time between academic work and lecturing to officers at the Joint Defence College.

With its syllabus saturated with total strategy conceptions the Joint Defence College is actually no exception to the general rule that national war colleges, from Latin America to Asia, play a primary role in the dissemination of national development strategies by military institutions.[76] The function of the College in inducting SADF members into total strategy is, however, also facilitated by a variety of institutions and individuals within Defence Force ranks who are either formally or inform-ally concerned with institutional socialization in the military network. These include the Directorate of Civic Guidance attached to the Chief-of-Staff, Personnel (responsible, *inter alia*, for the 'spiritual welfare' of recruits); the Military Psychological Institute (whose work in identifying leadership potential stretches out into a number of ancillary directions); the in-house media of the SADF, *Paratus, Uniform* and (to a lesser extent) the technical publication *Militaria*, all of which bombard their readership with simplistic analyses of the 'total onslaught'; and military intelligence and Defence Force personnel seconded to the Department of Foreign Affairs as military attachés designated for service abroad. The role of the military attachés does not of course encompass organizational socialization. They are nevertheless important in the flow of doctrine between the various international military establishments with which the SADF enjoys cordial, if often furtive, relations and the military intelligence section of the SADF stationed in South Africa. Military intelligence has, as a subdivision of the SADF, experienced remarkable elevation in status in recent years in accord with Beaufre's injunction that a major determinant in effective strategy is, in the words of the SADF, 'an outstanding intelligence service ... to forecast the action of the enemy'.[77] Today, many of the total strategy concepts appearing in the deliberations of the Defence College or in the pages of local military journals originate in the ruminations of personnel attached to this section. The intelligence section also plays a more direct role in the process of disseminating total strategy through officer ranks by its policy of recruiting staff and line officers on a temporary basis and then returning them to their original regiments. The whole elaborate internal communications system is maintained by – and, indeed, could not function in the absence of – a relatively small group of younger higher officers who are particularly interested in defining the role of the military in South Africa's turbulent and dynamic conditions and who occupy strategic positions at the epicentre in the Defence College, Intelligence, the Chiefs-of-Staff and, in particular, the Ministry of Defence headed by General Malan (previously Chief of the South African Defence Force). The military as a whole is not uniformly intense in its commitment to total strategy: the more administratively-oriented staff officers are noticeably less enthusiastic than the higher line officers and combat generals, while the Army leads the way over the other three major service divisions in projecting the total strategy framework. Yet there is a basic cadre for total strategy and it is to be found in a loose collection of officers made up of some lecturers at the Joint Defence College, a number of Chiefs-of-Staff attached to Defence Headquarters, top combat officers predominantly drawn from the Army (and, to a lesser extent, the Air Force) and virtually the entire staff component of Military Intelligence. Since this group enjoys access to the Minister of Defence, General Malan (who, as we have already noted, functions as a keystone in the patron–client system between the military and the executive arm of government), it is directly connected to the main communication channel of influence and information running between the military and civilian leadership. Since this small but critically placed group occupies a central spot within the military hierarchy it also tends to dominate the flow of strategic and political information moving both laterally and horizontally through SADF structures.

Total strategy, it is important to note in conclusion, is not an ideology in the sense of a tightly integrated set of universal ideas with a distinctive eschatological dimension. As an intellectual construct it is of a much lower order – essentially a counter-revolutionary programme devised by a particular group of power-holders as a self-protective device through the distilled combination of their own historical and cultural background with the practical experience of others in the art of containing revolution. Total strategy nevertheless performs a number of functions in contemporary South African society directly reminiscent of the roles of ideology in general. While the total strategy projected by local political and military leaders lacks the intellectual refinement of a fully articulated ideological construct, its richness in aggressive metaphor and symbolism, its repetitious emphasis on total onslaughts and communist imperialism is perfectly suited to the semi-paranoidal state of white South Africa. Indeed, it is precisely because the overwhelming majority of the white elite responds so favourably to the gut-level thrust of total strategy that total strategy has in its turn emerged as one of the most potent tools in the state's armoury of political mobilization. Total strategy, it should be added, has become an important instrument for stifling political criticism in South Africa, on the part of the white elite and, to a considerably lesser extent, on the part of isolated elements among the subject races, in the Indian and Coloured communities and among the urban black middle class with developing stakes in the perpetuation of some version of the present discriminatory system. Total strategy, like most successfully operationalized political programmes, has the innate ability to reduce the complex vitality of social and political existence in South Africa today to a few easily graspable and stereotype formulae which not only feed upon the inherited historical and racial prejudices of the average white South African but actually confirm them and update them to the modern era. Backed by considerable technological support, within the institutional boundaries of the Defence Force or through the projections of the mass media to wider society, total strategy selectively interprets the world in the narrow, dialectic and melodramatic terms with which white South Africa is so familiar, confusing communism, nationalism, dissidence, subversion, racism and imperialism into an interpenetrable mélange from which only the security of the white state emerges as constant and paramount. Total strategy, needless to say, mystifies and obscures reality in a manner entirely appropriate to what the ideologue terms 'false consciousness'. It writes off the internal problems of South Africa as external manipulation and, where it is unable to find persuasive evidence of the 'total onslaught' on South Africa, it falls back on the fabricated series of perils historically so effective in activating the white *laager* mentality – the old 'black peril', the 'red peril' or, on the infrequent occasion when some meagre evidence of its existence can be detected in the further reaches of Southern Africa, be it Zambia or Angola, the 'yellow peril'. Out of this glittering kaleidoscope of colours, none of which is so definite as to be pinpointed with any precision, emerges a climate perfectly commensurate with the way the government and its military allies legitimate virtually any claims to appropriated civil power. In essence, the logical conclusion of total strategy is a more perfectly defined and streamlined version of South Africa's already authoritarian climate. Total strategy legitimizes this development, it engenders the psychological and institutional atmosphere conducive to the growth of a garrison state and, through a series of mechanics, brings the idea of such a state into operation. It is to these mechanics, the subtle mixture of 'interior' and 'exterior' manoeuvres at the centre of counter-revolution as conceived of under total strategy, that we now direct our attention.

3

◇◇◇

Exterior manoeuvre: the dynamics of militarization

States of society are inherently resistant to precise measurement, and the resistance increases as one moves from the small-scale to conditions and relationships characteristic of whole societies. Hence the democratic nature or revolutionary potential inherent in a society can never be specified with any degree of mathematic accuracy over and above the loose inferences drawn by observers from the workings and institutions of the political process. Some political systems are apparently more democratic, some observably more revolutionary – but it is always impossible to express the exact difference given the complexity of the phenomena under observation. The same principle and problems of inaccuracy arise when we attempt to specify militarization. Because militarization can take an infinite number of social and political forms ranging from what is concrete and institutionalised to relatively intangible developments in the minds of men, we can see, but never entirely prove the existence of, a so-called 'garrison state' – certainly not with the degree of precision called for by scientific criteria. Garrison-statehood becomes a convenient and often, one might add, ideologically-manipulable label applied by social scientists to situations where there is strong suspicion that considerable political influence is wielded by the military.

The complex flow of political influence in society is not in itself easily measurable given the variegated nature of its components. Hence there is always an incentive for civil–military analysts to fall back on hard and relatively cogent statistical facts – particularly facts related to the distribution of the national budget – as a means to demonstrate the actual political clout wielded by military institutions in the formal allocation of the material resources of society. This search for rough and ready indicators to the political power of the military is no less marked in the case of South Africa than in any other. Militarization, we are increasingly told, is indicated by the 'take-off' of the South African defence budget over the last twenty years, by the increased amount of public money steered into

2 *Defence Expenditure, 1958–83*

Financial year	Rands
1958/59	36,000,000*
1959/60	40,000,000
1960/61	44,000,000
1961/62	72,000,000
1962/63	129,000,000
1963/64	157,000,000
1964/65	210,000,000
1965/66	229,000,000
1966/67	255,000,000
1967/68	256,000,000
1968/69	254,000,000
1969/70	272,000,000
1970/71	329,000,000
1971/72	327,000,000
1972/73	358,000,000
1973/74	481,000,000
1974/75	692,000,000
1975/76	1,043,000,000
1976/77	1,408,000,000
1977/78	1,712,000,000
1978/79	1,759,000,000
1979/80	1,857,000,000
1980/81	1,970,000,000
1981/82	2,465,000,000†
1982/83	2,668,000,000†

* rounded to nearest R million
† estimated

Sources: South African Institute of Race Relations, *Annual Survey of Race Relations*, 1968– (South African Institute of Race Relations, Johannesburg); *Republic of South Africa*, White Paper on Defence, 1965– (Pretoria: Department of Defence); National Union of South African Students, *Total War in South Africa: Militarisation and the Apartheid State* (Johannesburg: Allied Press, 1982) p. 11

defence channels. South African soldiers, it is widely argued, have a corporate stake in the annual defence budget as a measure of their social status and their professional self-esteem and, while it is specious to compare the SADF to their Latin American counterparts who have developed interventionist motives in reaction to apparently inadequate budgetary support, South African soldiers have nevertheless developed the political means to influence distinctively the way in which the state allocates its financial resources.[1] Indeed, the ability of the Defence Force to accumulate progressively the public money necessary to meet the material and symbolic values of the military establishment is, in itself, a measure of the growing political influence of the soldiers in the constellation of political forces making up the white power structure.

There are certain irresistible patterns in the South African budget of recent years which statistically support the notion of the Defence Force as a politically influential consumer of public resources. To the extent that gross defence expenditure figures are indicative of the rising political stars of militaries, the political importance of the South African military has increased enormously. In the 1958/59 financial year a mere R36 million was allocated for defence purposes: by 1982/83, twenty-five years later, this has risen to close on R3 billion (see Table 2). In reality, South Africa's defence spending has doubled over the last six years and is more than ten times greater today than it was twelve years ago. To the extent that distributions of political influence have anything to do with hard allocations of national finance, the ability of the South African military to influence national decision-making has grown in a direct and linear manner subject to two major accelerations – between 1960 and 1964 (following the initiation of a major expansion programme at the beginning of the period) and again since 1974, when a second major modernization programme was accorded priority. By the same token, putting into operation the 'exterior manoeuvre' envisaged by total strategy has made progressive demands on the gross national product and patterns of state expenditure. In 1960/61, 0.9 per cent of the GNP and 6.6 per cent of state expenditure was steered in a defence direction; by the 1979/80 financial year these proportions rose significantly, to 5 per cent of the GNP and 14.3 per cent of state expenditure. Since the beginning of the eighties roughly 20 per cent of total government expenditure has been fed into the Defence Force.

It is however extremely dangerous, if not somewhat simplistic, to infer distributions of political influence from sheer economic statistics. However accurate these statistics might be, the fact is that the militarization of any society involves much more fundamental alterations in social and institutional relations than those occurring within the public decision-making nexus on issues of budget distribution. Indeed, as I will attempt to show in the remainder of this chapter, militarization in South Africa (or in any other context, for that matter) is an all-embracing social activity involving major institutional shifts within and between the public and private sectors of society, new dimensions in state power, and new psychologies in the process of interaction between state and society. In the imperfectly identifiable atmosphere of garrison statehood, elites stake out new political claims in relation to each other, social and political obligations are redefined, major power shifts take place in the influence network supporting public decision-making, and conventional political relationships are reworked to take account of altering social circumstances. Defence budgets – the South African defence budget no less – are in any case always questionably accurate indicators for subtle social and political issues, this is even more true when (as in the South African case) the underlying arithmetic is open to differing interpretation. Conclusions regarding militarization in the South African context must, for example, be tempered by the fact that there are numerous sets of annual figures on defence spending, all of which are technically official but many of which differ according to their individual arithmetic inclusions or exclusions. The costs of intelligence-gathering, for example, are incorporated under the Treasury rather than the Defence Vote in parliament and in some years this is added into the global figures issued by the Department of Defence to the legislature, but in some years it is not. Parliamentary figures on defence spending – the stuff out of which most analysts infer the growing political influence of the military – sometimes include expenditures incurred by governmental bodies working for the Department of Defence (such as the Department of Community Development responsible for military housing), but in other instances they exclude from their aggregate calculations the role of such important state bodies as the Armaments Corporation (Armscor), responsible for providing the Defence Force with military equipment. This distinction can make a significant difference, as for example in the 1974/75 financial year where the R692 million allocated to the Department of Defence (representing 3.2 per cent of the GNP) would rise to R707 million (or 3.3 per cent of the GNP) if this extraneous or auxiliary expenditure were included.[2] From a strict statistical point of view, defence expenditure prior to the 1976/77 financial year is also not readily comparable with later annual allocations because of major alterations in state accounting procedure: prior to 1976 the state budget was divided into two separate accounts, the Consolidated Revenue Account and the State Account – thereafter this pattern was discontinued. Finally, and perhaps most importantly, the politically indicative quality of the defence budget is skewed by the fact that a considerable proportion of South Africa's defence expenditure is actually laundered through a secret Defence Special Account, under the direct authority of the prime minister and beyond the realms of state audit. Originally established in 1952 to facilitate the purchase of arms on the world market, this initially small fund has escalated in size to the point where today, in sheer quantitative terms, it enjoys the status of an unofficial defence budget. In 1974 a Defence Special Account Act was passed by parliament with an eye to rationalizing secret defence expenditure and two years later, in the 1976/77 financial year, R11.8 million was already being channelled in this direction. This amount has progressively increased to the point where, in 1980/81, R1.2 billion (out of the total annual budget of R1.97 billion) was allocated for Special Account purposes.[3] What these 'purposes' are, it should be added, remains a matter for speculation. While it seems reasonable to assume that a good proportion of Special Account moneys are allocated to (unspecified) military purposes, there is also some evidence to suggest that some of it is steered in a distinctly political direction related to the interests of the government and the ruling National Party. Defence Special Account money seems to have played some role in financing the activities of the now defunct Department of Information and, indeed, it was in the wake of the so-called 'Information scandal' that Finance Minister Owen Horwood assured the public that greater financial control would be exercised over Special Account resources. In practice, however, the Account still operates beyond parliamentary control and supervision in a way which continues to allow the executive to inflate and allocate defence expenditures without publicly appearing to do so.

Any balanced view of the political significance of the defence budget must also look to the purposes of defence expenditure against the long-term historical background of military finances. Most analysts equate the pattern of budgetary increases with the rapid expansion of the Defence Force, with arms procurement policy and with corporate action designed to advance the political interests of the military in the domestic constellation of power. At the same time it should be borne in mind that the SADF has almost always operated on shaky financial foundations. With the natural exception of the two world war periods, defence financing has almost always been chronic. After World War I, during the late twenties and in the Depression years of the following decade, the then Union Defence Force came perilously close to disbandment on a number of occasions. Personnel retrenchment, cutbacks in equipment, stores and training facilities, and demobilization of units was very much the order of the day.[4] Similarly, the spurt of organizational growth during the six years between 1939 and 1945 was followed by a period of reduction and decay: between 1946 and 1960 the SADF tended to fall back on its British connexion and no new equipment was purchased during this whole fourteen-year period, barring a few Centurion tanks in 1952 and two squadrons of Sabre aircraft three years later.[5] The natural result of this situation is predictable: with the severance of the Commonwealth tie the SADF found itself with little except worn and antiquated equipment in the face of an increasingly hostile international environment. The growth in defence expenditure in the last twenty years represents a concerted attempt to alleviate this deleterious situation under conditions where the global and regional strategic and political balance of forces have progressively tipped against South Africa. Retooling, renovating and generally modernizing the military to meet the accumulating pattern of external threats has become the imperative, the other side of the coin of expanding defence expenditure. In practice, there is a direct correlation between the sense of insecurity experienced in top military circles, defence spending, and political developments within the southern African region. It is not coincidental that the present wave of defence force expansion initiated in 1974 coincides with major deteriorations in the strategic position of South Africa on the subcontinent. These have been instigated by the collapse of Portuguese colonialism immediately followed by the emergence of Zimbabwe and the appearance of Cuban troops on the Angolan salient. It is also quite conceivable that increments in the defence budget have less to do with the military appropriating public policy influence, as part of a wider thrust towards militarizing society, than with an enhanced sense of social role and responsibility under circumstances of endangered national security. Nordlinger, for example, notes that 'all militaries tend to adhere to more demanding standards of national security than do civilians ... Given the soldier's defence responsibilities ... it is better to err on the side of additional safety by spending more on men and weapons'.[6] The military establishment in South Africa today may be better placed to attract state revenue not because it has more political influence but rather because civil leadership is more easily impressed by military demands for social resources in the discharging of their functional responsibilities in an increasingly stressful situation. It is important, finally, to draw clear distinctions between expenditure on arms procurement and expenditure on operating costs. This distinction is normally ignored by those in a hurry to demonstrate that the SADF is frantically rearming as part of its policy of securing political predominance in South African society. While arms expenditure absorbed the greater proportion of the defence budget in the early years following South Africa's withdrawal from the Commonwealth and the subsequent decision of the SADF to embark upon a rapid modernization policy, the pattern has since then changed as the Defence Force has reached optimal force levels. The international arms embargo has undoubtedly played a role in depressing arms expenditure in relation to operating costs, yet all the available evidence points to a real levelling-off of financial outlay on armaments during the 1977–80 period. In the 1979/80 budget, operating costs accounted for 55.6 per cent of expenditure. Official Defence Force projections anticipate this figure rising to 66.7% in the 1982/83 allocation and to continue to move upwards for the next five years.[7]

When cast in a comparative light, defence spending by South Africa is not extraordinarily large, nor may it be as great a drain on the national economy when viewed within the broad context of contemporary economic development. Defence spending today is undeniably a hundred times greater than it was in the 1958/59 financial year, and the R8 million per day lavished on the Defence Force is certainly *an* indicator of both the importance attributed to strategic issues by the present government and the ability of the soldiers to steer public financial distribution in a distinctly military direction. Yet, as the Minister of National Education has accurately pointed out, defence expenditure is still less than the annual parliamentary vote for education, and under universal conditions the 4–5 per cent of the GNP allocated annually by the South African government to defence is substantially smaller than the double-digit percentage of the GNP expended on military purposes by most Third World countries. The proportion of the GNP fed into South African military channels also compares very favourably with the United States (5.4 per cent per annum), the Soviet Union (12 per cent per annum) and Britain (4.4 per cent per annum).[8] In addition, any realistic and balanced appraisal of the money fed by the South African state into defence channels needs to be adjusted to the rising rate of inflation, not only in the local economy but, more importantly, in the international arms market where South Africa is forced to seek out obscure, quasi-legal (and expensive) sources of arms with a South African Rand which fluctuates in its convertibility. In practice, most analysts of the South African military present defence expenditure in gross terms (and then infer political consequences from these statistics) without giving very much credence to the important fact that much of the story of the SADF's rising expenditure stems from the situation of a military institution seeking to keep pace with the eroding value of its money. To some extent the SADF has managed to cut economic corners by diverting arms procurement into local channels. Nevertheless, it still remains active as a far from lavish buyer in the international market where the South African Rand is often under pressure and where the price of complex and sophisticated military technology has been known to quadruple in the course of a single financial year. Dealing with South Africa in the sensitive area of armaments is also a politically dangerous act from the point of view of the international market, and South African arms buyers attached to Armscor are often forced to cover these risks in the form of prices substantially higher than those paid by relatively more legitimate members of the international community. On the local front there can be little doubt that in certain sectors the development of an indigenous arms industry has had a stimulating effect on the national economy; yet under recessionary conditions the SADF is still forced to pay more for its basic equipment than it would have some years ago. Ironically this is partially because investment in the defence sector has the global effect of inducing inflationary pressure. Indeed, when viewed from the perspective of the real (as opposed to gross) spending power of the Defence Force, the amount of state revenue flowing to the military is far less pronounced than at first appears to be the case and, in certain respects, proportionately lower than recent past experience. With due allowance for the devaluation of the Rand the 1976/77 budget should be R1,356 million at constant 1976 price levels. If due allowance is made for a reasonable 15 per cent inflation rate the increase in defence expenditure between the 1979/80 and 1980/81 financial years is negligible. This led military planners to actually project a 9 per cent decrease in real defence expenditure for the 82/83 budget.[9] Defence expenditure has not, in general, held up against the recessionary tendencies in the current South African economy: much as in the arduous economic years of the early sixties, the SADF has been forced to defer replacement and expansion programmes and reduce stock levels in the face of national economic pressure. This has led to a decrease in the proportion of the GNP allotted to defence (from 5 per cent in 1979/80 to a projected 4 per cent in 1982/83) and warnings by the military that 'under more favourable economic conditions in the future the allocation of funds to the SADF will have to be increased accordingly if its required defence potential is to be maintained'.[10]

When seen in this light the defence budget appears as a far from perfect index of militarization: given our inability to penetrate the Defence Special Account, changes in the money market and inflation rates and the different arithmetic and accounting procedures used to compute defence spending, the proportion of public money allotted to the Defence Force may tell us far less about militarization in the Republic than legions of analysts have led us to expect. In the last analysis, the general, if marked, growth in the defence budget may enable us to say that more money is being spent for military purposes and precious little more. Total strategy is, moreover, 'total' in demanding, as P.W. Botha has put it, 'interdependent and coordinated action in all fields – military, psychological, economic, political, sociological, technological, diplomatic, ideological and cultural'.[11] This clearly implies that the building blocks of South Africa's garrison state are far more complex, wide-ranging, diverse – and, one might add, insidious – than the relatively simple and publicly visible process of soldiers tapping the public coffers for a mixture of motives ranging from corporate to national interests. As Beaufre himself notes, 'exterior manoeuvre' as part of a broad counter-revolutionary package involves major changes in social relations and institutions, and the intricate competition surrounding the allocation of national revenues is a single if important part of such changes. This means that if we are to appraise realistically 'exterior manoeuvre' in the South African context, if we are to indicate clearly the social and political consequences of total strategy inasmuch as it has captured the attention of the local military mind, we need to take our analysis of militarization from the defence budget to the deeper structural reaches of South African society.

Militarization, it is widely recognized, has innumerable implications for the working of the national economy. The rise of military institutions to public and political prominence can conceivably stimulate economic growth in the industrial sectors linked by production and technology to the national war machine. Alternatively, as is argued in some quarters, it can do irreparable damage in the short term to the national economy by diverting resources from the more energetic sectors of production or, more indirectly, through fueling inflation. Echoes of this complex economic debate can be detected in contemporary South Africa, in the various formulae brought by economists and politicians to strategies of economic development, and in the context of party competition. Hence, the defence spokesmen of the official opposition – Harry Schwartz and subsequently Philip Myburgh of the PFP – have frequently deplored the growth in the defence budget as both politically and economically dangerous, as a poor substitute for social reform and as a magnet for attracting national resources into an inherently unproductive area of economic activity. At the same time there can be little doubt that the political rise of the Defence Force has shaped the South African economy in important military directions independent of whether or not this is desirable from a growth or development point of view. As the garrison state has taken a hold on the psychology and organisation of local society, so we find today many of the ingredients of what Wright-Mills has labelled the 'military–industrial complex' in the South African context.[12] With growing international isolation and the increased efforts of the state to achieve some degree of self-sufficiency in the face of internal pressure, military demands have come increasingly to set the pace for local economy which is in turn increasingly bent to the varied requirements of the national war machine. Whether this development is comparable in intensity, articularity and institutionalization with other military–industrial complexes which have arisen in other countries in times of war or threats to the security of the state is still a moot point. Certainly there is no perfect alignment in relations between the South African military and businessmen who, as we shall see below, bring substantially different institutional imperatives to the process of interpreting and applying total strategy within the garrison context. Nonetheless, it is an undeniable and clearly visible fact that the tentative organization of the South African economy on a permanent or semi-permanent war footing has today stimulated a greater degree of political mingling between economic, military (and governmental) elites than at any previous time in South African history. The South African military today is 'not only an army of soldiers ... but an army of industrialists, financiers, economists and other business personnel'.[13] Indeed, as the international arms embargo has forced the South African military inwards to explore domestic sources of both soft and hard military technology, so private enterprise in its industrial, financial and commercial manifestations has become increasingly geared to meeting the appetites of the military for products ranging from uniforms and boots to the most modern and sophisticated types of armaments. As governmental authority has in turn become sensitive to the importance of communication and cooperation between the military and business sector as a crucial ingredient in state security – the Defence Force, after all, needs to know the productive capacities of the economy, and the entrepreneurs the material requirements of the military – so it has in turn moved in to support and develop what is today a highly complex and articulated tripartite network supporting a wide variety of war-type military–private-sector transactions.

Many of these transactions integrating military needs, industrial production and government action are highly sensitive matters of state and are therefore kept secret. As a result it is impossible to document accurately the growing number of meetings and decisions taking place in the offices of government, in the Defence Force or in proverbially smoke-filled corporate boardrooms. One of the more obvious foci of the three-way government–business–military network, one of the major points of contact, is the Defence Manpower Liaison Committee established as a channel of communication between large-scale employers of white labour, the Defence Force and the Department of Manpower Utilization and Development. Composed of the Chiefs-of-Staff, Personnel of the four arms of the SADF and representatives of twenty-one employer organizations throughout the Republic, the Manpower Committee has emerged as an important (if not necessarily perfect) instrument for coordinating Defence Force recruitment policy with the demands of an expanding economy persistently short of skilled white labour. Both the Defence Research and Development Council and the Defence Advisory Council are also important links in the military–industrial network, the former as a vehicle for integrating the specialist knowledge of the private sector into defence research and development activities, the latter as a forum within which military and business leaders discuss total strategy in relation to armaments policy. The Defence Advisory Council, whose purpose it is to examine the internal operations of the Defence Force in relation to the local armaments industry, is a veritable index of influentials in the South African corporate world: established in 1980 along lines similar to those of a previous Defence Council created in 1968 to integrate leading representatives of state and capital, its thirteen original members included Mike Rosholt (Chairman of Barlow Rand and presently Chancellor of the University of the Witwatersrand), Gavin Relly (then Deputy Chairman of the Anglo-American Corporation), Dr Johannes Hurter, Fred Du Plessis John Mackenzie and Frans Cronje (representing South Africa's major Afrikaner and English banks, Volkskas, Trust Bank, Standard and Nedbank respectively), Willem De Villiers and Basil Hersov (top executives of General Mining and Anglo-Transvaal Consolidated), Jaap Wilkens (President of the South African Agricultural Union), Richard Lurie (President of the Johannesburg Stock Exchange) and leading executives of South Africa's major brewery and sugar-producing conglomerate.[14]

South Africa is also a long-standing armaments producer, with private enterprise and the state cooperating in the development of the local armaments industry. With the outbreak of World War II, shells, cartridge cases and bombs were locally manufactured as part of the Allied war effort under the directing auspices of an Advisory Committee on Defence Force Requirements established in 1940 to advise the Minister of Defence on all matters concerning the acquisition of armaments.[15] The recommendations of this body were to lead to the establishment of half a dozen armaments factories spread around South Africa during the war years and, four years after the conclusion of the war, to the creation of a Board of Defence Resources as a more permanent and institutionalized mechanism for the direction of national armaments policy. This body was in turn superseded in 1951 by a Munitions Production Office established as a section of the Department of Defence. It was under the influence of this body that South Africa's first rifle factory was set up during 1953. By the early sixties, moreover, as the threat of an international arms embargo on the Republic became more imminent, the MPO was in the process of being expanded. The year 1963 also saw the creation of a National Rocket Institute at the Council for Scientific and Industrial Research charged with the development of a ground-to-air missile system in conjunction with local industry.[16] This was to result in the first of a subsequently long stream of selected South African scientists proceeding abroad to acquire specialized knowledge of production techniques in the armaments industry.

These first efforts at building a local armaments industry were to reach an important milestone in 1968 with the first testings of locally produced missile systems near St Lucia on the Natal north coast.[17] Indeed, by 1964 some R33 million was already being ploughed into the development of local armaments as opposed to a mere R315,000 four years earlier.[18] The early sixties in general form the background to South Africa's present-day Armaments Corporation (Armscor) – currently the major institutional contact point between government, business and the South African military, the veritable foundation and epicentre of contemporary efforts to build an explicitly coercive and armed dimension into total strategy. In the early sixties South Africa shifted from the importation of arms to the acquisition of arms technologies necessary to support local production. In 1961 alone, no less than 127 licences for the local manufacture of military equipment were negotiated with a wide range of overseas sources.[19] At the same time the state began to encourage foreign investment in the still nascent arms industry and in 1964 a successor-body to the MPO was established – the Armaments Production Board, whose task it was to integrate state with private sector activity in the arms area and to procure whatever armaments might be necessary for the immediate and long-term aims of the Defence Force. In the first four years of its existence the Board was to establish the essential infrastructure of what is today the world's tenth-largest armaments export industry and the largest in the southern hemisphere. Activity at this level included the securing of plans and blueprints for most of the weapons systems currently the standard issue of the SADF, extensive contact with local industry with the aim of encouraging it to invest capital and expertise in arms production as a counter to the United Nations embargo, and the exchange of technical knowledge and personnel with overseas organizations, both in the public and private sector, involved in the manufacture and marketing of armaments. In 1967 P.W. Botha, then Minister of Defence, visited armaments factories in Portugal as part of an in-depth investigation into various models for local arms production.[20] In the following year the powers of the Armaments Production Board (renamed simply the Armaments Board) were extended to oversee all phases of production and procurement and an Armaments Development and Manufacturing Corporation (the present-day Armscor) was established as a fully fledged state enterprise to manufacture South African armaments.

The basic role of Armscor, according to the enabling legislation of 1968, is to meet, as effectively and economically as possible, the armaments requirements of the Republic. To this end the Corporation is directed, *inter alia*, to 'promote and co-ordinate the development, manufacture, standardization, maintenance, acquisition or supply of armaments by collaborating with, or assisting or rendering services to, or utilizing the services of, any person, body or institution or any department of State'.[21] The Corporation is also imbued with power 'to develop, manufacture, service, repair and maintain, on its own account or as the representative of any other person to buy, sell, import or export or through advertising or otherwise, to promote the sale of, armaments, including armaments required for export and firearms, ammunition or pyrotechnical products required for supply to members of the public'.[22] Very little information is publicly available on precisely how the Corporation fulfils this complex variety of tasks: most Armscor activities are shrouded in protective legislation rooted in the Armaments Development and Production Act whose 1980 amendment 'prohibits the disclosure of any information in relation to the acquisition, supply, marketing, importation, export, development, manufacture, maintenance or repair of, or research in connection with armaments by, for, on behalf of, or for the benefit of the Armaments Corporation or a subsidiary company'.[23] It is nonetheless clear that in the fifteen years of its existence Armscor has proved an almost unattenuated success – in developing the South African arms industry to a high degree of self-sufficiency in the face of international sanctions and, of no lesser importance for domestic politics, in locking together the military, governmental and economic elite into a tight tripartite network in support of apartheid policy. Today, as the only official body coordinating the production, procurement and marketing of armaments for the Defence Force, Armscor is at the node of communication between the military, private enterprise and government regarding the conception, planning and implementation of armaments policy. Both the Corporation's chairman and chief executive have direct access to the highest realms of public decision-making through their membership of the Defence Planning Committee which brings together Defence ministry officials and top SADF personnel. The board of the Corporation, which varies from seven to twelve directors serving for a maximum three-year period, draws on the Republic's bureaucratic, business and scientific elites as well as the office of Director-General of Finance and the Chief of the Defence Force. In complying with the provisions of the Armaments Development and Production Act, that 'it meet as effectively and economically as may be feasible the armaments requirements of the Republic', Armscor has succeeded in increasing its assets from approximately R200 million in 1974 to R1.2 billion, making it allegedly today one of the three biggest financial undertakings in South Africa (along with Barlow Rand and Anglo-American).[24] With the annual expenditure on arms manufacture rising from R315,000 (in 1960/61) to R140 million (by 1972) and then to R1.54 billion in 1981, Armscor is estimated to have experienced fivefold growth since its inception.[25] The Corporation also ranks as one of the Republic's largest all-round employers of labour, in a way reflecting the increasing complexity and enormous growth of the local arms industry from its simple origins at the beginning of World War II. At the apogee of the war years an estimated 12,000 people were directly involved in armaments production and related activities. By way of contrast, Armscor employed 18,973 persons in 1978 and in the region of 29,000 a mere three years later.[26] Of this number a minority are attached to Corporate Headquarters with the overwhelming remainder of the workforce distributed throughout the network composed of the Corporation's twelve subsidiaries. These 'affiliates' include the giant Atlas Aircraft Corporation (sited near Jan Smuts Airport and engaged in the manufacture of Impala trainers, Mirage fighters and a variety of light military aircraft), Pretoria Metal Pressings and Naschem (ammunition and bombs), Somchem (originally a subsection of African Explosives and Chemical Industries and now an important local source of explosives and propellants), Lyttelton Engineering (cannon and mortars), Eloptro and Telcast Engineering (electro-optical and metal castings) and Kentron with its two factories producing a variety of guided missiles. Since it is also Armscor philosophy to maximize use of the private sector through a dense network of contractors and subcontractors engaged in the manufacture of every conceivable type of military hard and software, at least 100,000 South Africans must today be considered working elements in the defence industry.

Many people and institutions undoubtedly benefit from their Armscor connexions, either directly or indirectly. In 1978, for example, 43 per cent of Armscor employees were 'non-whites',[27] and today Armscor is an important source of employment and technical upgrading for this sector of the South African population, particularly for Coloured women who are a major component of the Corporation's 'non-white' workforce.[28] Most of this group are confined to low-grade administrative and production roles (although some of the Corporation's subsidiaries, for example Naschem, are officially opposed to the principle of job reservation). Black workers nonetheless draw certain material benefits from participation in the armaments industry by virtue of Defence Force policy to extend rewards to its more compliant black affiliates and members. Armscor is also sensitive to internal shortages of skilled labour in a manner reflecting current structural problems in the South African economy as a whole. Thus, political and technological factors reinforce each other to produce a fairly benevolent set of policies for the black workforce. It is probably out of this mixture of motives that the Corporation decided to extend its generous housing subsidy to its black employees at the end of 1977. Both Naschem and Somchem have embarked on projects to construct houses for their substantial Coloured workforces while in 1981 Pretoria Metal Pressings embarked upon a R176 million expansion project, part of which included the development of a Coloured training centre. Armscor does not recognize the formation of trade unions among its members but, in a way which mirrors the subtleties of political control in wider South African society, all its personnel have full and equal coverage through its medical aid scheme (Krygmed), equal pension facilities and equal access to loans of up to 95 per cent for private housing development.

Both the state and private enterprise benefit directly and perhaps less ambiguously than blacks in the armaments industry by virtue of its existence. From the point of view of government the development of an indigenous arms industry represents a major saving of foreign exchange and an important stimulus to the national economy at a time of recession and world-wide inflation – particularly in the arms market. Defence Force personnel also view Armscor as a boon due to its ability to generate military equipment at prices which are competitive or even lower in some cases than those in the international arms market. To many top soldiers this is particularly important as long as the Defence Force is under some degree of public pressure to tailor its claims to the annual national budget. To both civilian and military leadership Armscor is of inestimable strategic value in that it has played a crucial role in allowing South Africa to circumvent United Nations arms sanctions and to reduce, if not necessarily to totally break, the country's previous almost total dependence on foreign sources of armaments. This is not to downplay the enormous contribution of the external sector to the military perpetuation of apartheid, particularly the much-bemoaned role of the multinational corporations as conduits for contacts between the South African and international arms industry, and as sources for technology and finance which are of direct assistance to South Africa in acquiring the 25 per cent of its weapons which it still cannot produce locally.[29] The impact of the United Nations arms embargo was also by no means immediate and for a number of years after its initiation the Republic was able to avoid the international stranglehold with the working out of long-term contracts concluded prior to the embargo. It was in this way that the Republic continued to acquire helicopters, transport and supersonic jet aircraft from overseas sources (plus the personnel to service and maintain the additions to her armoury) well into the present era. Many governments, needless to say, have adopted a cavalier attitude towards the flow of military material and technology and personnel towards the Republic despite their publicly stated aversion to apartheid. Both Britain and the United States continued to supply the Republic with basic weaponry into the early sixties, although the arms procurement pattern has now diversified to include West Germany, Italy, Canada, Belgium, Holland, Spain and Taiwan.[30] All of these countries have, to differing degrees and at different times, met the military requirements of the SADF although most of those transactions remain relatively invisible from public scrutiny given the fact that South

Africa makes its payments under the Special Defence Account. It is well known however that French state and private concerns played a crucial role in the initial efforts of South Africa to develop its missile capacity and that as late as 1971 French armaments manufacturers were still contracting with Armscor to construct Mirage III and F1 jet aircraft – albeit under the palpably transparent argument that this equipment could only be used for external defence purposes.[31] Israeli military specialists have also seemed to play some role in more recent developments in the South African missile industry, although this is difficult to assess with any precision given the veil of secrecy over Armscor activities and the fact that most states are far more sensitive to being labelled transgressors of the embargo than was the case some years ago. Contracted foreign manpower, it should however be added, is still a visible component in South African arms production, particularly in the military aviation industry centred on the Atlas Aircraft Corporation. While the foundations of the industry were laid well before either Atlas or Armscor (Westland Wapiti aircraft were being manufactured under licence at the Aircraft and Artillery Depot at Roberts Heights as early as the twenties), foreign technicians undoubtedly play an important part in manufacturing the Impala, Kudu, Bosbok and Mirage aircraft on the Atlas production line. This reflects the fact that, according to a recent estimate, foreign contracted labour makes up 10 per cent of total Atlas staff.[32]

With due reference to the international input it can still truly be said that in the absence of Armscor South Africa would not, in all probability, have attained its current level of military capacity. While, as we have noted, South Africa's most technologically sophisticated military needs are still partially serviced through the importation of equipment and personnel, the SADF has managed to achieve total self-sufficiency in multiple areas as Armscor has moved from its original research phase through the production of weapons used for counter-insurgency purposes to the more technologically advanced realms of conventional armaments manufacture.[33] Today the South African military is fully supplied through domestic production with artillery guns and rockets, artillery fire-control equipment, short-range guided missiles, mini-computers, detonators and mine-resistant vehicles, operational and armoured vehicles, tactical telecommunications equipment, arms and ammunition, anti-personnel, anti-vehicle and programmed ground mines.[34] Armscor has also played an important role in pioneering and adapting available military technologies to the particular defence needs of the Republic. The Ratel ICV and Eland armoured car, the 127mm multiple rocket launcher, the 155mm G5 field gun, the R4 assault rifle and the Olifant tank (a modified version of the British Centurion) are some of the advanced products in the local Armscor catalogue, although it is difficult to relate the exact contribution of imported technical assistance to each specific project. In practice many Armscor products synchronize local and international expertise in a single activity. An example of this is the Defence Force's latest showpiece, the G6, 155mm motorized cannon, marketed as a result of extensive cooperation between the Corporation and some fifty companies in South Africa's private sector, but actually based on a variety of technologies supplied by the American Space Research Corporation assisted by a number of Western European countries.[35] The local content of Armscor production, measured in men or material, is nevertheless increasing with passing years and as the Corporation has moved to higher levels of production and scale the international arena has actually taken on greater importance – no longer as a source of imported technical and capital resources, as has been the case through much of South Africa's recent history, but as a potentially vast market for high-quality exports manufactured in South Africa. Today, as Armscor officials readily admit, the measure of the Corporation's success lies in the fact that the internal market is now too small in relation to the output of the arms industry. With the SADF having sufficient stockpiles of weaponry to meet any conceivable contingency in the forseeable future, this means that the continued expansion and diversification of the South African arms industry depends on aggressive salesmanship in the international arena – particularly in the arms markets of South America, the Middle East, the Far East and some African countries.

Armscor is nevertheless a sound and highly dynamic enterprise and from the point of view of the some 5,600 business operations linked into the defence establishment as Armscor subsidiaries, contractors or subcontractors, association with the Corporation is a lucrative and satisfying activity. While some elements in the private sector complain of technical difficulties experienced in relations with the Corporation – its regulating and pricing policies, its procedures for formulating orders or its ostensible failure to discriminate against companies directed by non-South African nationals – the basic fact of the matter is that virtually all of South Africa's leading corporations (and many subsidiaries of well-known international firms) form part of the estimated network of roughly fifty main companies who are primary contributors to Armscor production of hard or soft military equipment, who assist the Corporation in marketing its manufactures, or who provide specialized personnel or managerial skills to the Corporation along the lines of John Maree, seconded to Armscor from Barlow Rand and generally regarded as one of the main architects of current Armscor interactions with the private sector. Some segments of local and multinational capital are fairly prominent and visible components of the military system (although all would deny that their activities are geared in any direction other than the civilian market). These include such domestic and internationally reputable companies as Sandock-Austral (who manufacture armoured vehicles and high-speed naval patrol craft), Erikson-Ford (responsible for the mine-resistant Ribbok truck), Fuchs (a supplier of radar and communications equipment to the SADF), Barlow Rand (whose tractor division also manufactures armoured vehicles), Barlow and Grinaker Electronics (both suppliers of telecommunications equipment), Daimler-Benz and Toyota (suppliers of vehicles to the Defence Force), Siemens (electronic components), Sperry-Rand (aerospace and communications equipment), AEG-Telefunken (communications systems), Messerschmidt (radar equipment), IBM (computers) and Shell and B.P. (both active as sources of oil products). Both Sasol and Iscor are also linked into the defence establishment through their planning organizations and through sales to the security forces and other state organs.[36] For the most part however the majority of recipients of what one source has euphemistically labelled 'the not inconsiderable benefits of the armaments industry'[37] are small-scale enterprises, roughly 400 subcontractors supplying mainstream military components and a further 1,500 firms involved in the supply of the 'nuts-and-bolts' of the local war machine – the producers of military uniforms, boots, plastic rifle butts, shelving systems, food, stationery, furniture, canteen cutlery and ration packs – all hidden from immediate public sight by a dense and intricate pattern of contraction and subcontraction extending to the furthermost reaches of the national economy. In 1977/78, for example, Armscor placed no less than 5,636 contracts with the private sector, 89 with unit values in excess of R1 million, 383 worth more than R100,000 each and the remainder under R100,000 in individual value.[38] In 1975/76, in a fashion which indicates the massive reorientation of defence spending from foreign to local channels (and the comparable growth of the arms industry), R184 million of the total R534 million annual defence allocation was invested locally, R59 million directly in the private sector, the rest through Armscor and its associated subsidiaries.[39] When seen against the background of the fact that prior to the establishment of Armscor in 1968 an insignificant proportion of public money was being diverted into arms procurement and production on the local front, the degree of change is quite astounding. In these circumstances it is also hardly surprising that many segments of the private sector are today either directly or indirectly dependent upon Defence Force contracts. The SADF is one of the largest consumers of the products of South Africa's textile industry while both the local electronic and mechanical engineering industries have been economically boosted through their involvement with Armscor. In a way which doubtless typifies the position of many South African business concerns operating in conditions of recession, military contracts have become a primary source of capital for the building industry, an integral ingredient in its survival under currently difficult economic conditions. The present prime minister, P.W. Botha, drew heavily on private sector advice during his tenure as Defence Minister and since a 1977 meeting at the Rand Afrikaans University, which many analysts regard as the 'take-off point' of the local military–industrial complex, Botha has frequently expressed the desire to 'unite business leaders behind the South African Defence Force'.[40] The state in general goes out of its way to cement the resources of the private sector into the military system by streamlining Armscor relations with the business community and generally designing investment in the arms industry as attractively as possible. As part of this process the Treasury was no longer required to approve every Armscor purchase after 1974 and the production and procurement activities of the Corporation were effectively merged into a single operation three years later. Potential participants from the private sector are also encouraged by Armscor's relatively efficient tendering procedures, particularly the willingness of its Tendering Committee to consider all offers for production and investment. Particularly congenial from the point of view of the business community is the Armscor policy of giving maximum rein to the productive capacities of the private sector through the principle that its own subsidiaries produce only special strategic equipment (or material whose production would be uneconomical for private business), leaving the rest of the field free for local enterprise. The structure and management design of the Corporation is also specially geared to private participation – in the practice of appointing local business leaders to the directorates of Armscor and its subsidiaries and in the constant encouragement given to specialized private personnel to involve themselves in Corporation operations on an ad hoc or consultancy basis. Although the standards of quality control imposed by Armscor on its contractors and subcontractors are exceptionally rigorous, those enterprises who succeed in acquiring tenders immediately enjoy a wide variety of benefits including easy access to government subsidies, research facilities and technical assistance. South Africa's history as an arms exporter dates back to the R18 million of products sent to Rhodesia during the 1972–76 period,[41] and today, when an estimated R77 million of arms are exported annually, the marketing division of Armscor (Nimrod) is also of considerable use to South African arms manufacturers, negotiating sales on favourable terms to local industry and in identifying potential markets. In the last analysis, most elements in the private sector see Armscor as a unique para-statal organization, managed largely by private enterprise and working for the benefit of private enterprise, relatively untrammelled by the notorious mass which is the South African bureaucracy. They may publicly bemoan total strategy and militarization but in a period of economic recession where international isolation feeds a relative decline in foreign investment few can afford to resist the lucrative temptations offered by the defence industry.

The general receptivity of the private sector to militarization reflects the wider movement of the military establishment into the civil realms of South African society, initiated in the late sixties and taking on accelerated momentum in the subsequent decade. As the industrial base of South Africa has been adjusted to the imperatives of arms production so, in a broader social sense, the application of total strategy has made its own human demands on both the body and spirit of white South African manpower. In a sheer physical sense the number of white South Africans exposed to military roles and values is now greater than at any time in previous South African history. The civil elite is today in the process of being directly and rather bluntly incorporated into the military realm, into the world of military norms, institutions and principles of social behaviour in an historically unparalleled fashion – arguably with more intensity and reinforcement than during the two occasions in the twentieth century when the country has entered a world war. The extension of the national conscription system with the development and crystallization of South Africa as a garrison state is significant. Today, with growing internal and international threats to the state it is virtually impossible for any physically capable white male under the age of sixty-five to legally avoid some sort of physical commitment to the Defence Force – through the Citizen Force, the Commandos or the 'controlled' National Reserve envisioned under amendments to the Defence Act made during the parliamentary session of 1982. In contrast to the situation prevailing some twenty years ago where only a small proportion of white males over the age of eighteen were swept into the military net, virtually every white male is today considered a component part of what the Defence Force has described in the unremitting language of total strategy as the 'struggle for national survival'. The 1982 amendments to the Defence Act are in effect corrective measures for what Defence Force planners see as imbalances in the 'national' defence effort, most notably the fact that defence commitments have until now been carried by a disproportionate 25 per cent of the 17–60-year-old age category of the white male population.[42] Subsequently, the registration age for national service has now been extended to 55 in accord with SADF policy to place 'particular emphasis on the greater majority of citizens who for some reason or other have as yet never made a contribution and have so far been members of an uncontrolled National Reserve'.[43] The number of men conscripted for national service on an annual basis has also naturally increased as the military has projected its increased force level demands into civil society: whereas a mere 11,759 men were mobilized in the Citizen Force during 1962 the annual intake had more than doubled to 26,357 eight years later.[44] Since national conscripts are eligible for a two-year period of service this means that the Defence Force has over 50,000 Citizen Force recruits in training at any one time.[45] This increase in numbers necessarily reflects changes in the selection procedures feeding the national service system. In 1960, for example, national servicemen were recruited through a ballot system for a three-month period of military training. However, shortly thereafter, in terms of the report of the Groenewald Commission created to propose revisions in national service structures, the ballot system was scrapped in entirety to be replaced by the principle of universal (i.e white) national service as built into the Defence Act and its various amendments. The result is that it is now, as the Defence Force describes it, 'the duty and privilege of every young white male citizen of the Republic' to render national service.[46] In terms of major changes made to the national service system during the sixties this 'duty and privilege' has been extended, from three to nine months service, from nine to twelve months (in 1972) and then in 1977, to a two-year period of duty – despite innumerable complaints from national servicemen that they are not fully employed or utilized during this lengthy training period. The training period for the Citizen Force has been held constant into the present period, yet the obligations of Citizen Force members to the military after they have completed their training has been progressively extended in line with Defence Force policy to maintain continuity with its part-time members. According to the legislation of 1972, each Citizen Force member was annually obliged to render nineteen days service for five years after the initial training period; in 1977 this was upped to 30 days service given annually over an eight year period. According to the 1982 amendments to the Defence Act, however, it is no longer possible to discharge these commitments through three tours of operational duty. Indeed, as of January 1983, each member of the Citizen Force having completed his national military training will be required to serve a further 720 days spread over fourteen years, he will then be transferred to the Active Citizen Force Reserve (where he serves twelve days annually for a further five year period), then the Commandos (where he renders a further twelve days service per year until the age of 55), before finally being placed on a National Reserve for a further ten-year period. In addition to demanding this life-time commitment to the Defence Force on the part of whites the new legislation also makes provision for 'area defence' in terms of which local militias can be called upon to contain civil violence and insurrection in specific areas as the need arises.[47]

Defence Force spokesmen have dismissed public criticism of the new system as unnecessary total mobilization with the argument that the 1982 proposals should be seen as a set of contingency plans designed to bring individuals into the military network when and if necessary. At the same time, military officials have begun to move outwards into civil society to appropriate a variety of civilian roles in the process of revitalizing the old kommando-related notion of the citizen-soldier. This is not to say that today's professionals in the SADF specifically welcome the idea of their being transformed into functioning as part-civilian, part-military elements. The modernization of South African society, the state and its armed forces precludes the reinstitutionalization of the old kommando in any strict sense and South African military leaders see themselves, in the last analysis, as technically proficient experts in the 'management of violence', to use Laswell's famous phrase, to the benefit of the state apparatus. Nonetheless, the South African military has a long tradition of participation in the social, if not necessarily political, affairs of white society, literally built into the prescribed regulations of the SADF which is directed to 'render assistance in exceptional cases to government departments, administrations, private organizations and even individuals' in times of crisis. There are numerous examples of the SADF fulfilling this civil commitment in recent history – during widespread flooding in the Cape in 1974 and 1975, in the more recent Laingsburg floods where the Army supplied tents and transport to a wide variety of displaced persons, and in frequent air–sea rescue operations undertaken by the Navy backed up by Air Force Shackletons, Albatross search aircraft and Frelon helicopters. As total strategy has taken hold of the military imagination, as its prescriptions for counter-revolution direct soldiers to new and relatively unfamiliar areas of social action, so the SADF has built on this tradition of rendering assistance to the civil realm – so it has, in a nutshell, given it more political explicit meaning.

Civic action on the part of the military is today a vital component in the application of total strategy, a characteristic feature of military participation in South Africa beyond the strategic realm and a critical lever in the process whereby civil–military boundaries have shifted appreciably in recent years in a military direction. The purpose of civic action as conceived by the military authorities is basically psychological in its contribution to the foundations of total strategy: its purpose, according to Major-General Lloyd, head of the Northern Command and previously Chief of the South West African Territorial Force is 'to secure through administrative and socio-economic action, the goodwill, support and cooperation of the local population by alleviating friction points, grievances and dissatisfaction, improving their standard of living, giving them something worthwhile to defend in the revolutionary war'.[48] In pursuit of these objectives civic action was made part of the South African counter-insurgency programme in Namibia during 1974. In 1978 the principle of winning the hearts and minds of the popular masses was transferred directly to the Republic with the establishment of a civic action subsection in the Defence Force under the energetic leadership of Major Phil Pretorius, an expert in psychological warfare and therefore adequately equipped to conduct 'Burgersake', that is, the cultivation of a favourable public image of the Defence Force as a vital component of total strategy. Selected military personnel are today exposed to a special civic action course, and they subsequently materialize in special positions in the state bureaucracy – in education, engineering, administration, tourism, the legal, agricultural, financial and health services of the state for which there is no white manpower readily available. In this context where shortages of white skilled labour intersect with the psychological thrust of total strategy, the SADF has become an important source of semi-permanent or temporary bureaucratic labour. In the Department of Inland Revenue, SADF accountants are active as sales tax inspectors and in the Department of Cooperation and Development military doctors and agronomists have emerged as important, if seconded, elements in the process of 'homeland' development.[49] Acting on the somewhat peculiar logic that 'a healthy civilian population is a sure bulwark against Communism',[50] military doctors have played an important preventative and containing role in the treatment of disease in South Africa's numerous drought-stricken areas, particularly in cholera-infested regions of the eastern Transvaal and in the Nduma region of northern Natal. The Department of National Education has also made periodic if generally unsuccessful use of militarymen in the role of schoolteachers in the black townships – although this practice is constrained by the fact that urban black leaders prefer to tolerate shortages in teaching personnel rather than use soldiers who are regarded as intelligence-gatherers for the government or propagandists for Bantu Education policy. During February 1979 for example, a mass meeting in Soweto resolved to initiate a school boycott along the lines of 1976 and 1977 unless soldier-teachers were removed from various posts in the townships.[51] This parallels the experience in Namibia where black parents have generally resisted civic action programmes geared to primary and secondary education.[52] The result is that the educational authorities do not use military personnel as instructors in black schools unless the black communities explicitly request their presence.[53] Soldier-teachers are nevertheless used fairly extensively in some of Johannesburg's Coloured schools, and in the homelands where the teacher crisis is far more acute than in the township areas. In Kwazulu for example, military educationists are accepted in principle provided they teach out of military uniform.

The military are also an increasingly important source of specialized white manpower in a way which cuts across accepted civil–military boundaries. The SADF may be reluctant to invest time and energy in training civilians, yet as South African military institutions have modernized in a fashion which places a premium on technically competent manpower, able to use complex and sophisticated military equipment, so the Defence Force has been obliged to upgrade technically its manpower, be it in the form of Permanent Force members or conscripts transitionally within the SADF in the course of working out their national service obligations. The result is that many young whites are technically and educationally improved during the course of their military service. They may conceivably use these newly acquired skills within the military framework, or, as is more often the case, carry these skills back to the civil society on their completion of military service. The result is a growing pool of white manpower who can employ their capabilities on an interchangeable basis in accord with civil and military functions. In addition, as the South African military undergoes modernization, so it also becomes to some degree dependent on skilled manpower drawn from the civil sector on a seconded basis. During 1956–66, for example, the number of civilians employed in the Permanent Force increased from 1,298 to 1,912 and today some 20 per cent of all SADF personnel are civilians.[54] As noted in the 1982 White Paper on defence, 'the civilian component of the SADF forms an important part of the administration and management of the Defence Force... [Civilians] render a valuable contribution especially in the administrative, financial, technical and medical branches of the Permanent Force'.[55] Since the performance of numerous tasks by civilian personnel frees regular military men for operational service, plans are currently afoot to expand the number of civilian posts in the Defence Force structure.[56]

Military demands for highly specialized manpower always lead to intimate relations between the defence establishment and the scientific community, and this is no less the case in South Africa where the SADF and local scientists have a long history of cooperation in the development and production of military technologies long preceding the establishment of Armscor and the subsequent take-off of the local arms industry in the late sixties. As early as 1926, in a move foreshadowing the creation of the Atlas Aircraft Corporation forty years later, the South African Air Force was drawing on local technical skills to produce military aircraft, Wapitis and later Avro Tutors and Hawker Hartebees, with British engines and instruments but otherwise local content.[57] Today, only a mere 2 per cent of the Defence Force budget is devoted to research and development. Yet, civilian scientists drawn from the private sector, academia or other institutions in the governmental network have come to play a vital role in the development of the local arms industry to its present point beyond self-sufficiency. Working through the network of the SADF's Directorate of Projects and Combat Development, Armscor's National Institute of Defence Research and the project steering committees of the Defence Research Council, South African scientists are a vital element in a multivarious research programme into virtually every aspect of military hardware – from techniques for rapid airfield construction through the production of combat clothing to the manufacture of plastic materials suitable for use in Defence Force weaponry. In a climate where 'all the resources and full capability of the SADF are placed at [their] disposal',[58] local scientists have engineered a number of technological breakthroughs in the manufacture and development of armoured vehicles – the locally produced Buffels, Ratels and the modified Olifant tank – mechanized artillery, most notably the new G6, 155mm mobile cannon, and surface-skimming, ground-to-ground and ground-to-air missile systems. In the field of military telecommunications local scientists have been instrumental in successfully developing mobile tropo-telecommunication systems and highly sophisticated ultra-high-frequency-hopping radios. The potential suitability of all these products for the international market attests to the ingenuity and depth of cooperation of the military and scientific establishments in the face of the international arms embargo. Joint consultation and planning between the SADF, the Atomic Energy Board and the Council for Scientific and Industrial Research (whose president sits on the Defence Research Council) has also doubtless played some role in the development of South Africa's controversial nuclear capacity. While the local nuclear industry is not officially geared to the production of weaponry, it is generally accepted in most knowledgeable domestic and international circles that South Africa has the ability to either manufacture nuclear weapons or rapidly to convert its nuclear stockpile to military purposes. In either eventuality, the link between the military and South Africa's scientists is bound to grow as the local arms industry moves into the production of naval vessels, submarines and other high technology military equipment.

It is not readily apparent whether today the Defence Force is militarizing the values of white civil society or whether the civil sector is more significant in civilianizing the military establishment. What is quite clear however is that the military is perhaps better situated to influence civil opinion than at any previous time in civil–military history. This is particularly true in relation to the growing number of white recruits passing through the military network at any given point in time, the national servicemen who have to be deeply educated in the norms, code and values of the Defence Force if they are to be forged into a relatively professional fighting unit with the ability to contribute to state security. With the constant movement of civilians into military ranks the various decisions by the SADF to extend the obligations of its national servicemen are as much based on the desire to contain contamination of institutional values by civil influences through a system of follow-up commitments to the Defence Force as they are rooted in calculations related to manpower requirements. From the official point of view the use of political propaganda is not considered a central component of the training programme of Permanent Force and national service recruits. Yet in the course of psychologically conditioning its recruits as defenders of the state, the SADF, much like any other military institution, is obliged to communicate information of definite political character. The result is a contradictory situation in which top officials of the SADF deny that the Defence Force politically indoctrinates its recruits in the relative isolation of the barracks, while readily admitting that 'our soldiers are however motivated against subversion and communism through the medium of our civic guidance program.'[59] In effect the SADF regards it 'as absolutely essential that every member should know our enemies and be able to identify them'.[60] Today it is Defence Force policy to 'make fullest use of the opportunities afforded by the National Service System to promote the physical and spiritual preparedness of our youth',[61] and in recent years a number of institutional mechanisms have been created within the military to advance this specific objective. During 1967, for example, a psychological section was established in the Medical Service, ostensibly with the role of testing Permanent Force personnel and potential national service leaders with an eye to suitable posting. These tasks were subsequently transferred to a fully fledged and newly established Military Psychological Institute which currently devises various programmes for institutional socialization as well as screening recruits with the purpose of identifying leadership. The military authorities also display considerable interest in the way recruits utilize their leisure time and they have created a Leisure Time Utilization Unit with subsections attached to each of the nine commands in the Republic whose purpose it is to see to the 'cultural enrichment' and 'spiritual defensibility' of the young soldier.[62] While the programme of the unit also covers a variety of mundane and practical matters from road safety to environmental studies, particular attention is given to 'citizenship' and 'constitutional development' as a means of 'giving our young men a clearer understanding of national issues ... to ensure that they are not only equipped with military preparedness but spiritual preparedness [as well]'.[63] In this regard the work of the LTU parallels that of the Civic Guidance Programme originally established to cultivate 'a positive approach to citizenship',[64] although the two instruments of institutional socialization have now been separate entities for some years. In practice, institutional socialization in the Defence Force has become increasingly rationalized and supported by sophisticated communications technology developed by the Defence Force's College of Educational Technology (responsible for instructor training), and the fifteen instructional media centres located at the various training schools of the three major service arms. Today, internal education in the SADF is reinforced in its persuasiveness by television programmes, audio-visual aids and multi-media learning packages, most produced exclusively by and for the military. While a good deal of these facilities are geared to routine technical training, it is by no means apparent that the desire of the SADF to provide its recruits with what it calls an unbiased 'knowledge of such subjects as ideological tendencies and world trends, a deeper insight into the problems of Africa and the part the Republic of South Africa can play in it' is sufficiently objective to meet the requirements of a well-rounded education.[65] On the contrary, even a cursory glance at the handbooks produced by the Directorate of Civic Guidance and Leisure Time reveals a content vigorous in its use of crude racial and ideological stereotypes, dangerously selective in its interpretation of historical data and fundamentally hostile to any information critical of either the Nationalist Party or its apartheid policy.[66] The use of material of this nature to 'enlighten' recruits has led to numerous charges by the official parliamentary opposition that the SADF is less a politically neutral instrument of the state than a propagandizing creature of the ruling party.

The Defence Force utilizes both the state controlled media and a network of favourably inclined civil organizations to propagate total strategy and the military ethic outside of its immediate institutional sphere. The SADF has, of course, developed its own internal media with the purpose of 'promoting the image of the SADF and instilling a sense of pride in every member of the Defence Force'.[67] During 1980 the military produced some twenty different types of publication at a cost of R349,000, including *Warrior* (for 'non-white' soldiers), *Paratus*, the official organ of the SADF, and *Militaria*, devoted largely to technical aspects of military history and science.[68] In addition the SADF 'spares [no effort] to cover the many facets of Defence Force activities through the various public news media' as a complement to its in-house publications.[69] In 1980, for example, Johannesburg's *Sunday Times* produced a Defence Force pamphlet entitled *Psychological Plans: Defence Budget Debate* signed by the head of the military's civic action directorate which instructed military departments to manipulate the public media in order to influence the outcome of the then ongoing parliamentary defence debate. While the Defence Force then sought to cover itself by the argument that the pamphlet was 'unauthorized' – technically speaking, all documents concerning party politics are vetted by the Chief of the Defence Force – a new pamphlet entitled *The Reason Why* soon appeared in order to propagate National Party policy and discredit their opponents.[70] It is also Defence Force policy to consult with newsmen on a reasonably frequent basis and there seems no doubt that there is official liaison between the military and South African Broadcasting Corporation decision-makers regarding radio and (in particular) television coverage of Defence Force activities.[71] This results in the South African television-viewer being saturated with highly selective documentaries designed to emphasize the 'total onslaught' and portray the role of the SADF in combating it. Given the tendency of the advertising industry to jump on the military bandwagon in the process of marketing a wide variety of consumer goods, frequent military parades and rigid censorship of military matters, the average South African is confronted by a veritable psychological barrage directly designed to stimulate an emotional climate conducive to total strategy. This is additionally assisted by the activity of numerous civil organizations which idealize military service either consciously or inadvertently. Foremost among these is the Southern Cross Fund whose 250 branches throughout the Republic raise money for the military on a full-time basis. The Fund is linked to the military through the SADF's public liaison office which, in turn, channels Southern Cross money into the official SADF fund, the so-called 'Brandwag'. As of May 1981 an estimated R5.5 million had moved in this direction.[72] While these moneys are used for humanitarian purposes, particularly to provide aid and comfort to soldiers in the operational area, the actual affect of Southern Cross activity is to market militarization in a way which encourages public identification.

Akin to other nationalist movements, Afrikaner nationalism regards the youth as a critical transmitter of group values, and virtually since its emergence as an organized political movement Afrikanerdom has sought to galvanize its young into defence of the national homeland. As Afrikanerdom has monopolized institutional political power so the tradition of the youth as a bulwark against threats to national and racial survival has been extended to the point where today so-called 'youth preparedness' is regarded by top decision-makers as a vital component in any strategy to offset the 'total onslaught' against the state as it is presently constituted. In current terms, the militarization of the youth, both English and Afrikaner, is effected through the cadet system which has been established in many white state and private schools and which requires all pupils at secondary level to devote a certain proportion of their weekly time to marching and other neo-military activities. While the whole system is often written off as a waste of precious time by parents, particularly parents of English students in the urban areas, cadet training services a number of distinctly useful purposes when viewed from the perspective of the military. It periodically exposes young men to martial routines, it serves as a nursery to national service, it stimulates patriotism and, according to its more ardent defenders, cadets 'create a favourable climate in respect of national defence'.[73] In present terms there is extensive liaison between the Defence Force and the Department of National Education on the integration of military training into the curricula of the white schools, either through the Director for Cadets at Army Headquarters, the Committee of School Principles, or the Inter-departmental Cadet Committee, established as a channel for the SADF and the educational authorities to communicate on the design and implementation of cadet programmes. Much of the so-called 'youth preparedness' programme designed for the consumption of secondary school students stems from these diverse sources. As a result of cooperation between the military and educational authorities the whole cadet system has been progressively extended through state schools, although privately-operated schools partially free of government subsidies have displayed markedly less enthusiasm at the prospect of subjecting their pupils to pre-national service training. Thus, in 1976, there were only 24 cadet detachments in private schools as opposed to 567 in government schools: of the 67 detachments established since 1970 none was in a private educational institution.[74] Despite this lacuna, a new revised cadet system was put into operation in the same year with the aim of putting a total of 100,000 schoolboys into uniform within a twelve-month period. As a result of the new intensified system the number of cadet detachments had grown to 626 involving 154,000 by the end of 1979. It was hoped to raise this global figure to 200,000 by the end of 1982.[75] The teaching staff of secondary schools are also regarded as an integral part of the process whereby scholars are imbued with military values prior to their actual incorporation into the Citizen Force on reaching the age of eighteen. Teachers are therefore selected to attend courses at the Danie Theron Combat School concerned with the training of Commandos, and are then, after a period, seconded to Army Headquarters as cadet officers of the SADF.[76] There are also plans afoot to extend cadet training to white schoolgirls and Indian and Coloured students although it is not readily apparent whether this move will go unresisted among Indian and Coloured leaders who have traditionally refused formally to render military service to the state short of being guaranteed full political participation. In the meantime a major proportion of young white males continue to be subjected to military education even before actually entering military service. This tendency is particularly marked among young Afrikaners who supplement their cadet training with membership of various nationalist paramilitary organizations such as the so-called 'Voortrekkers'.

With increased urban and rural activity on the part of the clandestine African National Congress in recent years the SADF has lent its assistance to government in developing a nation-wide civil defence system to function as an ancillary to the military establishment. Civil defence is, of course, not an unfamiliar realm of action for South Africa's soldiers. The military was an important source of aid during widespread flooding in the Cape in 1974, 1975 and, more recently, in the case of the Laingsburg floods where the Army supplied tents and transport to a wide variety of displaced persons. While long-range rescue operations and maritime reconnaissance are often inhibited by the growing obsolescence of the SAAF's Shackleton aircraft, Albatross search aircraft and Frelon rescue helicopters of the Air Force and Navy undertake land and sea rescue services on both a day-to-day basis and during specific periods of national disaster. Assistance of this type is an important part of the SADF's public relations: it projects an image of public concern and vigilance and basically maintains the military in the public eye. From the point of view of the Defence Force civil defence also has the added advantage of relieving military manpower from a variety of commitments, particularly in the task of providing security at the 633 'key point' non-military installations identified since the early seventies by the National Key Point Committee as vital to the safety of the state.[77] The growing number of sabotage attacks launched by the ANC on railroad installations, power stations and major oil refineries such as that as Sasolburg have highlighted the importance of a concerted civil defence effort to guard facilities which 'render important services or manufactured products of such national importance that destruction or damage to them could cause serious harm to South Africa, handicap the state in its war effort and thereby seriously prejudice law and order'.[78] The so-called National Key Points Bill is actually one of the latest legislative devices in the government's civil defence programme first initiated following the political disturbances of the early sixties. In 1963 a Civil Defence Organization was established under the aegis of the Department of Justice with the task of developing a 'national survival' plan to be integrated into the functions of government at all levels.[79] Following the Civil Defence Act of 1966, the CDO was removed from the Department of Justice, and during 1968/69 incorporated into the SADF as the Directorate of Civil Defence responsible for planning and coordinating the entire operation in direct collaboration with military authority.[80] Following a further reorganization in 1970, the Civil Defence Section of the SADF was directly attached to Army Headquarters in Pretoria, and today, with each of the nine Army commands responsible for activating and advising local authorities and ensuring satisfactory standards of preparation, civil defence is firmly within the military ambit. By February 1977, 657 local authorities had been identified for civil defence purposes including city and town councils, Bantu administration boards, area committees and peri-urban boards, 94 of which had received 'A' gradings from the SADF – meaning that their emergency plans had been finalized, tested and approved by the Army command concerned.[81] In a manner analogous to the extension of the national service system, the manpower net for civil defence personnel has also been extended in recent years: today, while the Civil Defence Act excludes members of the SADF, the South African Police and Railway Police, Prison Service, Armscor and Department of National Security members from civil defence, all employees of local authorities, all members of the National Reserve, the Reserve of Officers, the Citizen Force Reserve and the Commando Reserve who have served for more than five years in each Reserve are liable for civil defence duty.[82] The legislative foundations of civil defence have also been developed into a tight network integrating the SADF and local provincial authorities under the centralized control of the Minister of Defence. In terms of the Civil Defence Act of 1977, the SADF remains responsible for the overall control and coordination of civil defence, for activating the provincial and local authorities and assessing their efforts.[83] In addition, however, the Minister of Defence may proclaim a three-month 'state of disaster' in any area if he considers that 'extraordinary measures are necessary to assist and protect the Republic and its inhabitants and to combat civil disruption' or if he believes such a situation might arise. The Act defines 'disaster' to include 'an act of God, the influx of refugees into the Republic or any consequences arising out of terrorism as defined by the Terrorism Act of 1967'.[84] In such circumstances a provincial administrator 'may, in consultation with the Minister, take any steps he deems necessary in terms of the relevant ordinances', while the Minister is empowered to 'take over, after consultation with the administrator concerned, any power or duty conferred by any civil defence ordinance of any Provincial Council'.[85]

The centrality of the military in upholding public order through the civil defence system is paralleled by growing involvement by the SADF in domestic police work, although, as befits a professional body of soldiers, the military is careful to maintain distinctions between its own role in protecting the state against its internal enemies and that of its sister organization, the South African Police Force. In general the police have been in the forefront in combating political unrest since the establishment of the Union, black political unrest in particular. Nevertheless there are numerous instances in twentieth-century South African history where the Defence Force has been used, either alone or in conjunction with the police, in quelling domestic insurrections on the part of either blacks or whites. These include the 1914 rebellion and the 1922 Rand revolt when the fledgling Air Force, in one of its first acts, bombed rebel concentrations to the east of Johannesburg, in Brakpan and Benoni. The new air arm subsequently went on to assist the suppression of the Bondelswart Hottentot uprising in the same year, the Rehoboth Baster rebellion of 1925 and the Ovambo uprising seven years later. Today the legacy of these actions is statutorily recognized in various Defence Act amendments including Act 77 of 1963 in which provision is made for the use of Citizen Force units and Commandos in support of domestic control work by the SAP.[86] In terms of Act 1 of 1976 the Defence Force may be used in time of war, in connexion with the discharge of obligations of the Republic arising from any agreement between the Republic and any other state, for the prevention and suppression of internal terrorism and in a fashion justifying preventative actions by the SADF across the Republics's regional boundaries, 'for the prevention or suppression of any armed conflict outside of the Republic which, in the opinion of the State President, is or may be a threat to the security of the Republic.'[87] There is in fact an entire tradition of the police and military being used on an interchangeable inter–external basis to defend the interests of the South African state.[88] South Africa's initial involvement in the military defence of Namibia was originally a police operation, from 1966, with the first incursions by SWAPO guerrillas, to the point where the police were replaced by the military in the operational area during 1973. South African assistance to the beleagured Rhodesian government during the war against the Patriotic Front also took the form of a police contingent, while there is some evidence supporting the notion that both the South African Police and the Defence Force are involved in providing support for MNR dissidents in post-independence Mozambique. Since the creation of the Union the SADF has been regarded as a so-called 'second line of defence' against internal insurgency and as police manpower has been increasingly stretched thin during the seventies so this second-string role for the military has become progressively activated. At present there is considerable military–police cooperation in the pursuit of crime, particularly in controlling the growth and transportation of narcotics: military aircraft and helicopters are often on hand to assist the police in detecting so-called 'dagga' growing areas and then subsequently destroying them. During 1976 the military were placed on standby but were not subsequently used to control riots in Soweto and other black townships where police force proved adequate.

Since the 1976 disturbances, however, the military have been directly employed as a force for riot control in the Coloured townships of Johannesburg while soldiers are frequently found alongside the police manning roadblocks and conducting spot-searches on the main transport routes between Johannesburg and its adjacent black townships. In terms of its commitment to protect the civilian infrastructure of the Republic the SADF also collaborates with the South African Police and the South African Railways Police in counter-insurgency operations in the rural areas, either in the form of supporting ground units or in the form of aircover provided by Air Force helicopters. Cooperation between the Air Force and police is particularly close, the former having devoted some two thousand hours of flying time to supporting police operations over the course of the last two years.[89] Military–police cooperation also extends to Namibia so that while the current war effort is dominated by the SADF the police still do regular stints of operational duty, either in regular units supported by Ovambo police or in the specially-trained COIN counter-insurgency unit.[90] Counter-insurgency training generally adds to the obscuring of the functional divisions between police and military. Many of the cues for SADF tactics in Namibia today are drawn from earlier police experiences on the Angolan border, while the crack counter-insurgency units trained by the police at Maleoskop in the northern Transvaal are assisted in their development by military personnel and technical information produced by SADF units engaged in research and analysis of counter-revolutionary war. Many Joint Staff Courses at the South African Defence College are attended by police officers from the regular police or the railways police subsection.[91] According to reputable sources there is also considerable liaison between the Security Police, DTI (military counter-intelligence) and DMI (Directorate of Military Intelligence).

Militarization is always measured by the appearance of soldiers as public decision-makers and the growing influence of the South African military is finally, and perhaps most importantly, reflected in the penetration of top government institutions by Defence Force personnel, on either a formal or informal basis. The South African Defence Ministry, for example, has always been a poor relative of the more prestigious office of the prime minister and/or the Ministry of External (Foreign) Affairs and this has tended to make it very much an imperium of military rather than civilian authority since the creation of the Union. Originally established as a subsection of the Department of the Interior, the Department of Defence did not actually emerge as a separate institution until 1912. Thereafter its early history was dominated by considerable strain between its military and civil sections, with the military normally emerging in a position of institutional predominance. In 1922 the offices of Secretary of Defence and Chief of the General Staff were fused into a single position. Although this arrangement was reversed in 1933, only two of the six defence ministers prior to 1960 had not seen active service at some time during their lives and many were men of military title. Already in 1949 pressures for the complete and final abolition of the secretaryship of defence had been set in motion: in 1966, following the recommendations of the Verster Committee established to investigate relationships and work within the Secretariat, the offices of the Commandant-General of the SADF and the Secretary of Defence were once more fused into a single appointment by the then Minister of Defence, P.W. Botha.[92] Shortly thereafter, in May 1967, the secretaryship was finally abolished with all the functions of the office being transferred to the Chief of the Defence Force. In October 1980, with the appointment of the Chief of the Defence Force, General Malan, to the office of Minister of Defence the process of institutional absorption was taken one step further.

The subordination of the Department of Defence to military influence must be seen against the background of the common interest of both executive and military authorities in rationalizing state structures in support of total strategy, overlaid by the close personal links between P.W. Botha and top military leaders forged during the former's tenure as Minister of Defence, to produce a degree of mutual trust and confidence rare in the annals of South African civil–military history. Growing military intervention in the highest political struggles over state policy since 1977 is also, however, a direct result of growing internal and interstate conflict in South and southern Africa, the effect of which has been to propel strategic issues to the forefront of the public-policy agenda. In the field of foreign policy formation, in particular, the South African military has ridden the crest of demands for its special strategic expertise and thereby accumulated political influence in the higher realms of national deliberation. As the geographic noose on the Republic has tightened so that regional policy is today very much a matter of military survival so the Defence Force has emerged as a crucial source of foreign policy influence on international issues in both the subcontinent and further afield. In Namibia, which is virtually a military fiefdom, it is questionable whether any important political or administrative decisions are taken without reference to the military. During the 1978 elections military personnel acted in an important support capacity to the Democratic Turnhalle Alliance – displaying DTA stickers, maintaining order at DTA rallies and allegedly disrupting the rallies of its opponents.[93] Top ex-military officers have begun to appear in the upper ranks of the diplomatic corps as ambassadors, most notably, General Neil Webster, the Republic's representative to Iran under the Pahlavi monarchy, and, more recently, General Dutton, formerly

Chief-of-Staff, Operations, and then South Africa's first ambassador to Chile. Defence Force personnel are also increasingly prominent in negotiations and meetings between the Republic and its immediate neighbours. Today it is almost self-evident that General Malan or, to a lesser extent, General van der Westhuizen (Chief-of-Staff, Intelligence) will accompany the prime minister and Minister of Foreign Affairs on high-level diplomatic junkets, be they negotiations between South Africa and the Western contact group on Namibia, meetings with Zimbabwe's President Mugabe, or, as was fairly recently the case, at the historic Botswana meeting between P.W. Botha and Zambia's Dr Kaunda.[94] In the last analysis the entire destabilization exercise in the process of being implemented as a cardinal element in South Africa's regional policy is entirely unintelligible apart from the political weight wielded by Defence Force 'total strategists' at the highest levels of foreign policy conception.

The ability of the military to influence high-grade foreign policy decisions reflects the wider fact that the Defence Force is highly prominent in the so-called 'national security management system' centred on the State Security Council and its surrounding network of interlocked interdepartmental, working, planning and joint management committees. While this network operates in extraordinary secrecy and while the State Security Council (established in 1972) is not a military creation, it is fairly well known that the Defence Force has played an important role in upgrading, overhauling and developing the state security decision-making apparatus as part of its interest in rationalizing state structures under the prescriptions of total strategy.[95] After South Africa's involvement in Angola in particular, the military was perhaps the most important pressure group acting for the transformation of the Council from an ill-defined to a primary element in national security affairs, from a loose advisory body to a highly centralized pool of public policy.[96] Today when the Council (SSC) is at the apogee of public decision-making by virtue of its legal character, exclusive membership, comprehensive support network and chairmanship by the prime minister, military officers are a distinct and important factor in its activities. It has been claimed that SADF officers take part in all interdepartmental meetings within the state security system 'regardless of their subjects or whether direct SADF interests are involved' and that military advisers sit on all fifteen interdepartmental committees.[97] Be this the case or not, both Generals Magnus Malan and Constand Viljoen are 'primary', that is, permanent members of the State Security Council by virtue of their respective positions as Minister of Defence and Chief of the Defence Force. The State Security Council Secretariat (SSCS), responsible for planning and coordinating total strategy (as well as providing administrative services to the Council), is also headed by General van Deventer, formerly Chief-of-Staff, Finance; the joint management centres of the national security system (the GBS – Gesaamentlike Bestuursentrums) responsible for carrying total strategy from the centre to the periphery correspond exactly to the areal commands of the Defence Force and contain a heavy dose of military officials in their membership. Given the wide brief of the Council to 'advise the government on the formation of national policy and strategy in relation to the security of the country',[98] militarymen are in general placed at strategic points to influence virtually every aspect of public policy. This influence has progressively increased since 1980 as Botha and his military allies have moved to an ever more embracing conception of 'national security' which penetrates into virtually every aspect of political, economic and cultural life and as the powers of the legislature have been eroded to the advantage of the office of prime minister and the state security network in the formation of national policy.[99] The future, it should be added, is not likely to see a diminution of military influence at this particular level. Indeed, under the highly centralized arrangements envisaged under the government's new constitutional dispensation, the power of the executive and the military to take determining public decisions on virtually every issue, domestic or international, is likely to increase rather than diminish.

The growing role of the military in the State Security Council must also be seen as the institutional framework for major shifts of political influence in the national intelligence community. According to the State Security Act of 1972, the Council is responsible for determining national intelligence priorities. Hence, access to the Council immediately gives the Defence Force leverage to collect and interpret information subsequently incorporated into the decision-making process. In addition, however, the military is influential at the intelligence level in the State Security Council Secretariat, through its appropriately named Total Strategy Branch, its National Intelligence Interpretation Division – fed by military intelligence and the National Intelligence Service – and, one assumes, through the third of its three main branches, whose activities and very name are veiled by official secrecy.[100] On the whole, the Botha years have seen a veritable revolution in the national intelligence community with the Bureau of State Security (the precursor of NIS) having been basically displaced by military intelligence organizations as sources of information closest to the prime minister. This is particularly important in the light of the chequered history of DMI (Directorate of Military Intelligence) as an institution; formed originally in 1961 it has since then been constantly shifted between the authority of the Chief of the South African Defence Force and the Chief-of-Staff, Operations, while at the same time being locked in combat with civilian intelligence organizations, the Bureau of State Security in particular. Today, following the recommendations of the Potgieter Commission established to coordinate state security, DMI has clearly come into its own as an authentic and independent element in the intelligence community, with direct access to both the head of the Defence Force and the office of the prime minister. The exact dynamics of the process whereby the Bureau of State Security (now renamed the National Intelligence Service) has been downgraded to an instrument for processing routine information under the auspices of the State Security Council will, in all probability, never be known. Undoubtedly the present predominance of DMI reflects the association of the Bureau's former chief, General van den Berghe, with the now discredited Vorster government, the involvement of the Bureau with the so-called 'Information Scandal' and the antipathy between van den Berghe and the present prime minister. Nonetheless, the intelligence area is today clear for DMI operations.

Any description of militarization in South Africa must conclude, at some length, with the extension of the military network to include members of the subject race groups as active participants in Defence Force ranks. This development, arguably one of the most important developments in South African state structures, represents the culmination of numerous social forces, both political and economic.[101] On the one hand it represents in microcosm the cooptive thrust of the contemporary South African state and the partial shift from racial and ethnic techniques of political control to those where class criteria come to constitute the standards for membership and participation in the polity. The opening of Defence Force ranks to Indians, Coloureds and (to a more limited extent) blacks must be seen against the broader background of limited attempts to deracialize South African society – in both the labour and political fields – with a view to perpetuating its present cardinal features in some modulated and refined form. Hence, the appearance of Indians, Coloureds and blacks in the lower echelons of the military in recent years is intimately intertwined with the process whereby apartheid is streamlined through the creation of buffer groups between the masses and the white elite, be it in civil or military society. Inasmuch as total strategy prescribes the maximum use of manpower resources for military purposes and the creation of national armies in the process of counter-revolution, recruitment of 'non-whites' is also directly linked to the basic strategic and ideological thrust of the polity.

The recruitment of 'non-whites' into the Defence Force is also a reaction to manpower problems in the military which, although far from crippling the SADF in the performance of its internal and external tasks, are still sufficiently serious as to cause policy-makers to re-evaluate the role of 'non-whites' in the state security network. The officer ranks of the

Permanent Force, it should be emphasized, are still adequate in relation to present requirements, the numbers of servicemen taking up employment in the SADF still exceed those leaving the service, so much so that the military can still afford to maintain screening procedures which exclude almost half of the personnel applying for permanent service. The increasingly sophisticated technologies used by the SADF also tend to shift pressure away from the quantity to the quality of available manpower. It is nonetheless a fact that since 1969 personnel losses in the ranks have progressively exceeded gains and that the gap between personnel appointments and losses in the officer corps is gradually and negatively narrowing.[102] Since personnel figures formulated in global terms also tend to obscure the fact that a good proportion of personnel shortfalls are offset by the recruitment of women, many in a purely temporary capacity, there are distinct indications of serious manpower problems in the foreseeable future. This problem has been identified by military analysts in the Defence Force who have begun to lobby for what is described as 'a special effort ... to restore the balance in terms of the present conservative expansion in the establishment tables'.[103] According to manpower development plans extended into the 1990s, such an effort need not necessarily be confined to the use of 'other sources of manpower, such as white females', but could, and indeed should involve 'members of other population groups ... [working in the SADF] in a meaningful manner'.[104] In a nutshell, the military has come to recognize clearly that unless it dilutes its traditional policy of excluding 'non-whites' from its active ranks, it cannot realistically hope to meet the minimum manpower requirements of total strategy projected into the indefinite future.

There are many elements in the Defence Force who do not in principle support the extension of recruitment to 'non-whites' for a mixture of strategic and ideological reasons (which will be dealt with in more detail in the following chapter). Some members of the officer corps, backed by right-wing elements in the National Party, would clearly prefer to keep the military a racially reserved institution, despite the fact that the military competes unfavourably with the private sector in the white labour market, and despite the fact that any serious attempt to reverse the process in favour of the Defence Force would involve a variety of economic and political costs for the white elite which could conceivably cut into its unity and its capacity to expand the system in the process of maintaining power. It is a reflection of the internal influences of these elements that the SADF has given considerable attention to the recruitment of white women and permanently resident immigrants to South Africa as an alternative – a last-ditch alternative, it seems – to the inevitable option of bringing greater numbers of 'non-whites' into the military establishment.

In reality, attempts to win women and immigrants to military ranks have proved largely unrewarding, or at a minimum, problematic, given the needs of the Defence Force. Women have a tradition of service in the SADF dating back to World War I when many were first recruited as nurses. During World War II close on 90,000 women saw national service in various auxiliary roles.[105] In 1971 the Civil Defence College at George was transformed into a fully fledged South African Army Women's College and a consistent attempt was begun to integrate women into the Defence Force as a means to release male members of the SADF for operational service. By 1975 the Women's College had produced 325 female officers and 571 members of the ranks to supplement the growing number of women working as Defence Force personnel in the form of nurses, administrative officers, flight controllers, signallers, caterers and clerks.[106] Yet despite a massive rise in the female component of the SADF between 1973 and 1977 – from 0.6 per cent to a full 7 per cent[107] – the notion of transforming the military into a multi-gender force along classic Israeli lines has remained seriously constrained by a general lack of interest on the part of women in the civilian community. On the whole, there is no deeply ingrained tradition of female soldiering in South African civil–military culture, neither in the Afrikaans community where women's primary responsibility is seen to lie in the direction of the family, nor in the English segment where women are accustomed to comfortable domestic existence or professional careers in the private sector. Attempts by the SADF to encourage women to enlist, let alone to propose the conscription of women, tend to confront strong resistance from Afrikaner women's organizations associating female service with familial, moral and social disorganization, or from their English counterparts who are disinclined to take SADF proposals too seriously. Since the military itself is geared neither psychologically nor organizationally to a large intake of female recruits, the female option in meeting manpower problems is likely to remain largely impractical for the foreseeable future.

Military attempts to swell its ranks by recruiting non-South Africans, mercenaries, expatriate white Zimbabweans, or, above all, members of the large immigrant community permanently resident in the country, are also of dubious merit in the short run. The sense of patriotism and professionalism in the SADF tends to counter any policy of recruiting foreign mercenaries on a cash basis quite apart from the international political costs involved in any attempt to bolster recruitment in this way. While there is some evidence to suggest that military intelligence is connected to the global mercenary network, the recent abortive coup in the Seychelles (with its undertones of SADF involvement) has reinforced the general aversion of the military to working with mercenary elements.

White migrants resident in South Africa are also not a viable source of manpower although the number registering for military service has progressively increased over the years, from a mere 1,122 in 1971 to 1,919 in 1979, 2,206 (1980) and 2,259 during the 1981 calendar year.[108] While the South African military and government authorities have officially refused to incorporate entire ex-Rhodesian army units into the SADF, a good proportion of the foreign component of the Defence Force is made up of former members of such regiments as the Imperial Light Infantry or the Selous Scouts who have joined the SADF as individuals and who are now reportedly being used to train black units in the security-sensitive border areas of north-eastern Transvaal and northern Natal.[109] At the same time, the overwhelming majority of migrants to South Africa are clearly not motivated to enter the Republic by the prospect of a military career – in either a professional or in a conscript capacity. Relatively few have taken advantage of the provisions built into the national service system since 1967 which allow non-citizens domiciled in the country for five years 'to perform military service shoulder to shoulder with National Service Citizens',[110] and more frequent are the cases where permanent residents have explicitly refused citizenship after their five-year trial period in order to avoid military service. In practice, the increases in their numbers in military ranks has as much to do with SADF pressure on migrants to involve themselves in military activity as it has to do with a newfound sense of patriotism. In 1978, for example, an amendment was made to the Defence Act which makes all young white aliens liable for military service should they fail to take out citizenship within two years of becoming eligible for it. Plans have also been mooted to increase the tax burden on permanent residents who fail to take out citizenship as a means to avoid the national service system. There are, however, fundamental constraints on attempting to derive manpower from this particular source. The number of new white South Africans is, for one thing, far too small to make more than a marginal contribution to Defence Force needs on an annual basis. The real possibility of conscription would, above all, cut into immigration figures at the very time when the economy is increasingly dependent on imported skilled white manpower.

In these circumstances the Defence Force has been forced to fall back on 'non-white' manpower, reluctantly, but with the awareness that on past occasions when blacks have been called to render military service to the white state they have done so with a degree of courage and loyalty often far in excess of military expectations. While it cannot be assumed with any degree of certainty that these qualities will be replicated in today's climate of harsh racial polarization, the tradition of 'non-white' military service is still of considerable importance. Even though the Defence Act of 1912 specifically bars non-Europeans from military service without express approval of parliament, both before and after the creation of the Union the subject race groups have frequently been used to render military support to the white state on a pragmatic basis.[111] In reality the official use of Coloureds in a military role dates as far back as 1795 when half-castes and Hottentots were levied for service.[112] Despite the harsh racial climate of the Boer Republics, President Kruger adopted an Act of the Volksraad in 1883 which provided that 'the Coloured people – and persons whose father and mother belong to one of the native races of Africa or Asia until and in the fourth generation – who are able to be of service in war may be called up'.[113] Blacks were used as auxiliaries in massive numbers by both contestants during the Boer War, although it was accepted implicitly by Boer and British that neither would use 'non-whites' in an active military capacity.[114] In 1915 a Cape Corps (composed of Coloureds) was formed to assist the South African war effort and again during World War II Coloureds played an important role in South African army operations in both North Africa and southern Europe. While the Coloured element in the Union Defence Force was officially non-combatant it nevertheless performed an active military role as the practicalities of the situation demanded. As Neil Orpen has noted in his refutation of the widespread idea that the Coloured forces were mere auxiliaries: 'The Cape Corps, re-formed originally as non-combatant ... in fact permeated every branch of the service ... 45,015 men altogether served in the Cape Corps during the war, and of the 2,678 who became casualties outside the Union no man can say how many were actually killed or wounded in action as combatants.'[115] White South Africa, no less its Defence Force, has always understandably approached the arming of the racial majority with considerable caution, not only for fear that they might use their arms to overthrow white domination, but also because military service has tended to have a distinctly politicizing effect on blacks integrated into the SADF, along lines similar to other countries. Feelings of this nature, which persist to the present day, were clearly voiced in the so-called Black Manifesto issued by the extreme Afrikaner nationalists of the Ossewa-Brandwag shortly before the 1942 election, while the social activism displayed by many members of the Cape Corps after World War II was certainly a factor in the decision of the National Party to disband the unit as a part of the SADF shortly after its coming to power.[116] At the same time, contemporary leaders of the SADF have for some years expressed admiration at the ability of the South African Police to quietly yet quite effectively resolve manpower problems similar to their own by bringing blacks into the ranks, albeit in a carefully controlled manner.[117] Others have noted the important military role of black soldiers in the Rhodesian army during the war following UDI leading to Zimbabwe's independence. Drawing on both experiences, SADF policy since the beginning of the 1970s has been carefully orchestrated to recruiting black manpower on an experimental basis, particularly for use outside the direct public eye, either in the rural areas, or, more importantly, in the Namibian theatre of operations. To a large extent, the calculation that blacks can be used as effectively in defending the white state today as in the past, has borne fruit. Speaking in October 1977, when it was estimated that already more than 20 per cent of South African forces in the Namibian operational theatre were black, either South African regulars, or South African-trained local armies, General Malan was obliged to compliment these forces on what he described as their 'outstanding work'.[118] Today, many white commanders on the borders wax enthusiastic over the fighting capacity of their 'non-white' soldiers, be they blacks or Coloured members of the Cape Corps Battalion.[119] Others, with a note of surprise, point to the ability of their non-white recruits to mingle freely and effectively with their white counterparts in the combat zone despite the apartheid injunction that social intercourse and physical proximity between the races inevitably leads to friction and conflict.

Military institutions are often among the first state organizations to be officially desegregated and with the passing of the years and the expanded operational requirements of the SADF the role of the subject race groups in its ranks have been proportionately expanded. This is especially true of the Coloured community, both because of its tradition of military service and its relative proximity to the dominant white group in South Africa's racial hierarchy. Since the re-establishment of the Cape Corps in 1963, numbers of Coloureds in the Defence Force have grown quite rapidly, although, it should be added, the Coloured component of total Permanent Force membership is still quite modest. Nevertheless, while there were only 527 Coloured soldiers in the Defence Force in 1966, there were no less than 2,737 volunteers for the two-year period of military service prescribed for the Corps during January-February 1982 alone, of whom 1,456 were subsequently accepted.[120] Coloureds, originally enlisted into the revitalized Cape Corps to fill purely auxiliary roles, today perform numerous functions in the varied facets of the SADF network and have actually been brought into the combatant mainstream. Already by 1975 Coloureds were to be in the Anti-Aircraft regiment at Youngsfield Air Base near the Cape Corps training depot at Elsies River near Cape Town, as personnel in the SADF's ordnance and electronics workshops, in supply and transport services, and as students in the military's main training institutions, the Military Academy at Saldanha Bay, the Infantry School at Oudschoorn, the Engineer School at Kroonstad, and the Danie Theron Combat School in

Kimberley.[121] In 1972, moreover, the Cape Corps (now formally entitled the South African Coloured Corps) gave birth to its first specific combat unit, seven of whose soldiers were given the rank of lieutenant during 1975 – the first black officers in Defence Force history. In 1977 it was announced that an infantry unit for Coloureds was to be established as an integral element of the Citizen Force and in the following year the first Coloured infantrymen began training as paratroopers for deployment in the operational zone of Namibia.[122] Since 1977 when the Coloured Corps first appeared for duty in Namibia, members of the unit have spent most of the second year of their two-year period of service in the operational area where they have emerged as an important component in the Republic's war effort. With the added use of Coloured personnel by Naval Command at Simonstown the 'Coloured man', in the words of one commentator, is truly 'once again in uniform serving on land and sea'.[123]

Indians and blacks have also been incorporated into the Defence Force in line with the belief inherent in total strategy that all population groups be militarized in defence of the state. In neither case is the degree or diversity of mobilization comparable with that of the Coloured group. The insular features of South Africa's Indian community tend to undercut enthusiasm for service on behalf of the state quite independent of state discrimination against the Indian population, while black leaders and a good proportion of the black public are vigorous in condemning military service in the absence of civil and political rights for the majority community.[124] While black leaders differ in their reactions to the state according to their relationship with it, both radicals and moderates tend to cohere in the opinion that it is illogical and unethical for blacks to assist in the defence of a South Africa under apartheid. Chief Lucas Mangope of Bophutatswana has expressed the view that black military service is conditional on the black majority being given a real stake in South Africa – as he has put it, 'We are prepared to lay down our lives in defence of our country ... [but] we do not want anybody to get the impression that we are prepared to defend the country for the privileged position of others and the disabilities and inequalities that we are subjected to.'[125] Similar views have been expressed by Dr Cedric Phatudi of Lebowa, and, above all, by Kwazulu's Chief, Buthelezi. At the same time, the number of Indians and blacks willing to serve in the SADF on a voluntary basis has increased in recent years, as has the willingness of the military to accept assistance from the politically disincorporated. In 1974 an Indian Corps composed along the lines of the Cape Corps was established at SAS Dalsena on Salisbury Island near Durban and although its training is undertaken by the Navy in terms of an agreement between the now-defunct South African Indian Council and the SADF it is clearly intended that Indian volunteers will move into a variety of forms of military service.[126] Despite the fact that the SADF is not considering the conscription of blacks 'until such a time as the citizenship question of blacks is resolved',[127] there is still a substantial pool of black manpower upon which the military can draw in meeting its recruitment requirements – a pool far in excess of present SADF requirements. In the first six months of 1980, for example, 458 blacks (and 300 Indians) came forward to volunteer for service in the SADF of whom 228 and 153 were subsequently accommodated.[128] The number of blacks seeking positions in the Defence Force as soldiers has subsequently also increased with great rapidity: in January 1981 alone, 816 black recruits came forward (of whom 518 were accepted for service); in January 1982, 918 (of whom 672 were taken into the ranks).[129] While the greater number of black SADF personnel are still civilians, clerks, storemen and chefs in the Auxiliary Service, greater moves have been afoot since 1971 to train black soldiers in the mainstream of the SADF along the lines suggested by the Coloured and Indian communities. In 1974 the first black unit was formed of San Bushmen in north-eastern Namibia, followed by the first black Permanent Force unit in 1975.[130] Today, eight years later, a good proportion of South African counter-insurgency operations in Namibia and within the territorial Republic are conducted by specially-trained black units such as 111 and 113 Battalions composed respectively of Swazis and Shangaan stationed at Amsterdam in the eastern Transvaal, 112 Battalion (Venda) at Madumbo (near Phalaborwa in the far north-eastern Transvaal) and 121 Battalion (Zulu) affiliated to Natal Command and deployed at Jozini. An estimated five thousand blacks forged into similar ethnic units operate in conjunction with South African security forces in the Namibian–Angolan theatre, for example, 701 Battalion, originally the Caprivi Battalion, operative in the area since 1979 and stationed at M'Pacha.[131] This use of ethnic armies composed of subject groups to defend the state is not of course a uniquely South African phenomenon, and understandably, the local civil and military authorities prefer to create ethnic rather than multi-ethnic units in accord with the traditional apartheid policy of dividing and controlling along distinctive communal boundaries. However, 'multi-national' black battalions are also in the process of creation, most notably the elite 21 Battalion stationed at Lenz near Johannesburg. This unit, composed of selected individuals drawn from the regional ethnic units as well as recruits from the urban areas, has tended to emerge as a show-case for black soldiers in the South African army. Its members, following 27 weeks of basic and specialized training, have been deployed in Namibia since 1978 where, according to all reports, they have acquitted themselves well in combat, in liaising with the local population and in intelligence gathering on the basis of common racial affiliation.[132] Finally, blacks serve in a support capacity to the SADF through the 'homeland' armies developed by the Defence Force in each of the 'independent' homeland areas and equipped with a mixture of South African manufactured and imported weaponry. The Bophutatswana National Guard, with over 1,000 men, stationed just north of Mmabatho, was, for example, a subunit of the SADF command centred on Potchefstroom before being converted to its present 'national' status. Its training, however, is still conducted by seconded SADF officers acting under the Bophutatswana Ministry of Defence which is in turn headed by a former South African Defence Force officer. The Transkei Defence Force is also tightly tied into the South African military network in terms of its planning and development, although some of its approximately 1,750 men are equipped with French arms and commanded by ex-Rhodesian army elements. Both the Bophutatswana and Transkei armies are officially directed to defend the territorial integrity of the two 'independent' states, but the particular emphasis placed on counter-insurgency since the beginning of the eighties suggests that the two forces are being groomed essentially to cope with internal dissidence. A similar orientation towards domestic as opposed to external control is also evident in the training programme and equipment of the relatively more recent Venda and Ciskeian armies.

The militarization of the bantustans is part of a wider and ongoing process whereby the political predominance of South Africa's racial elite is becoming increasingly dependent on an interlocking but diverse security network composed of non-white elements. In the Transkei in particular, some 2 per cent of the 'national' budget (R11 million) is currently devoted to defence, plans are afoot to develop a complex military infrastructure composed of aerial, naval and engineering units to complement the present mixture of infantry and special strike forces and, equally important, to Africanize the military and reduce its present reliance on imported white manpower. As a result, the present head of the TDF, Lieutenant-Colonel Reid-Daly, is due to be replaced within the next few months by a black Transkeian citizen. South African military leaders for their part are aware of the importance of black soldiers in extending the life-span of other white African regimes – particularly that of the Rhodesian regime – and they have indeed taken many of their cues from the historical example of nearby Rhodesia in designing the incorporation of blacks into the Defence Force and in rationalizing the desegregation of the military to the white South African public. Not all of this public is unequivocal in its support of the idea of arming the 'non-white' majority in support of the racial status quo. Indeed, militarization along non-racial lines, the progressive if still partial tendency to bring the subject race groups into the military mainstream as a means of propping up apartheid, may be one of the most important developments in recent South African history – conceivably of more consequence to the long-term future than the present pattern of constitutional change from which most current commentators draw their key indicators. This is not to diminish the importance of political developments in both black and white society at the foundations of present attempts to redesign the constitutional order. Yet, much of South African politics involves an interplay of force, a balance of violence between incumbents and contenders for state power, in which the nature of the state security apparatus – its membership and internal influence patterns – can be absolutely decisive. As we have previously emphasized, developments within the Defence Force, including the still narrow and circumscribed pattern of race relations within the military establishment, stand at the nexus between evolution and revolution in the South African context.

A good proportion of contemporary South African politics is concerned with attempts to extend the legitimacy of the state, and the degree to which the subject race groups can be encouraged to identify with the activities of the Defence Force may be one of the most important issues in the complex of support-building activities of which cooption and constitutional change are integral parts. At present, few blacks recognize the SADF as a legitimate institution. The deep sense of illegitimacy attached to the white state carries over to its agents, and this is likely to continue into the forseeable future despite the various leadership changes in the military which have allowed it to be partially transformed from an instrument of pure violence into a more genuinely social and civil institution concerned with action to win the hearts and minds of the majority black population. Civic action, it is readily if privately conceded by Defence Force leaders, has not yet succeeded in winning the allegiance of most blacks (or Indians and Coloureds) along the lines prescribed by total strategy: only a miniscule proportion of South Africa's 'non-white' population is genuinely receptive to the rhetoric and symbols of 'total onslaught' designed, *inter alia*, to project the Defence Force as a national or people's army. Many Coloureds and Indians were initially reluctant to join the Defence Force with the reinvigoration (and founding) of the Cape and Indian Corps, yet the fact of the matter is that today the time has passed when SADF recruiters were forced to visit Coloured schools and Indian cinemas in order to win 'non-white' recruits to military ranks.[133] Today there is an 'internal' group of applicants for Defence Force service composed of Coloureds and Indians (and black manpower) which is willing to enter the white military establishment and, in many cases, is eager to take advantage of the material opportunities proffered by the Defence Force, despite its elementary racial character. This reflects the deeper fact that to some members of the subject race groups – their precise number cannot be determined with any degree of accuracy – the white military establishment has a distinct instrumental value. Given the limited number of channels available to upwardly mobile blacks in apartheid society, the Defence Force, the South African Police and the state bureaucracy are important career outlets for individual members of the subordinate race groups who are prepared to live off the system – particularly at a time of economic recession and rising black unemployment. While serving the white state as a military or bureaucratic functionary involves a variety of ethical and social costs when viewed from the perspective of the Coloured, Indian or South African black, the decision to do so is not entirely irrational in terms of the material rewards made available to those willing to make such a commitment. A rural black of reasonable age, with a primary school education and without rights to live in 'white' urban South Africa has precious few life-chances in apartheid society, least of all at a time when economic recession and intensified application of influx control laws combine to keep him poor and outside the cities. As a member of the Defence Force, on the other hand, he is able to acquire a substantial salary relative to his counterparts in the open labour market and, unlike the common black worker, he is able to enjoy a number of ancillary benefits and 'perks' in the form of on-the-job training, housing, free medical and dental care, uniforms, thirty days of annual vacation and a guaranteed pension on retirement at the age of sixty. The SADF is also an important means for rural blacks to ingratiate themselves with tribal headmen and local chiefs (many of whom act as informal agents of the military in the homeland areas) and the Defence Force, being a relatively encapsulated institution, is also able partially to shield its members from the unrequited racism of wider South African society. The military authorities have in fact made considerable use of positive incentives in relation to black recruits in recent years, both to ensure their loyalty and to bolster the image of the Defence Force as a non-racial institution. Considerable effort, for example, is taken in catering to the ethnic and cultural sensibilities of non-white recruits insofar as the ethos and practical requirements of the SADF as a predominantly white institution will allow. This means observing the religious and dietary habits of Indian recruits at SAS Jalsena, respecting Zulu customs in the case of 121 Battalion, and in the case of white officers in command positions in the various ethnic units, learning the appropriate native language. In the process of assisting the institutional socialization of 'non-white' recruits Defence Force authorities have taken a number of fairly radical steps (relative to the wider context of South African society) to promote a degree of racial equality within military ranks. The Navy, in particular, has made an extended effort to use and upgrade Coloured personnel on the basis that maritime activity is a traditional occupation for the Coloured community, many of whom continue to live on or close to the coastal areas.[134] In reality, navies normally precede air forces and armies in integrating their ranks in multiracial societies particularly in cases like South Africa where the threat to the state is seen as essentially landward and where, as a result, the navy is perhaps the least sensitive of the service arms in the security network.[135] In either eventuality the South African Navy has led much of the way in breaking down institutionalized barriers to 'non-white' advancement: while Coloureds have traditionally been employed in the Navy as mechanics, stewards, storekeepers and so forth, the Navy was the first of the major combat arms to admit Coloureds to mainstream combat duty and the first to publicly declare that merit will in future be the only criterion for Coloured and Indian advancement. Even in the more conservative ranks of the South African Army, however, moves have been afoot to improve internal race relations through a measure of non-discrimination. In 1975 the Defence Act was amended in the light of the appointment of the first Coloured officers in the Cape Corps so that all white officers are not obliged to salute 'non-white' officers senior to themselves. 'Non-white' soldiers are not only plentiful but also cheap labour in a manner reminiscent of blacks in the productive sector of the economy: in 1977 black soldiers in the Defence Force were receiving only 54–63 per cent of the salaries of white soldiers in comparable positions.[136] The Defence Force has since addressed itself to narrowing the wage gap between the various population groups in the military and has achieved complete parity in the salaries now paid to Indian, Coloured and white officers. Salaries paid to non-commissioned officers are closer to parity along racial lines than ever before and the SADF is officially committed to ironing out remaining inequalities in the foreseeable future in accord with the stated policies of the Public Service Commission. Blacks, as the least reliable racial group in the state security network, have not shared in many of these benefits. Only black chaplains are paid an equal rate to whites although the prime minister has given his assurances that the future will see more equity in the salaries of all race groups in the Defence Force.[137] In the meantime blacks are able to rise to the rank of staff sergeant in the Army while the possibility of allowing blacks into the permanent ranks of the Navy is currently being investigated. Many lower and middle-ranking white officers in all of the service arms have a vested stake in assisting Indians and Coloureds (and even blacks) to move upwards in the military hierarchy since this means their own upward mobility in terms of South Africa's conventional colour bar. Hence, it is often widely argued, the more 'non-white' lieutenants, the more white captains, majors and colonels.

Finally, there is evidence of some degree of social intercourse between white, black and brown soldiers in the operational zone of Namibia in a way which suggests the breaking down (or temporary weakening) of the racial barriers between soldiers in the harsh crucible of combat.

One must of course exercise considerable discretion in inferring social and political consequences from these developments. The various efforts to improve race relations within the Defence Force may have less to do with the intrusion of 'liberal' influences into the military decision-making process than with institutional imperatives and functional necessities related to the smooth operation of the military establishment. Since the rewards of service offered by the SADF to its Coloured, Indian and black recruits are in the context of a command system which remains exclusively white in character, it does not seem unreasonable to suggest that the whole pattern of improved service conditions is part of an elaborate and calculated process to cement the 'non-white' recruit into the Defence Force system in a way which allows the state to manipulate his manpower for its own racial purposes. The rewards extended by the SADF to its black recruits actually run in tandem with an elaborate system of controls – the basic purpose of which is to ensure institutional cohesion and obedience. All Indian, Coloured and (in particular) black applicants to the career ranks of the SADF are rigorously screened at the point of admission. In the case of 21 Battalion this is exemplified by the use of the recommendations of government-sponsored bodies – the 'homeland' authorities and the now-defunct Indian and Coloured Representative Council – in separating out possible recruits from 'undesirables'.[138] While a primary school education is technically sufficient to ensure admission to the black regional armies, recruits to elite units such as 21 Battalion must conform to more rigorous criteria of age, physical fitness, language proficiency and social track record. Even then, black volunteers do not become fully fledged members of the Permanent Force until they have served a full twelve weeks in the operational area of Namibia where their capabilities and loyalties are fully tested. Ethnic and racial diversity in the Defence Force are naturally encouraged as a technique of social control since Coloured, Indian and black tribal units are separated from each other by function and differential treatment within the context of a unified white command structure. It is, one might add, quite apparent that a significant number of 'non-whites' join the Defence Force not through a 'comprehensive understanding of communism and terrorism' or a 'desire to fight for their country' (as Defence Force rhetoric would have us believe),[139] but for more mundane and instrumental reasons related to the state of the labour market and the economy. Not only are many black and Coloured recruits linked to the state apparatus by familial ties (they may have relatives in the white bureaucracy,[140] the police or the homeland leaderships), but many come from deprived rural areas – blacks from the underdeveloped homelands, Coloureds from the poor farming areas of the Eastern Province and north-west Cape. Attempts to create urban commandos to 'help and protect' areas such as Soweto have not proved particularly successful since their introduction in 1978 – considerably less so in attracting 'non-white' manpower than the mainstream ranks of the military with their attendant benefits and services.[141] This suggests that 'non-white' recruitment into the SADF is still very much related to what one analyst has called 'an economic draft' and that considerably more remains to be done in the process of converting the instrumental allegiances of 'non-white' recruits into more substantial diffuse identifications with the military if it is to attain its objective of a genuinely popular Defence Force.

The blend of reward and control built into SADF polity regarding 'non-whites' must also be seen against the background of the fact that the progressive militarization of South African society must inevitably change the racial arithmetic in the military establishment, in gross material terms, and in terms of the distribution of influence and status within the Defence Force, as Indians, Coloureds and eventually blacks move in greater numbers into non-commissioned and officer ranks. 'Non-white' numbers in the SADF are presently small and, admittedly, increasing relatively slowly. 'Non-whites' are unlikely to be admitted en masse into military ranks as long as the white elite remains dubious of their commitment to defend the white state, or at least until the questions regarding 'non-white' citizenship in the polity are resolved in a way which creates a legal basis for conscripting blacks into the military establishment. The number of applicants for military service among 'non-whites' is also likely to shrink in the face of growing racial polarization and it is not readily apparent that the SADF has the organizational resources to deal with a significant influx of raw black manpower, either in the form of volunteers or as conscripts under an extended national service system. There are nevertheless equally strong, and, I would argue, preponderant forces, working towards the racial dilution of the SADF in the foreseeable intermediate future. For one thing, the Defence Force is already fairly close to its saturation point of absorbable white manpower and there seems no reason to believe that South Africa will prove the exception to the universal rule that ethnic states dilute their criteria for admission to military service as a last resort in the face of social crisis. The private sector (as we will note in more detail below) certainly encourages the replacement of scarce white manpower by black recruits in military ranks, and its incentives to racially dilute selected areas of the military establishment would certainly increase if the perennial shortage of skilled white labour in the civil sector began to take on the dimensions of major economic crisis. It is Defence Force policy to gradually enlarge 'non-white' numbers in the military: in the recent past the SADF has pragmatically bent its recruitment policies to meet its institutional appetite for manpower and it is likely to extend this tendency in the foreseeable future as the state is brought under growing internal and international pressure. Even if this does not occur, the present pattern of constitutional change with its emphasis on incorporating Coloured and Indian into the white body politic must inevitably spill over to produce racial changes within the ranks of the Defence Force. As these two minority groups are brought into the political system as citizens they will become technically and legally available for military service: they will become a new pool of available manpower which the military must eventually mobilize in the process of meeting its functional and strategic obligations.

I do not wish to speculate about the implications of these developments except to say that as the military becomes decreasingly white in its overall composition changes must take place within the military establishment which must in turn affect relations between the South African military and the remainder of the white polity. I do not foresee a dilution of the tradition of white control over the military nor do I conceive of a Defence Force with Coloured, Indian and black generals – short of a revolutionary overthrow of the white state and social order. Nor do I envisage 'non-whites' even rising to upper-level command situations, to colonelcies and brigadierships, except in stringently controlled and critical situations. Nonetheless, as 'non-whites' move into the lower and middle ranks in the various ethnic and racial units in the SADF they must inevitably come to constitute a force within the Defence Force to which its leadership must respond in the interests of institutional solidarity. Today, some 40 per cent of the SADF and the South West African Territorial Force (SWATF) are 'non-white'. This may or may not mean that the subject race groups are being used as the cannon-fodder of the white state as alleged by its local and overseas critics. What it does mean is that the white state is becoming increasingly reliant on 'non-white' manpower some of which, Indian and Coloured, is bound to be propelled into middle-officer ranks in the course of time – for institutional and strategic reasons peculiar to the Defence Force and for political reasons related to the progressive incorporation of Indian and Coloured minorities into the broad political system. There are pressure groups within every military establishment, and in the SADF, as within any complex military organization, the numerically growing 'non-white' component could emerge as a source of intra-institutional demands whose claims white leadership must address if it wishes to maintain its organizational integrity and the commitment of its members. In this process engineered by middle-level Indian and Coloured officers at the nexus between the white command and the blackening ranks there could conceivably be considerable spillover of a reformist type across the civil–military boundary. Assuring the reliability of its 'non-white' members may even involve the SADF pressing more actively for a better political and economic deal in the context of wider South African society.

Reliability is indeed the touchstone by which militarization across racial boundaries needs to be measured. It is by no means certain that the mixture of material inducements and institutional controls presently at the heart of SADF attempts to involve 'non-whites' in the building of the garrison state will prove adequate to maintain their allegiance under the shifting political and economic circumstances of the future. Improvements in the South African economy enabling potential recruits to seek out more lucrative, less dangerous and considerably less controversial career opportunities could well eliminate the 'economic draft' at the basis of today's movement of 'non-whites' into the SADF. Increased racial conflict will also test the commitment of 'non-whites' to the Defence Force: racial polarization could raise the social risks 'for non-white' participation in the military apparatus of the white state along the lines of 1976, when the families of 21 Battalion were evacuated from Soweto for fear of their personal safety. Such conflict could also give reality to the nightmare scenario of many white South Africans who see black soldiers ultimately turning their weapons on the state structures they have been armed to defend. The issue of reliability is also at the heart of many of the current debates within the Defence Force between, on the one hand, technocratic and pragmatic elements who regard the recruitment of 'non-whites' as an organizational necessity which can be carefully monitored by the socialization techniques and instruments of internal control in the hands of military leadership and, on the other, more ideological and tradition-minded officers who are culturally resistant to the principle of arming black soldiers and are sceptical as to whether it is possible to develop their commitment to the military from one based on expediency and reward to a deeper sense of identification and allegiance. Militarization, it should be emphasized, has bred a variety of conflicts and cleavages within the defence establishment, between General Malan and his managerially-minded followers who compliment blacks for their 'outstanding performance' in the operational area and those officers not entirely sure that recruiting non–whites does not open up a Pandora's box of institutional and political problems which must ultimately undercut the protective and inherently racial role of the Defence Force. Militarization, the building of the garrison state along the lines prescribed by total strategy, has indeed bred a variety of differences of interest and opinion throughout the white elite constellation. The admission of 'non-whites' to the security system is but one pale but important reflection of this.

4

◇◇◇

Militarization and conflict in the siege culture

Militarization in South Africa is a source of both social conflict and coherence. Coherence stems from the integrating and homogenizing forces set in motion through purposive attempts by the state to create a garrison atmosphere and institutional network appropriate to the prescriptions of total strategy. Conflict stems from the fact that garrison states in the process of their development are always to some extent imperfectly unified entities within which different social formations compete in carving out their respective stakes in the new social order. South Africa, despite thirty-five years of authoritarian rule, is still a highly dynamic and pluralized society within which various social fragments – in government, business, the bureaucracy and even in the military – diverge in their political perceptions and interests despite their common and transcending interest in the perpetuation of the racial order. Members of these different fragments – the expression of a complex, differentiated and intrinsically modern South African society – are not uniformly intense in their identification with total strategy; they differ in their understanding of the meaning and social implications of militarization in a way which reflects specific institutional imperatives and some of these fragments are actually sceptical as to whether applied total strategy represents a viable response to South Africa's political problems. Hence, as militarism takes root and generates pressure from a homogeneous society, in the very process by which South Africa equips itself strategically, economically, politically and psychologically for a siege situation, conflict begins to swell within and around the elite constellation as its constituent elements jockey to protect their prerogatives and their claims to social resources in the face of shifting civil–military boundaries. It is this particular quality of militarization in South Africa, with its roots in the institutional history and political culture of local society, which has inhibited the rapid transformation of South Africa from a limited parliamentary to full-blown praetorian state up to the present time. Under certain social conditions to be identified in the following chapter, the same forces of social plurality could conceivably act as a brake upon further changes in civil–military boundaries in the foreseeable future.

In reality, there are numerous entities in current South African society whose reactions to militarism range from the hostile to the mildly equivocal. Some of these interests, as we shall note, have both the will and the political capacity to give substantive support to the traditional 'liberal' conception of civil–military relations in South Africa, others can register little more than verbal protest against the resurgent kommando ethic in South African society. The subject race groups are of course in the forefront of opposition, although there are significant differences of emphasis between Black, Indian and Coloured within the universal perception that militarization, with its baggage of total strategy and onslaughts, represents a new and more systematic dose of white authoritarianism. The calls for 'national solidarity' in the face of 'communist imperialism' do not generally find a receptive audience among politically disincorporated 'non-whites' who are understandably sceptical of interpretations of society and politics emanating from governmental authority. Yet the subject race groups are not politically disincorporated to the same degree, least of all at the present time when the National Party's new constitutional dispensation seems to hold out a slight possibility that Coloureds and Indians will eventually be brought into the mainstream of South African political life as reserve elements in the elite minority. In such circumstances the political and military appeals of the state tend, as a broad generalisation, to find greater receptivity among South Africa's repressed racial minorities than among members of the black majority who feel no moral or material obligation to assist the state to ensure its survival.

Within the subject communities, attitudes towards militarization range between two extremes. On the one hand are to be found the 'collaborative' element – Indians, Coloureds and, to an understandably smaller degree, blacks who are prepared to serve as functionaries of the military establishment, as employees in the armaments industry or, more directly, as volunteers in the small but growing number of 'non-white' units in the South African Defence Force. At the other extreme lie the proponents of the underground liberation movements, most notably members or sympathizers of the African National Congress whose policy it is actively to encourage draft resistance and desertion among military personnel in conjunction with armed revolutionary violence directed against military persons and property. Expressions of this most radical reaction to militarization are to be found in the Committee of South African War Resisters (COSAWR) founded out of the British Anti-Apartheid Movement and the South

African Liberation Support Committee during 1979 and the increasingly frequent attacks by ANC activists on South African military (and police) property. Between the underground and quisling elements lies the broad majority of urban blacks, most of whom see the SADF as an integral part of the complex of institutions making up the repressive state apparatus. This view has been strengthened as the Defence Force has emerged as an active participant in township control alongside the police in the period since 1976.[1] Whether or not the problematic nature of South African military intervention in Angola acted as a catalyst for the 1976 disturbances, as alleged in some circles, SADF setbacks in any form tend to feed what one recent observer of black politics has termed the climate of 'political exhilaration' to be found in urban black communities in the wake of the riots.[2] At the same time resistance to militarization is not a black prerogative – even though dissident members of the white elite have neither the material nor psychological incentives to oppose the growing role of the Defence Force with the same fervency as those opposed to the fusion of military and state power in the black community. Much of the spirit if not the activism of radical black opposition to militarization is replicated in the English church and academic communities which have today emerged as one of the primary focal points for opposition to total strategy – despite the authoritarian climate of the present-day South Africa where mild criticism of the SADF can be technically construed as an offence against the state with revolutionary connotations. With the extension of South African military activity in Namibia and across national boundaries in the region, the issue of conscientious objection has, in particular, generated crises of conscience in the white liberal community and today, with growing frequency, questions related to the ethical and political implications of military service have emerged as an important vehicle for projecting the wider issue of militarism into the local public debate. Conscientious objection has in fact become one of the primary factors fueling the tension between church and state in South Africa, although the origins of this political conflict long predate South African military claims on political power. From a purely technical point of view objection to military service is not an offence under South African law provided the refusal to serve in the Defence Force is rooted in bona fide and long-standing religious convictions and provided the erstwhile objector is prepared to accept non-combatant status in SADF ranks. This is the essence of the 1957 Act which provides that 'a registering officer shall as far as may be practicable allot any person who to his knowledge bona fide belongs and adheres to a recognized religious denomination by the tenets whereof its members may not participate in war, to a unit where such person will be able to render service in the Defence of the Republic in a non-combatant capacity'.[3] The military has also recognized certain 'churches of peace', including the Jehovah's Witnesses, the Plymouth Brethren, the Christadelphians and the Seventh Day Adventists.[4] Nevertheless, many conscientious objectors have refused to serve in the Defence Force even in a non-combatant capacity and the severe punishment exacted on these individuals has fed the burgeoning conflict between the apartheid state and the various elements in the ecclesiastical community who find it difficult to reconcile the social order with Christian tenets of human dignity. In 1974, in the so-called Hammanskraal Resolution, the South African Council of Churches called on its member churches to consider 'whether Christ's call to take up the Cross and follow him in identifying with the oppressed does not, in our situation, involve becoming conscientious objectors'.[5] Both the Anglican and Roman Catholic churches have also denounced Defence Force policy to prosecute conscientious objection under military and civil law as 'destructive of human integrity and incompatible with Christ's Gospel'.[6] Nationalist politicians have also tended to aggravate the issue by public pronouncements characterizing objection as unpatriotic and tantamount to subversion. Since this lack of sensitivity coincides with a period in South African history where a significant proportion of both the English and Afrikaner church community is in the process of questioning civic obligation under the injustice of apartheid, the state, its soldiers and the clerics become locked into a mutually reinforcing spiral of conflict.

It is important not to over-estimate the actual political influence wielded by the anti-militarist lobby in the English churches, the universities or even – at this point in time – the 'non-white' communities. While blacks, Indians and Coloureds may well provide much of the manpower of the SADF in the intermediate future, with social and political implications which remain to be discussed, their present pariah status in the white South African political world largely excludes them from exercising any real and direct influence on the formation of political and military policy – except in the sense that they are the immediate objects of national security concern. The activist anti-militarist groups in the churches and the largely English-speaking universities appeal to a very small and select community of liberals and mild radicals, many of whom are politically demobilized by the contradiction between their material commitments to the white state and their moral and philosophical repugnance at it. At the same time, many of the attitudes of the subject race groups, white academics and church groups towards militarization are filtered into public debate through political party channels. It is important to emphasize that all of the parliamentary parties, including the National Party, have vested if differing stakes in opposing militarization which must inevitably lead to a diminution in party political competition and in the social status of the various parties. While it is difficult for party spokesmen to avoid bending to the rhetoric of total strategy, particularly towards the right of the political spectrum, there is an acute realization, even in National Party ranks, that militarization means the centralization of political power in executive institutions – such as the State Security Council – beyond legislative control and access. As we shall note in more detail below, the tendency of these executive organs to admit members along strict techno-cratic criteria already poses a threat to many of the traditional institutions and power-broking patterns in the ruling National Party. White party leaders of all persuasions are also sensitive to the fact that bringing the military into politics means bringing politics into the military in a manner which could conceivably cleave a major instrument of white state control. There are, as we have noted, various points of conflict in the South African military establishment (with which I intend to deal in more detail) and, as numerous politicians appreciate, these still largely sub-surface differences might emerge into full-blown divisions in military ranks to the extent that Defence Force leadership is transformed from a 'non-political' agent of the state into an increasingly active participant in conceiving the formulating state policy. This fear that the politicization of the military could undercut its unity and effectiveness as a protector of white interests has acted as an important brake on even more assertive action by the executive to draw the military into policy-making. The same factor lies behind frequent pronouncements by the Defence spokesmen of the PFP that it is in the 'national interest' that the Defence Force be kept 'above politics'.

The Progressive Federal Party has in fact been the foremost parlia-mentary critic of militarization although, as behoves a coalition organiz-ation of its type, there is a good deal of inconsistency in the PFP's official approach to military matters. The shadow defence ministry has always been controversial among the various offices in the party and even today it is still regarded as one of the more difficult major portfolios, where the latent tensions within the party tend to come together. Towards the right of the party, opposition to militarization is essentially instrumental and turns on the mechanics rather than the principles of total strategy in a fashion reminiscent of the opposition voiced by the New Republic Party (NRP), the smallest of the English white opposition parties, and the one closed to the Nationalists. In these circles the dominant issues are the size of the annual defence budget and the impact of SADF recruitment policies on the availability of white manpower in the labour market. Basically, the PFP favours political reform over increased defence spending as the best available means to ensure national security and favours an enlarged professional and permanent military establishment based on volunteers and career soldiers as opposed to the National Party notion of mass mobilization through the medium of the Citizen Force. As one moves from the centre to the left of the PFP, its anti-militarism takes on more distinctively moral and philosophical coloration as the relationship between militarization and the quality of political life is tested through such issues as the political neutrality of the Defence Force and the degree to which parliament can exercise effective control over its actions. While the party on the whole is sceptical of the 'total onslaught' described in government propaganda, those on the left of the PFP, mainly supporters of the old Progressive Party rump of the organization, are particularly critical of governmental rhetoric rationalizing total strategy and militarization on the basis of an imminent communist threat to the country. While conservatives in the PFP are inclined to grant the Nationalists the benefit of the doubt on these issues, and subsequently to support government claims for the defence budget as a matter of patriotic duty, the leftist element in the party is inclined to dismiss the analysis of prevailing political conditions contained in total strategy as a rather imperfectly objective assessment of political reality. In these circles total strategy is widely regarded as a manipulative device designed to justify the National Party appropriating more power or, at minimum, a paranoidal construct derived from the fears and fantasies of its decision-makers. This results in the view that total strategy is, at best, an artificial framework for stability and change, or, at worst, a dangerously authoritarian means to further centralize power in the prevailing political and military leadership of the system. The PFP is also sceptical of the political neutrality of the SADF, and virtually all of its members would welcome greater public and parliamentary scrutiny of its activities in accord with the normal tenets of the liberal-democratic process. While some of the PFP's more right-wing spokesmen are inclined to accept Nationalist assurances that the SADF is being held in political isolation in accord with the best traditions of liberal constitutional theory, the mainstream of party opinion is understandably perturbed at the increasing number of indications that the political role of the SADF is expanding under the Nationalist aegis. The PFP, for example, has frequently condemned organizational socialization practices in the SADF where recruits conscripted under the national service system are forcibly subjected to propaganda either glorifying the role of the National Party or reinforcing the worst of racial stereotypes.[7] In the face of Nationalist insistence that the internal affairs of the military are best left to the soldiers themselves, the PFP has initiated numerous moves to open the SADF to public enquiry in cases where its actions are believed to be detrimental to the national interest as defined by parliament. The recent involvement of high-ranking SADF officers in the abortive Seychelles coup, ostensibly without the approval of either the government or the military leadership, constitutes one of the instances where the PFP has, with notoriously little success, sought to bring the Defence Force under the discipline of public authority. Above all, the PFP (and the NRP) has resisted the Special Defence Fund originally established in 1952 as an extra-parliamentary account to facilitate the purchase of defence equipment, and subsequently broadened in scope to finance Armaments Board activities during 1964. As allocations to this fund have grown to subsume a significant proportion of the entire defence budget, as its expenditures have become more secretive and increasingly centralized in the Ministry of Defence, the Armaments Board, the Chief of the SADF and its Comptroller, so parliamentary control over the military has emerged as a major bone of contention between the National Party government and its official white opposition.

Conceived in these terms militarization evokes considerable parliamentary opposition despite the ability of the ruling Nationalist Party to extend a protective veil over SADF activities through the use of various instruments of state security legislation designed to stifle questioning and public criticism of the mechanics of state control as exercised through the medium of the police and the Defence Force. Criticism of total strategy and its Defence Force progenitors emanating from the left of the white political spectrum has moreover received added, if ironic, reinforcement in recent years as elements to the right of the National Party, in the Herstigte Nationale Party, the Conservative Party and right-wing members of the official National Party itself have lent their support to the movement against increasing military influence in politics and the public decision-making process. This is not to suggest the possibility of an alliance between the PFP and the Afrikaner right centred on the issue of militarization: the ideological differences between the two entities, the one looking towards a gradual multi-racial future for South Africa, the other representing a nostalgia for a simpler and more purist Afrikaner past, preclude such a possibility. Yet there are points of political contact between the polar regions of the white political spectrum on the issues of militarization which are important in their loose combined effect to act as partial constraints on official National Party policy. The PFP and the Afrikaner right differ on the philosphical and practical desirability of admitting larger numbers of 'non-whites' to the ranks of the SADF, yet, in a way which mirrors their essential hostility to the developing technological and managerial thrust of public policy articulated by the Botha executive and its military cohorts, both are opposed to the principle of centralizing political power along the lines of the prescriptions of total strategy. In a certain sense, the PFP, the HNP and the CP are all in their different ways populist and ideologically-minded political parties. While the PFP opposes the growing executive–military alliance for fear that it will lead to a new authoritarianism which will compromise the attainment of a multiracial society, and while the Afrikaner right adopts the same posture for the different reason that such an expression of total strategy will threaten Afrikaner group identity, both have clearly vested stakes in inhibiting the Defence Force in acquiring increased political power.

Parliamentary opposition to militarization must be seen against the wider background of the fact that South Africa has no deep-rooted praetorian tradition, either in political culture or in the institutional experiences of society. In a way which is fundamentally different from many Latin American countries where militarism is an accepted element of political life and social thought, the relationships between civil and military society have neither material nor intellectual vitality. The coup d'état is an unfamiliar experience in the South African political tradition, so that the social and political roles of militaries have largely been pushed to the margins of local political thought concerning the nature of power in the social process. For the entirety of their history South Africans have been concerned – obsessively concerned – with the apparently more important nexus between race and politics rather than that between soldiers and politics, with the natural consequence that militarism is a low-ranked issue on the agenda of South African politics – both in its conceptual and practical implications. Vestigial elements of liberal ideology also continue to throw up cultural constraints on the development of a rapid and rampant domestic militarism in the South African context. While the institutionalization of apartheid has led to the material and intellectual erosion of liberalism in South Africa since the end of World War II, there remain various 'islands' of liberal ideas of politics and social organization in the surrounding sea of authoritarianism. The 'liberal' model of civil–military relations, with its emphasis on the predominance of civil over military authority in the process of public decision-making, is still deeply ingrained in the white South African collective mentality. This is the case not only in the minds of upper-level Defence Force personnel whose growing attachments to revitalized notions of kommando and the citizen-soldier are tempered by lingering attachments to the British military tradition, but also in the minds of the mainstream white public where it expresses itself in an inarticulate and occasionally stated feeling that soldiers playing politics is in some fashion undesirable and illegitimate.

In these circumstances where elite receptiveness to militarization is far from unequivocally enthusiastic, government and military authority intent upon the shifting of civil–military boundaries has to tread lightly if it is to avoid offending public sensibilities. This places a premium on the role of total strategy as a means ideologically to manipulate and socialize the white community into acceptance of greater political participation for the military as a facet of day-to-day social existence. Yet even though significant numbers of whites have absorbed the political messages of total strategy and internalized the accompanying psychologies of garrison statehood, there are still very few white South Africans who identify with the military in the powerful Brazilian sense of seeing it as 'o povo fardado' – essentially the 'people in uniform'. Most whites hold the Defence Force in high esteem for its role in upholding the state in the face of internal revolution, in protecting the national frontiers against the apparent southwards march of international communism. Most, to use the metaphor employed by white parliamentarians, see it as a necessary 'shield' for the Republic behind which order is upheld and possible constitutional reform can take place. The majority of whites, if not the majority of South Africa's population, also wax enthusiastic about Defence Force actions conducted over the national borders, such as Operations Sceptic, Protea and Daisy launched into Angola with the intention of disrupting the logistical system and command and control structures of SWAPO. As a measure of this esteem many whites support the SADF in the direct financial sense by purchasing Defence Bonds, although, it should be added, these instruments are also a relatively lucrative form of investment. Many whites living in the rural areas also benefit directly from the construction and expansion of SADF bases, whose consumer buying power and infrastructural demands can be an important spur to the economic development of more remote regions. The case of the South African Air Force base and its contribution to the economic growth of the Pietersburg region of the northern Transvaal is instructive. Yet, as even the prime minister and military chiefs are forced to concede, this is not quite tantamount to civil society willingly surrendering its political levers to the SADF or to civilian elements in alliance with it. All of the major political parties have expressed the fear that increased military involvement in civil society is bound to lead to the contamination of military ranks by party politics in a way which would undoubtedly cut into the unity of the major instrument of coercion under white state control. In general, white elite cohesion has not broken down in the face of internal and international pressure, nor has white public opinion reached the point where it has lost confidence in the capacity of civilians to identify and implement solutions to South Africa's political problems. The fragmentation of the ruling elite and the dilution of its sense of legitimacy and confidence are critical indicators of imminent political disturbance or, under certain conditions, of military intervention smoothed by a willing civilian surrender of its right to power. Yet while the South African elite is fairly deeply cleaved over the mechanics of maintaining racial domination, the principle of domination remains a basic transcending and integrating value.[8] Nor do white South Africans presently accept that their military can perform substantially better in the role of conflict resolvers and managers than the current civil leadership – independent of whatever qualms they might have regarding its composition. In such a situation where the notion of civil leadership remains an inviolable norm in the conduct of politics, there is simply little to no attitudinal legitimacy for uncontrolled militarization of the kind so readily evident in many Latin American societies. By the same token those in favour of militarization, in the ranks of the Defence Force or the executive, do not possess a clearly immediate and widely diffuse set of symbols with which to legitimize military penetration apart from those which can be instrumentally created. In this sense, total strategy, and its related concepts of total onslaught and total involvement, is basically part of an exercise to construct a language of images with which the military and its small but influential group of civil sympathizers can communicate with the remainder of the elite on a persuasive basis.

It must be emphasized that the restraining role of white public opinion is shaped as much by concrete demands made on the civil sector with increased militarization as it is by the vague if widespread feeling that the appropriate place for military activity is within the confines of the barracks. These demands go well beyond the tendency of defence spending to fuel inflation in a way which cuts into citizens' pockets. Only a small minority of whites are sufficiently versed in economic theory to appreciate the relationship between money spent on military hardware and the rising level of prices. What most English and Afrikaner whites are aware of however is that with the extension of conscription and increased military activity in the Southern African region they face the very real prospect of national service where life and limb are directly threatened. Organizations such as the Committee on South African War Resistance (COSWAR) in London and the South African Military Refugees Fund (SAMRAF) in the United States have attempted to exploit this sentiment by supporting conscientious objection, lobbying foreign governments to provide sanctuary for South African deserters, and by encouraging national servicemen to desert, emigrate or infiltrate the Defence Force in order to undermine it from within. It is largely the result of the activities of COSWAR that an estimated 1,000 South African objectors were granted political asylum between 1977 and 1981 in Britain alone.[9] At the same time it is dangerous to infer too much from these facts concerning the will of white South Africa to militarily defend the apartheid state. For one thing, there have been very few cases of draft resistance or desertion from Defence Force ranks for specifically political reasons. While the number of religious objectors languishing in military prisons today runs into the hundreds, in 1981 there was only one clear case of draft resistance founded purely on political motivations.[10] In part this reflects the weakness of organized draft resistance in the South African context: organized draft resistance in the Republic is naturally illegal and the international movements are technically unable to guarantee asylum to South African draft-dodgers in terms of the United Nations' 1978 Convention on Refugees, unless they are able specifically to link draft resistance to actual racial, political or religious persecution as prescribed in the earlier 1951 Convention.[11] At the same time the development of a South African version of the 'Vietnam syndrome' is also doubtless hampered by the fact that, unlike the case of the USA, military service is perceptibly linked to the survival of the white heartland, and by the motivated quality of most conscripts many of whom have internalized their role as fighters against international communism long before actually entering the military. Under garrison state conditions avoidance of military duties also tends to induce far heavier social sanctions than in communities where military service and national survival are not directly linked in the public eye. With the noteworthy exception of a few organizations and individuals, South Africa's white public displays little sympathy for conscientious objection. Nor are most of its members critically assertive with regard to the increasingly draconian measures built into recurrent amendments to the Defence Act regarding the avoidance of military obligations.

There are however a number of considerations which, if not necessarily pointing to cracks in the moral fibre of white South Africa to the point where a large proportion of its members would refuse to defend the elite political order, nonetheless indicate real areas of material conflict and tension between the white public and the military authorities. Motivation, as most military strategists realize, is an essential component of any effective fighting force. Thus, even small professional armies, such as the Israeli army, can be exceptionally well equipped in their role of defending the state provided they are constantly revitalized by an infusion of conscripts who identify with the military and whose movement across civil–military boundaries ultimately leads to the military being indistinguishably blended in with the civil component of society.[12] In South Africa there are certain factors working to support a similar process of civil–military fusion: the racially exclusive characteristics of the military and the state, the dissemination of virulent anti-communist images through the education system and the media, and the general beleaguerment of South Africa in the global community all work in the direction of producing individuals who have partially absorbed militaristic values prior to their embarking on formal military service, who regard their

3 *Incidence of courts-martial and convictions*

	Incidence	Convictions
1976	486	477
1977	595	588
1978	1,152	1,150
1979	1,669	1,636
1980	2,146	2,088

Source: Republic of South Africa, House of Assembly Debates, No. 6 (Questions and Answers, 8 March 1982. Col. 320. Pretoria: Government Printer, 1982)

period of conscription in strong patriotic terms and who generally see military service as a desirable part of their individual growth. At the same time it would be wrong to conclude that virtually every young South African white is unequivocally enthusiastic at the prospect of military service, least of all under present conditions where his obligations to the Defence Force are being progressively extended. The prime minister himself has admitted that only some 20–30 per cent of national servicemen are, in his opinion, highly motivated.[13] Within the Defence Force itself the number of courts-martial has veritably exploded – partly as a result of the pressures on discipline produced by the military's increased involvement with active combat duty in the operational area of Namibia, partly as a result of the extension of national service commitments (see Table 3). According to General Malan, 263 of 484 national servicemen in detention barracks at the beginning of 1982 were serving sentences for refusal to do duty.[14] Evasion of national service has also proved widespread enough to prompt the SADF to establish a South African Army Non-Effective Troops Section whose main aim it is to investigate requests for deferment of national service and to locate conscripted evaders. In general, it is estimated that a miniscule 3 per cent of Permanent Force personnel come forward on a direct voluntary basis.[15] The Commandos also experience considerable difficulty in attracting volunteers, particularly from the rural areas where potential enlistees are too deeply involved in the daily tasks of agricultural production to make themselves available for military service, least of all on the country's remote national borders. This had led the military authorities to baldly conclude that 'with the present limited numbers in the Commando Force, the Force is under strength and can therefore not fulfil all its obligations, particularly those in the rural areas. The number of volunteers has decreased considerably, and under present circumstances volunteers are a manpower element which cannot be guaranteed'. It adds that 'a large-scale allocation of national servicemen to the Commando Force is also not possible as there are not sufficient servicemen to supply the needs of both the Citizen Force and the Commando Force.'[16] Recruitment problems facing the Commandos in the rural areas – it is estimated that they are at least 37 per cent understaffed[17] – are not likely to diminish in the future as members of the white farming communities are drawn to the cities by economic incentives, or as it becomes increasingly dangerous to live in the northern, north-western or north-eastern Transvaal in the face of guerrilla incursions. The resistance of many farmers to strategic plans for the defence of the borders has already led to some tension between the agricultural sector and the military establishment. Some border farmers, even while arming themselves to act kommando-style against insurgents, find SADF attempts to coodinate defence efforts arbitrary and high-handed. Legislation introduced during 1978 empowering the military to enter private property within a ten kilometre border zone and to demolish or erect buildings or structures without the consent of the owner severely conflicts with the rugged individualism of Afrikaner farmers. The military, for its part, is deeply perturbed at the depopulation of the areas bordering Botswana, Zimbabwe and Mozambique, as farmers move in an urban direction under the combined effect of drought, guerrilla action and a shrinking agricultural market. The critical strategic importance of these areas – where nearly half of the farms are no longer occupied by whites – has prompted the military to press the state to intervene to reverse the flow of population. In November 1978 the Steyn Committee was formed to address the problem and in the light of its proposals the Promotion of the Density of Population in Designated Areas Act was passed in 1979 which provided the farming community with a variety of military and economic perks as rewards for remaining in or returning to strategically important agricultural areas. These included interest-free loans which would cost the state between R65 million and R80 million over a five- to six-year period, the establishment of fortified strong-points and free two-way radios. In return, however, the recipients of these benefits would be required to have their farms occupied and managed in accord with state purposes.

The still outstanding problem of white depopulation in the border areas raised the whole question of how intensely members of the racial elite have absorbed the precepts of total strategy and fully identified with its principles and purposes. The high rate of urbanization among the white farming community at least partly suggests that many critically placed whites temper their commitment to total strategy with a strong dose of instrumental motivation, despite the racial and patriotic appeals of civil and military leadership. This is echoed in the widespread bickering over the technicalities of military service in the civil sector. In a way which suggests something less than a blind enthusiasm for military duty, there are frequent complaints on the part of national servicemen that the pay-scales of the Defence Force are inadequate in relation to an initial two-year term of often dangerous duty far from the materially inviting conditions of 'normal' white society. While complaints of this type are common to the operations of every military establishment and do not in themselves indicate an extended philosophical aversion to military service, they do point to a distinctive difference in the way in which members of the civil sector and the military establishment view the purpose and utility of national conscription, particularly when interlinked with a variety of other technical problems encountered by young white South Africans in the course of their relationship with the military. There are, for example, frequent letters to the media originating in less than patriotic and ideologically motivated quarters which not only criticize the length of military service but which question the value of national service at all: numerous are the complaints on the part of conscripts or their immediate families that the entire national service system is totally unproductive from the point of view of individual development, particularly after the first energetic months of basic training. The SADF has sought to meet these criticisms by allowing national servicemen to continue their education on a part-time basis, yet many young white men continue to see their military obligations in specifically negative terms. These feelings are notably acute among the numerous young whites who are already economically active when called-up for military service, in the professions, farming or small-scale enterprise. Ultimately it is this group above all which disproportionately bears the burden of a situation where there are simply not enough whites to service the manpower requirements of a defence force thinking in terms of a total strategy. The same quantitative problems appear in a slightly different form in the process of the military allocating its available manpower. Because the Permanent Force component of the SADF constitutes a relatively small core, Citizen Force units are brought into actual military operations on a much more accelerated basis than in the case of militaries where the permanent professional component is large enough to handle any eventuality short of a full-scale war. In these circumstances, national servicemen face the very real prospect of border service under enemy fire relatively shortly after their initial induction into military ranks. This had led to numerous complaints that the Citizen Force is bearing an unfair share of the defence of sensitive areas along the Namibian–Angola border.[18] In these circumstances an increasing proportion of national service conscripts applies for exemption or deferment of military duty or actively seeks assignment to the Navy, Air Force or Medical Service as opposed to the Army.[19] In all of the major service arms however there are far fewer prospects for upward mobility in the Citizen Force in comparison with its Permanent Force counterpart: while Citizen Force officers can technically advance to the highest ranks, the professional bias in the permanent core of the military tends to exclude Citizen Force officers from positions beyond the rank of commandant. According to official opposition defence spokesmen there are very few cases of Citizen Force officers being promoted beyond commandant and numerous instances of 'commanding officers who have served for ten, twelve or fifteen years ... and who remain commandant with no prospects of promotion even though they are capable officers who in the ordinary course should get promotion'.[20] There are, finally, numerous problems confronting national servicemen returning to the mainstream of civilian life after increasingly frequent and protracted periods of military service. These problems are particularly acute for conscripts who are subjected to the stress of border duty, and for almost half of the national servicemen with low educational qualifications whose period of military duty places them at a relative disadvantage in finding jobs on the labour market. As periods of national service are lengthened many national servicemen find themselves pushed to the margins of civilian economic life on discharge from the military. As an official SADF report bluntly notes: '[Some] 55% of those national servicemen released in December 1978 were in fact workseekers'.[21] Extended national service also obviously takes a toll on social life, especially that of conscripts with wives and families. The decision of the SADF to establish a special personnel section dealing with the marital and financial problems of conscripts typifies the growing tensions experienced by the average young white South African torn between his military and civilian commitments.[22]

Popular white attitudes towards the military must also be seen against the backdrop of ethnic and cultural cleavage within the elite, historical differences in English and Afrikaner conceptions of patriotism and English reactions to Afrikaner domination over the state and military system. English South Africa, it must be stressed, has an undoubted pragmatic stake in the perpetuation of racial dominance and during the course of the years this has broadened out into a more genuine, deep and diffuse loyalty to (white) South Africa, despite many Afrikaner assertions to the contrary. At the same time the English community remains externally connected by virtue of history and culture in a way which its Afrikaner counterpart with its deep-rooted sense of indigenous nationalism is not. English South Africans do not on the whole identify with the country with the same degree of emotional intensity as the Afrikaners, and they are, from a psychological and often material point of view, less resilient in their social commitments in the face of social pressure. Emigration from South Africa, particularly since the disturbances of 1976, is a disproportionately and characteristically English activity, particularly among the urban middle- and upper-middle-class strata of the English community who have the educational and financial wherewithal to move to another country. While the motivations underlying emigration vary from the political to the most intensely personal it is significant that many of the younger white English-speakers are moved to action by the prospect of extended military service. English South Africa is, in addition, deeply ambivalent in its feelings towards the present Afrikaner monopoly of state power. While the English elite remains predominant in its control over the South African economy despite the incursions of Afrikanerdom into capital in recent years, such institutions as the bureaucracy, the police and the military are regarded as peculiarly Afrikaner preserves within which English-speakers have very little room for advancement or mobility. As Afrikanerdom has become more racially embracive and self-confident in exercising state power, its political leaders have sought to counter the communal image attached to these major instruments of the state. Yet all these instruments, the military included, remain overwhelmingly Afrikaner in ethnic complexion, and from the point of view of the competing English elite, basically unattractive as institutionalized focal points for social participation. The result is that despite the rhetoric of racial unity emanating from political and military circles, from civilian and military leaders, many English-speakers continue to filter their attitudes towards the Defence Force through an ethnic prism. Many, like their French Canadian counterparts in their reaction to an English-dominated military, have difficulty in conceiving the military as a genuine national institution as opposed to the military arm of Afrikaner nationalism.[23] Hence Defence Force claims on society are dismissed or opposed not because of any abstract attachment to the ideal of maintaining a distinction between the military and civil sector along classic liberal lines, but rather because militarization is seen, more narrowly, as intertwined with the progressive accretion of Afrikaner power. While there are no systematic surveys of English South African emigrant opinions, many of those who identify the possibility of extended military involvement as a reason for leaving are undoubtedly influenced by a reversed version of the historical experience of 1914 and 1939, when numerous members of the Afrikaner community could not proffer their full support of the Defence Force in its role of defending the interests of Empire. Today, apartheid is regarded by many English-speakers, somewhat disingenuously, as a particular Afrikaner creation, in which case it can be quite logically argued that the present English community, or its progeny, has little to no obligation to participate in its defence or, more pointedly, to smooth the social path for its primary defenders within the Afrikaner military establishment.

Relations between the military and the largely, if decreasingly, English private sector are also deeply ambivalent in a variety of respects – despite Defence Force dependence upon the local business community as a supplier of armaments and the reciprocal dependence of South African armaments producers on the local military market. This symbiotic locking together of soldiers and businessmen is likely to continue for the foreseeable future both because the international arms embargo on the Republic is unlikely to be lifted and because South African arms exports are unlikely to break into the highly competitive international weapons market on any significant scale in the short term. Militaries and private sectors are also often brought together by a common fear of communism,[24] and this is no less the case in South Africa where the business community supports the Defence Force's institutional and strategic stake in inhibiting the spread of any form of socialism as a means to protect its own interests in a highly profitable system of capitalist economic relations. A perpetuated war effort in Namibia, it is also sometimes argued, serves the profit motive of those fragments of capital with investments in the arms industry, as well as the Defence Force with its institutional and psychological stakes in the ongoing border war. Nonetheless, total strategy and private enterprise fundamentally differ in their perspectives on social and economic regulation, the former demanding a relatively homogenized and tightly structured society, the latter a competitive and free-wheeling social climate conducive to the accumulation of profit and capital independent of state control. Militaries, in general, have a strong statist orientation and many military leaders, in South Africa as elsewhere, tend to view the profit motive with distaste, in a fashion which normally sours the relations between soldiers and the business community. While this antipathy towards entrepreneurship is diluted in the case of some militaries by extensive contacts between top officers and the personnel of large commercial, industrial and financial enterprises, South Africa's own military leaders have very little accumulated experience in transacting directly with the private sector, basically because of their insulation from the mainstream of civilian affairs, at least until fairly recently. In the past, military–private sector contacts have either been mediated by government institutions or restricted to technical questions of armaments procurement. The result is that when the military and the business community today liaise on the mechanics of total strategy military officials are often seen by the entrepreneurs, not unjustifiably, as basically uninformed and insensitive to the intricate and subtle issues raised by the national economy. The tendency of the military to fall back on simple statist solutions to economic problems along the lines prescribed by total strategy is not entirely congenial to the largely English-dominated business community with its long history of contesting state control by Afrikaner government over the economy. While the private sector is clearly not a force for liberalization independent of profit considerations, and while it is undoubtedly favoured by the ability of the South African economy to generate cheap labour under apartheid arrangements, it has nonetheless emerged during the seventies, particularly since the so-called 'Carlton Summit' of 1979, as a powerful pressure group for national economic rationalization. From the standpoint of the business elite, political stability requires maximum economic growth over and beyond whatever claims the military may make on public resources, and economic growth in its turn is preconditioned by a relaxation of ideologically sanctioned state control over the employment and training of black labour, the siting of production and the organization of industry. Similar views are articulated by the Afrikaner business community which is apprehensive in the face of the growing number of state corporations and also by influential elements in government, in the executive and the bureaucracy, who have internalized a similar managerial and technocratic ethic. In practice, the increased involvement of the private sector in financing programmes geared to improving black standards of living in the urban areas represents the price it is prepared to pay for government policy leading to a diminution of public control over the economy. In these circumstances the desire of the SADF to impose greater state regulation on society, or the calls by its supporters in such institutions as the Armaments Board to 'rationalize and coordinate industry with specific reference to the field of armaments' does not rest easily with a business community newly anticipating that the state is actually in the process of loosening its grip on private initiative and action.[25] Government has sought to mediate between the military and business by creating consultative institutions, yet a variety of outstanding issues remain to be resolved before military and business interests are brought into a condition of reasonable alignment. One point of disturbance concerns the role of the private sector in providing security at strategic industrial installations in accord with the National Key Points Act of 1980 which, *inter alia*, allows the Minister of Defence to declare any building or installation a 'national key point' and subsequently to order the owner of the 'key point' to take security measures meeting with ministerial approval. In general the business community regards the responsibility of protecting the 633 'national key points' identified under the 1980 Act to lie with the state acting through the police and military. Military planners are not entirely persuaded that this is the case – particularly in the light of the increasing number of successful ANC attacks on Sasol, Secunda, Natref, the Koeberg nuclear reactor and the network of power stations in the eastern Transvaal. Capital and the military also differ on state procurement policy as defined by the National Supplies Procurement Act which allows the Minister of Defence the right to seize goods required for military purposes from any person or organization and to order the production of goods for military purposes. This Act, used for the first time during the 1976 invasion of Angola, has led numerous businessmen to fear subordination of production to military purposes. Above all, however, the militarymen and the business community have widely divergent institutionally conditioned perceptions of the issue of manpower utilization. From the point of view of the business community, state security is best served by economic expansion accompanied by political reform which removes the ideological constraints on production and allows for the optimal use of skilled labour. Most businessmen arguing from the logic of investment and profit have difficulty in identifying with the strategic scenario sketched by the military authorities. While the private sector has an equal stake with the Defence Force in upholding a capitalist South Africa, many of its members clearly do not attribute the same importance to the military ideals of mass mobilization and citizen-soldiers as a means for doing so. In the long run, it is increasingly argued in the business community, it may be far less costly, both economically and politically, to focus on the more substantial, if difficult, task of deracializing society, building a black middle class with access and vested interests in the political system – with the general effect of shifting the forces of social order and political control from racial to class channels. Yet this subtle prescription for perpetuating white domination does not resonate with impact on Defence Force consciousness – at least not to the extent businessmen desire – and the military remains, in the last analysis, occupied (if no longer preoccupied) with guaranteed force levels appropriate to the rather blunt strategic requirements of state security. Since top defence planners foresee future threats to the state emerging out of a series of nationwide area-based attacks, they are relatively unreceptive to private sector support for an enlarged professional army as an alternative to draining white manpower from the economic system. From the point of view of these planners anything other than an extensive nationwide pattern of military arrangements, with the capacity to call on the maximum number of available white citizens if and when needed, is a luxury which South Africa, with its white minority, cannot afford. With its shallow pool of 11,000 regulars and about 50,000–60,000 national servicemen in various stages of training at any given time, the Permanent Force, according to one commentator, is 'so small that [it] could not function properly without its national servicemen of various arms', mobilized, it might be added, on an increasingly frequent basis.[26] Whether or not this is actually the case is at the heart of the controversy surrounding the amendments to the Defence Act made during the 1982 parliamentary session. According to South Africa's economic leaders in the private sector, the newly proposed system with its intentions to add a further 800,000 men to the military network can only harm economic growth and political stability, and it is basically undesirable at a time when there is already a serious shortage of white skills in an economy in the midst of a recession period. Small companies in particular are affected by the drain on manpower and the PFP has been spurred on by their difficulties (as well as those of larger operations) to advocate an enlarged professional army in preference to the present situation of longer and more frequent terms of national service.[27] Outside of parliament this position has received added weight through pronouncements by government-appointed commissions and, curiously enough, by the more conservative white trade unions. The Wiehahn Commission has, for example, drawn attention to the tendency of conscription to prejudice the indenturing of apprentices in a fashion harmful both to the interests of labour and the national economy. Lengthy periods of national service, it notes, make it extremely difficult for apprentices to be allocated to industry on an optimal basis, given the fact that most employers are reluctant to indenture apprentices who have not yet fulfilled their military obligations. It subsequently proposes a system of remissions for apprentices designed to facilitate their access to the job market.[28] The official report of the Commission also points out that white trade unions are reluctant to support the removal of legislation constraining the training of black labour since this would lead to employers preferring to train and employ black apprentices as opposed to whites whose services are constantly disrupted by their conscription into the Defence Force.[29]

In the course of ongoing discussions between top management and senior members of the SADF the military has made numerous concessions on the issue of widening the conscription net. These include the SADF's acceptance of the principle that there be a six-month gap between the annual training camps which national servicemen are obliged to attend after completion of their formal military service, and the principle that Citizen Force members be employed for operational duty on an alternate year basis.[30] While the military supported an amendment to the Defence Act during the 1982 parliamentary session which would enmesh virtually every white male in some form of regular national service until the age of sixty, the SADF has subsequently backtracked to the point where it now seems that the implementation of such a system will be designed with a very careful eye to minimizing national economic damage and personal hardship caused by military service far from places of residence. The National Reserve limit has now been lowered to 55 years of age and in the face of public pressure it has been conceded that all call-ups will be adjusted to circumstance and necessity.[31] While the facilities of the new area system are technically limited to Commando members and 'that category of persons who are doing service in the Citizen Force and in respect of whom such circumstances may occur that continued service in that Force would lead to unreasonable hardship',[32] it is likely that the entire system will only be put into operation in certain regions on an emergency basis and then only if it can be shown that area servicemen can be productively employed.[33] At the same time the manpower issue still remains a source of tension between the military and the private sector, not only because each continues to define the issues in terms of their parochial interests and institutional requirements but, more basically, because it is impossible to design a national service system which will simultaneously meet the present-day needs of both local civil and military society. White manpower is in the last analysis concentrated in the dominant segment of society: this precludes the formation of an enlarged professional army adequate to meet the security needs of the state (relatively few privileged whites, after all, favour a career in the military) and it also means a concentration of skills in an arithmetically small number of the total population involved in the national economy. Either smaller numbers of whites can be conscripted for longer periods of national service, or larger numbers for relatively shorter periods of duty. In either eventuality the national economy must suffer through the withdrawal of skilled labour from the mainstream of economic activity – subject to an accelerated programme to train and integrate large numbers of blacks into the economy, or the conscription of significant numbers of blacks into the military on a substitution basis. These intrinsically political questions striking at the structural foundations of the South African system as it is now constituted form the stuff with which the National Manpower Commission must ultimately deal if it is to make any meaningful contribution to resolving the present competitive struggle between the military and business for the body and skills of white labour.

The whole manpower issue is aggravated by the additional fact that the military is basically uncompetitive in the open market for white labour. Despite its stated intention to 'reward each recruit with conditions of service and financial benefits as attractive as those offered by any other employer and in some respects superior to the best available in the private sector',[34] the overwhelming majority of career-minded whites still gravitate toward the relatively lavish opportunities and rewards offered by the private sector. In practice, South Africa does not fall into that small category of contemporary nations, notably China or Israel, where military service on behalf of the state is regarded as highly prestigious in the repertoire of careers open to upwardly mobile young men in a complex and highly differentiated modern environment. Young whites, as members of a highly privileged elite, are not in general attracted to the military when making professional commitments. Given their social, financial and educational advantages they can confidently lay claim to lucrative positions in the civil sector. While military officership carries some degree of status the same positions of influence can be realized far more easily and quickly when working through civil channels. This is not of course to say that there are no candidates for a professional military career, but they are mainly Afrikaans in social origin, and then largely confined to the relatively small Afrikaner lower middle class who regard an officer's commission as an upward step on the social ladder. To this group the opportunities for educational advancement provided by the SADF are particularly attractive, either in the form of technical training courses or, for the select few, enrolment at the Military Academy. Promotions in the SADF are also relatively rapid in line with the tendency of the Defence Force to move officers consistently upward through the ranks as a compensation for generally poor salaries. The result is a military organization somewhat top-heavy in colonels, brigadiers and generals. Promotions are also relatively frequent for white officers in the few black units of the SADF, largely as a means to allow the military to circumvent accusations that its policies violate the conventional colour bar. Yet the military faces shortfalls in personnel with each annual intake despite the fact that the number of careerists recruited on an instrumental basis are supplemented by some indefinite number who have enlisted for ideological and patriotic reasons. In the Citizen Force there is a shortage of senior officers, warrant and non-commissioned officers, while in the Permanent Force there exists what the Defence Force terms 'a real shortage of the leadership element (senior non-commissioned officers and junior officers), and among the ranks of instructors'.[35] There is also a considerable turnover of white technical personnel in all four service arms, particularly the Air Force, many of whose highly skilled pilots and technicians are regularly creamed off by civil aviation once they have completed their technical training.[36] The military's Directorate of Manpower Procurement has sought to remedy the situation by publicly marketing the SADF as a network of institutions offering a wide range of exciting careers, 'from submarines operating beneath the surface of the ocean to jet aircraft pilots roaming the skies'.[37] Plans have been mooted to attach military recruiters to educational institutions and employment agencies in the major cities with the objective that 'no school-leaver, student or potential recruit should be unaware of the outstanding advantage they may expect to enjoy under the greatly improved conditions of service now available in the Permanent

Force'.[38] The various advertisement campaigns and poster displays organized through the Directorate have been complemented by a tightly formulated contract system through which recruits bind themselves to a specific period of service prematurely terminable only upon payment of a hefty discharge fee. While there is some doubt whether this dose of coercion achieves its intended purpose (the Riekert Commission, for example, has argued that the contract system acts as a disincentive for recruits to join the SADF in the first place),[39] the SADF has also improved service conditions over recent years, progressively raising salaries and introducing a variety of fringe benefit schemes for its members. Unfortunately, salary scales in the SADF are controlled by the Public Service Commission which is reluctant to make special financial concessions to the military for fear of setting off an epidemic of demands throughout the network of bureaucratic organizations under its aegis. The result is that service in the military is disproportionately rewarded and relatively meagre in relation to the material rewards offered by civil society, particularly the private sector. In these adverse circumstances the military tends to fall back on its statutory powers of recruitment as a compensation for its lack of any viable alternative means to attract and hold white manpower. Given the institutional proximity of the SADF to the state and the subsequent ease with which it activates communication with government, this tends to engender added conflict with the local business community, many of whose leaders experience frustration at their own inability to gain comparable access to government decision-makers on vital questions of national service. While business pressure periodically influences government and Defence Force policy on manpower – the various concessions made by the SADF are indicators of this – the feeling prevails in the business community that the SADF is far more advantageously placed to capture the ear of government in the formation of manpower policies which will ultimately be embedded in legislation passed by the Nationalist majority in parliament. The result is a deep feeling of irritation on the part of business derived from its impotence to rectify a situation where production and profits are skewed as key personnel are constantly creamed off by an apparently over-bureaucratic, narrow-minded and arbitrary Defence Force.

The governmental sector is basically hamstrung in its mediating role between the institutional values of the military on the one hand, and those of the private sector on the other. This reflects the fact that the manpower problem at the heart of military–business tensions is a structural consequence of apartheid, about which very little can be done in the short term by the government or the private sector, acting alone or in conjunction. Until such a time as sufficient blacks have been trained to occupy the various positions in the economy traditionally reserved for individuals of white extraction, the private sector will continue to pitch its manpower demands in white labour terms, and the military will ostensibly continue to compete with it. In addition, the intermediary role of government is strongly compromised by the various similarities in interest and cognition binding the prime minister's office to the top leadership of the Defence Force. Their common intellectual and political investment in total strategy has caused many leading members of the business community to complain of governmental bias against the private sector in the process of including business and military interests in public policy deliberations. At the same time, the militarization of South African society has generated enormous conflict potential in the network of political institutions at the heart of the Afrikaner community. The Botha government has, on the whole, been sensitive to the institutional interests of the Afrikaner-dominated bureaucracy. Its preference for granting administrative exemptions under the existing racial laws rather than removing discriminatory legislation from the statute books is dictated largely by the realization that a substantial proportion of the bureaucracy consists of National Party supporters who depend on the sheltered employment generated by the complex apartheid apparatus. Botha has nevertheless forced through a radical rationalization of the public service, with an eye to the effective formulation and implementation of total strategy, which has directly touched on the prerogatives of various bureaucrats accustomed to the inordinately slow and hierarchical style of the country's inflated bureaucratic apparatus. This is not to ignore the fact that in South Africa, as in other areas of the world, certain technocratically-minded bureaucrats have little difficulty in identifying with the rationalizing thrust of military policy: there are some elements in the local civil service, particularly top bureaucrats linked to the executive office of government, who could conceivably function as political allies of the military in the task of streaming the political system subject to the proviso that the military could also attract a degree of civilian support in the process of doing so. For the rest of the bureaucracy however the tendency of the government to centralize major decision-making in a system of committees surrounding the prime minister's office is a source of considerable anxiety. This is exarcerbated by the fact that the hub of the system, the State Security Council, is basically dominated by military, civilian and bureaucratic personnel with demonstrably scant regard for established bureaucratic procedures. The attentive ear given by the prime minister to military advice, be it formally through the committee system or through informal social contacts, tends to compound the sense of threat felt by the many senior civil servants who have neither developed the high technocratic and management profile demanded by the government nor enjoy the access to public decision-making afforded by Defence

Force status. Militarization has in general contributed to inter-institutional tensions in the vast and sprawling South African bureaucracy as different organisations jockey for power and leverage in the public policy-making process. Tensions between the military and the erstwhile Department of Information under the Vorster government are notorious and it has even been suggested that leaks to the media concerning the misuse of funds in the Department were the work of military intelligence incensed at the loss of defence budget moneys to the Information Department secret fund.[40] Whatever the truth of these allegations, rivalry between the Defence Force and the Information Department seems to have played an important role in the ascendency of Botha to the office of prime minister, the dimunition of the Information Department to a subsection of Foreign Affairs and the rise to power in the national intelligence community of DMI to which we have already referred. There is also some evidence suggesting that top officials in the South African Police network experience some difficulty in adjusting to the growing monopoly of DMI over national intelligence. Leading elements in the Department of Cooperation and Development are frequently offended by Defence Force insistence that strategic considerations take priority over all others in the process of consolidating and developing the rural 'homelands'. The anxiety generated by the military's relatively scant regard for economic viability as a primary criterion for homeland development is shared by numerous economic planners in official circles – on the economics committee of the state security network and in the Department of Economic Affairs – many of whom also take issue at the growing size of the defence budget and military demands on scarce white manpower. In this regard, some top economic decision-makers link up with the various elements in the private sector who see the military as an insatiable consumer of national resources. South Africa's regional economic policy, in which both local capital and economic development planners have vested stakes, is also seen to be frequently compromised by SADF strikes across the Republic's national boundaries into neighbouring Southern African states. While the economists and businessmen carefully nurture the foundations of a regional 'constellation of states' through such instruments as the recently created Southern African Development Bank, military officials often act with scant regard for the political and economic consequences of their actions. As one commentator notes: 'Efforts ... at regional investment, trade and general economic cooperation are made more burdensome by an aggressive military posture toward neighbouring states. Economic instruments of foreign policy', he astutely notes, 'gain in effectiveness by a patient buildup of links and trusted relationships – they can be swiftly undermined by threats and open or clandestine military strikes into states with which, ostensibly, correct relations are sought'.[41]

The appearance of soldiers at the top of the public policy-making hierarchy, it should be emphasized, lends a distinctive strategic coloration to the decision-making process. Soldiers act as soldiers to push the non-military, political and economic variables of policy-making to the side. To the extent that they succeed in imposing their narrow and strategic world view on their civilian counterparts public policy becomes very much a matter of direct security calculations. In South Africa this is particularly the case in the foreign policy-making realm where the appearance of soldiers in the highest institutions of state has contributed to the downgrading of the Department of Foreign Affairs in the network of key institutions developed to formulate policy under the Botha government. The DFAI (the Department of Foreign Affairs and Information, as it is correctly called) has, as Grundy notes 'fallen on hard times'.[42] Indeed, while the Department continues to implement policy and fill out the details of policy decisions, the principles of foreign policy are today largely determined in the context of the State Security Council in which the Minister of Foreign Affairs is directly exposed to 'external' military influence. Militarization has, in effect, set off a vigorous process of bureaucratic competition on foreign policy issues in which the military, armed with strategic and military information on regional and international issues, vies with the foreign policy 'establishment' (the bureaucrats of the Department) in the setting of the foreign policy agenda. Total strategy, as Grundy notes, is 'an aggressive and not responsive strategy',[43] and South Africa's policy of destabilization in the Southern African region is a direct and natural result of military penetration into the foreign policy arena. This has been brought about, it might be added, in the face of quite substantial institutional resistance from mainstream career diplomats and foreign service personnel who have invested considerable time and energy in developing political and economic ties between the various Southern African states into a mutually interdependent and consensual system of regional relationships. While the ability of the Defence Force to project its strategic interpretations of regional developments into the foreign policy-making heartland is assisted by the prime minister's receptivity to its views, by his impatience with the Department as an inefficient and uncoordinated institution and by the predominant role of military intelligence in providing the information foundations for policy-decisions, many long-serving members of the foreign policy establishment continue to regard destabilization as ultimately contorted in its logic and harmful to the Republic's international image. The dialectic between strategic and political approaches to foreign policy action has also proved critical in shaping South African reactions to Angola and Namibia. In both cases, military leaders with access to top decision-making institutions have played 'hawk' roles in contrast to the Department of Foreign Affairs with its greater appreciation of inherent political considerations. In the case of Angola, the South African decision to retreat from military intervention during the 1976 civil war was the direct result of the ability of the DFA to impose upon the military leaders the view that a continued South African presence north of the Kunene would do incalculable harm to the Republic's image and interests in the West. While the Namibian question remains unresolved (and, as we shall note below, there are differences of opinion and strategy amongst SADF leaders), military opinion clearly leans towards a hard-line policy involving cross-border raids and unremitting defence of the territory, whatever the legal and political implications.

Internal conflicts within the South African bureaucracy are at least partially paralleled within the ranks of the ruling National Party where many politicians on the right of the spectrum have difficulty in reconciling the cardinal value of maintaining Afrikaner group identity with the rationalizing spirit of total strategy. Today's publicly prominent cleavages in the Nationalist ranks naturally predate the forces of militarization in South African society and they originate in far deeper social impulses and developments than those associated with the rise of the military to new positions of political power. Nonetheless, the elements of managerialism inherent in Botha's style of political leadership, his close association with civil and military technocrats with their urge to rationalize apartheid, and the prescriptions of total strategy with their emphasis on change in the form of a homogeneous social package are major irritants in the relations between *verligte* and *verkrampte* within Nationalist ranks. To the more conservative Afrikaner total strategy is anathema because of its inherently managerial and urban-oriented style of action. It derives in philosophy and practice from a managerial and specialized environment far distant from the rough and ready conditions of the incremental adaption which is so central to the rural and working-class setting of Afrikaner political culture. Total strategy and militarization are also unacceptable to the Afrikaner right because, on pure ideological grounds, no strategy, however total, is acceptable as long as it fails to make provision for protecting the ethnic foundations or group identity of Afrikanerdom. The tendency of the current batch of civil and military leaders to rationalize their actions with reference to 'free enterprise' and 'economic growth' generates anxiety among supporters of the HNP and CP. They fear that what is essential 'Afrikanerdom' and racial hegemony, is being lost in a political movement which overcompensates in its concessions to pragmatic adjustment or to English capital. The Afrikaner right takes exception in particular to the inclusion of 'non-whites' in the armed forces. Naturally enough, ideological resistance to total strategy is bolstered by hard functional and material interests. Afrikaner conservatives have resisted the centralization of political power in the executive branch of government since the time of the Vorster government not necessarily because it represents a violation of democratic principles – as is the publicly-advocated case – but rather because the subordination of the principle of party service to criteria of expertise which has occurred under Botha represents a fundamental threat to the conventional norms of power brokerage which have previously supported the distribution of political influence within the ruling party. Today, when political credibility in the National Party stems increasingly from links with the State Security Council, the old party hacks and institutions, the Broederbond and the provincial caucuses who have previously defined party policy are fading into insignificance. These tensions are replicated, it might be added, in the middle to lower reaches of the state bureaucracy which have traditionally lent support to the ruling party through a mixture of ethnic identification and as a repayment for sheltered employment. Today, many Afrikaner bureaucrats at the grass-roots level – such as in the Bantu Administration Boards in the urban black townships – simply ignore policy directives from the centre of the governmental and administrative system because these directives, formulated by what are perceived to be technocratic 'whizz-kids', are fundamentally at variance with standard (racially-contaminated) operating procedures, or, more directly, because the application of total strategy, with its emphasis on streamlined and rationalized apartheid, directly threatens the career prospects of the cohorts of potentially redundant officials.

Functional and ideological factors combine to create bureaucratic resistance to militarization even within the military despite the pronouncements of legions of commentators who represent the Defence Force as a social formation waiting eagerly in the wings with an acute eye to political power. If, as suggested by some commentators, it takes at least a generation to impregnate interventionist soldiers with civilian ethics in the form of a group tradition, then, by reverse logic, it is still far too early to expect the South African military to carelessly cast aside its liberal civil–military heritage and move with little compunction into the political process. While some of the younger generation of officers may dabble in political ideas and even go so far as to see themselves as distinctive contributors to South Africa's political future, the lingering legacy of liberal institutional socialization is still potent enough to dissuade the mainstream of the officer corps that the creation of a fully articulated garrison state – or some other radical alterations in the prevailing civil–military balance sanctioned by total strategy – is neither possible in the short run nor desirable as a long-term prospect. The process of transforming soldiers from obedient instruments of civil authority into political leaders in their own right can of course be accelerated – where civilian executive authority 'invites' the military to assume the mantle of political power, where civil political leadership meddles in the working of military institutions in a fashion which the soldiers consider a threat to corporate prestige and identity, or where the actions of civilian authority undermine the legitimacy of the system to the point where military intervention is necessary to save it from total degeneration. Yet none of these politically accelerating variables are important in South African civil–military relations at present. While there are points of convergence between the values and interests of the SADF and the Botha government, it would be wrong to assume that Botha and his immediate circle of supporters in the National Party or in the bureaucracy would welcome the opportunity of bringing the military into the heartland of policy-making on a more regular, potent and institutionalized basis. This is not only because the strength of white public opinion would oppose such a move except under dire crisis conditions, but for the more cynical reason that to do so could well constitute a first step in phasing civilians out of the political process altogether. Except in the event of a legitimating catastrophe where the white elite is prepared to sanction any action by its leaders in order to ensure its survival, Botha would require far more public support and far greater assurances that the military is politically controllable before taking the crucial step of 'inviting' its leaders *en masse* into the realms of civil government. Militaries, of course, often formulate their own invitations to political participation, particularly where civil leadership fails to win their respect by behaving in a way which tramples corporate pride or is visibly injurious to the interests of the state which soldiers are professionally obliged to protect. Yet Botha is held in very high regard by the military chiefs, not only because he has consistently advanced Defence Force interests largely without injecting political strife into the relations between the various power blocs internal to the military, but also because the public policies advocated by his government are a fair approximation of what the soldiers consider as necessary under total strategy. Many an executive has sown the seeds of his own political destruction by either ignoring the claims of the military to social resources, or by attempting to manipulate these claims in order to build political support among factions in the military. In the South African situation where the executive is deeply appreciative of the subtle distinctions between civil and military prerogatives along the lines described by classic liberal principles of civil–military organization, it has sought to curry favour among the soldiers by addressing itself to the interests of the military as a whole institution. The result is a situation where, from the military point of view, its relationship with the executive has proved to be both unobtrusive and rewarding. Since both the military and executive leaders in South Africa evaluate and design political strategy on the basis of the cardinal principle that whites have the legitimate right to rule, no executive or governmental action short of that visibly compromising white domination is likely to bring about the undermining of legitimacy which normally prompts militaries to take on a directly active political role. While there are conservatives in SADF military ranks who are receptive to rightist civilian criticism that the Botha government is in the process of introducing wildly 'liberalistic' policies, the overwhelming majority of soldiers are perfectly comfortable with both the rationalizing content and managerial style of civilian leadership. Since all except the most conservative elements of white public opinion are equally confident that the Botha administration is proceeding in basically the correct direction, there seems no real justification for the military to plunge into the whirlpool of civil politics in order to 'save' the nation.

The South African military may also currently lack the will to political power in relation to the costs and demands on military organizations moving into the civilian realm of politics. Soldiers are normally torn between feelings of arrogance and inferiority in their attitudes towards the politics of civil societies.[44] While the officer corps of many militaries tend to disparage political activity and take particular relish in denigrating political leaders in civil society, many also avoid politics or limit their political participation because of a basic lack of political experience and confidence in their ability to compete with civilians as equals. This is one of the main reasons why most Latin American militaries prefer transitional or caretaker roles over long-term rulership commitments in the political realm.[45] This factor is also a constraint on the politicization of South Africa's military where many top officers are not entirely comfortable in their political roles, the motivation of which is seen to lie in sheer circumstantial necessity. If the officer corps still regards itself as a servant of the state, this has as much to do with its members being unwilling to take on complex political tasks and responsibilities, as it has to do with professional and ideological ethics which see the appropriate place for the soldier in the confines of his barracks. This basic sense of political incapability is reinforced by the common belief among strategically placed leaders in the SADF that extended political involvement in the affairs of the civil sector will ultimately prove injurious to the institutional unity and identity of the Defence Force, with little in the way of compensating political returns. The South African military, as I have emphasized, is not, despite external appearances, any more of a homogeneous institution than its counterparts in other areas of the world: its officer corps is differentiated in generational terms and, within the overall structure, each of its service arms is a self-contained hierarchy. There are officers, particularly the younger officers, who are politically sensitive, and there are others who still strongly internalize the principle that professional soldiers must strictly abjure politics and remain subservient to civil authority. In these circumstances, as SADF leaders appreciate, interwoven generational, experiential and perceptual differences within the officer corps can only intensify as the military as a whole is increasingly drawn into civil politics. This eventuality is compounded by the correspondence between patterns of politicization among the officers and inter-service boundaries between the Army, Navy and Air Force. The South African military, it should be emphasized, is basically a landward-oriented defence force, both for geo-political and strategic reasons and also because it is relatively difficult to acquire expensive naval technology under the international arms embargo. While the international marketability of the Cape leads defence policy to feed considerable resources into defending the southern African sea route, the Navy tends to emerge as a poor third in the competition between the major services for slices of the annual defence budget.[46] Both the Navy, and, to a lesser extent, the Air Force, are still strongly British-oriented in their composition, traditions and perceptions of civil–military relations – certainly more so than the Army, which is not only more Afrikanerized, but more deeply involved in the formation and projection of total strategy. This obviously works to the advantage of the Army in gaining access to political authority, particularly to the executive with its managerial style of politics comparable in spirit to that of the army leaders themselves. Since managerialism tends to centralize power in military institutions, especially among service arms which adopt a managerial approach, more politics once more connotes more tension in SADF ranks in a manner inevitably harmful to corporate unity. Many SADF officers are also acutely aware that the current shift in civil–military boundaries is to a large extent a reflection of close personal links forged between particular, if strategically located, military leaders, and the incumbent prime minister. In these circumstances any surrender of professional code which the military is now prepared to pay as the price of greater political involvement may well be obviated in the future as a result of leadership changes, either in the military itself, or in the civil sector. Should Magnus Malan be replaced by a more traditionally-minded military leader, the SADF, having committed itself politically, would be obliged to reverse its stand and once more return to the barracks, its professional norms contaminated. Alternatively, should the Botha government succumb to a leadership group (of either the right or left) less susceptible to the appeals of total strategy and generally less dependent on the military for a political foundation, the SADF would be faced with the difficult choice between defending its political territory in the face of popular resistance or of losing corporate face by once more withdrawing from the civil realm.

There are already a number of issues fuelling conflict within the Defence Force, some of which carry over to compromise military–executive relations as well. On Namibia, for example, military opinion differs between some senior officers who see the Angolan border as the Republic's first line of defence (and who see military prestige as tied to decisive victory over SWAPO) and a counter-group in military leadership who are sceptical whether South Africa can ever achieve a decisive outcome and who see South African involvement in the territory as a basic holding operation. While 'hawk' opinion tends to elicit a stronger response from military and political leaders on most matters concerning Namibia, an increasing proportion of the military and political elite is today becoming attentive to the 'dove' argument that further military investment in Namibia represents wasted resources, that total strategy and South Africa's nationalist interests are best served by consolidation behind the Republic's shorter and more defensible natural frontiers, and, in the last analysis, that the corporate prestige of the military requires a speedy settlement negotiated between South Africa, the United Nations and representative elements of Namibia's diverse community. Government action in recent months in favour of an internationally recognized peace and its efforts to pressure the dominant DTA into accepting a broadly-based ethnic formula for the political future of the territory directly reflected the sentiments of many of the leaders of the military engaged in its defence. At the same time, despite the rough congruence of views among the SADF, the executive office of the South African government, and its Namibian Administrator-General, the military are generally less sensitive to the political implications of imposing an 'outside' settlement than are members of the Botha government. This is mainly because the latter are faced with a resurgent right in the Republic which is bound to derive considerable capital from any situation which even remotely appears as a 'sell-out' of white interests in the mandate, particularly if accompanied by demonstrable resistance on the part of its own indigenous white population. In a way which tends to confirm the notion that soldiers are often innocent with regard to the subtlety and complexity of civilian politics,[47] some of the more important South African military chiefs do not fully appreciate the conflicting pressures on political leadership. While the prime minister and his immediate coterie in the State Security Council are personally held in high regard, some of the generals have difficulty in coming to terms with the fact that South Africa's national interest is neither homogeneous nor obvious, but is actually composed in real terms of a variety of diverse interest groups with which political leadership must bargain and compromise if it is to ensure its own survival. Acting from the departure point of a heroic and martial institutional tradition, some of the military leaders privately feel that the executive is perhaps hypersensitive to the weight of public opinion and a little too irresolute in implementing the total strategy upon which the security of the state and the corporate interests of the military ultimately depend.

There is a fairly distinct feeling in the SADF that political leadership has not yet clearly formulated the defensible political goals required by a total strategy for national survival.[48] This derives not only from Namibia but also from other issues at the centre of contemporary South African politics where the executive finds itself in a cross-fire between the military and white public opinion, and where the military is itself divided over the burning questions of the day. While most officers present an image of unity when approached on questions of politics, and while most tend to demur on specific questions of political change (with the exception of those related to Namibia where they feel particularly experienced and qualified), there are clearly differences of opinion in officer ranks over the course which the executive is following. While many of these differences are matters of emphasis and revolve around fairly marginal issues, such as whether or not the executive is sufficiently assertive in marketing the internationally strategic significance of the Cape sea route, some of these differences are clearly on matters of principle and touch directly on the pace and pattern of political reform recently initiated by the civil author-ities. To some elements in the officer corps the actions of the Botha administration in rationalizing the political system are far too fragmentary and slow in relation to the urgency of the situation; to others, in a way suggesting the penetration of *verligte–verkrampte* dichotomy into military institutions, the political and economic innovations introduced by the Botha leadership are regarded as far too radical for comfort. Thus, while more conservative elements in the military regard the integration of blacks into the economy with a measure of anxiety similar to the right wing in the civil sector, there are more pragmatic if not necessarily liberal segments of the SADF officer corps who regard the dismantling of ideological barriers to black entry into the economy as distinctly in the interest of the nation and the Defence Force itself. Such policies, it is argued, facilitate the productive use of manpower in a way which strengthens the economic foundations of total strategy, frees larger sums of money for defence spending and makes available more whites for induction into military ranks without the added cost of antagonizing the private sector. On this basis, the 'left' in the military has quietly encouraged the work of the Wiehahn and Riekert Commissions and has given its backing to the prime minister's initiatives in the industrial relations field. The same sense of internal ambiguity permeates the reaction of the SADF towards the civil government's 'homeland' policy. On the one hand the more conservative soldiers regard homeland 'independence' as a complicating factor in the task of assuring South Africa's national defence: arguing from a strictly strategic position they see the fragmentation of the country into a number of tenuous mini-states as greatly assisting the access of guerrillas to the nation's geographic and industrial heartland. While they support SADF policy to assist homeland development technically, in the form of army teachers, doctors and agronomists, their interest in transforming the homeland economies stems directly from their desire to see the 'independent' black states firmly locked into the regional strategic network. More progressive elements in the military leadership are, on the other hand, more favourably disposed to the political development of the homelands since their 'independent' status allows the Defence Force to integrate homeland manpower into the national defence effort, albeit in the guise of inter-state cooperation between the SADF and homeland 'national' armies. This is regarded as particularly important in defusing white rightist criticism of the use of blacks in South Africa's white army. This circuitous attempt to meet the demands of national security forms the basis of SADF assistance to the independent homelands in the development of their own defence forces, particularly to the Transkei and Bophutatswana, both of whose political leaderships appreciate the benefits of indirect SADF support.

Many officers in the SADF do not in fact have clearly articulated political opinions even on the most potentially explosive political issue internal to the military, that is, the use in a combat capacity of Coloured, Indian and black manpower. With the exception of the coterie of top officers directly engaged in the development of total strategy as a counter-revolutionary doctrine, the bulk of middle and low level personnel seem to have given very little serious thought to the social role of the military or to the specific process of diluting the racial exclusiveness of the Defence Force. The universal tendency of those low in the military hierarchy to defer on matters of institutional policy to those in higher positions of authority reinforces the situation. In addition, conflict over the admission of 'non-whites' is diminished by the general consensus cutting across rank, generation and social orientations that the command structure of the SADF remain white and that 'non-whites' admitted to the military are incorporated on a highly selective and strictly controlled basis. Whether or not this unity of perception and purpose will continue into the indefinite future is however not at all clear – particularly with increases in the 'non-white' component. While most top officers would concur with

General Malan's assertion that this component has done 'outstanding work on our borders',[49] there is already some awareness in the Defence Force of the costs and risks that must be borne in the process of creating even an attenuated 'national' defence force. For obvious reasons, the arming of the subject race groups to defend the white racial order has always been a source of controversy and many of the traditional fears concerning 'non-white' soldiers have undoubtedly carried over to the more conservative members of the current officer generation who are uncomfortable with the compromises in convention and principle involved in the growing admission of 'non-whites' to military ranks. Policies of this nature, it is argued by technocratic and managerially-minded military planners, are a strategic necessity – for reasons we have already noted. Partially deracializing the Defence Force also has major symbolic and psychological value inasmuch as it allows the Defence Force to shift the image of its role from the racial to the ideological defence of the state. Hence the rhetoric today that the military is an institution of all South Africa's population groups engaged in an 'anti-communist' struggle. Yet these rationalizations are not entirely persuasive to those in the more conservative circles of the military who – like their right-wing counterparts in civil society – are not prepared to pay any price in the process of streamlining apartheid and attempting to build legitimacy into the state. The rationalizers may argue that the appearance of 'non-white' soldiers is perfectly attuned to present state policy to coopt compliant elements in the Indian, Coloured and black communities into a slightly modulated version of the present order. To the more conservative officer however, the admission of 'non-whites' is the Achilles heel of a wider process in which cooption and modulation must inevitably lead to the degradation of the whole racial order.

The controversy surrounding the incorporation of blacks into the Defence Force is basically one manifestation – if not one of the most crucial manifestations – of the fact that despite public appearances the South African military as a whole is not equally and unequivocally enthusiastic about total strategy with its multiple political, sociological and ideological consequences. In the upper reaches of the officer ranks among the technocratically-minded generation receiving its military and political education in the early and mid-fifties, the Malans, Viljoens and Geldenhuys, the philosophy and practice of total strategy as enunciated by a variety of local and international thinkers is a primary guide to social behaviour, both inside and outside the circle of the Defence Force. Within the institutional network of the Defence Force many of these ideas have filtered down into the second and middle-level grid of officers, the colonels, majors and captains who reached positions of reasonable institutional prominence in the late sixties and who have experienced command in the formative arena of the Namibian war. Yet the impact of total strategy doctrine in the SADF is basically conical in the sense that as one moves down though the command structure, from officers at the top whose views of the social and political world are dominated by managerially-minded concepts of strategic and political action, through a broader strata of middle-level officers who have limited experience in Namibia (or have failed to internalize these experiences in the form of specific social and political doctrines), to the non-commissioned officers and broad mass of recruits, the total strategy doctrines articulated in the top decision-making circles of the military, in the senior officer cliques, in the lectureship ranks of the military academy and in the heady seminars of the Joint Defence College take on progressively less meaning as a guide by which the members of the SADF interpret the workings of the Defence Force and the nature of the external political world. In the last analysis, total strategy, whether articulated by military or civil elites in the upper echelons of the National Party, is an intrinsically technocratic concept. Its emphasis is on planned and rational action, on effective decision-making, carefully managed social policy and, on the whole, a non-ideological brand of politics with which conservative South Africans, be they in the civil or military sector, do not feel entirely comfortable. The new 'whizz-kid' elements at the apogee of military power may have little difficulty in making adjustments in the South African economy, in the political system or in the policies of recruitment into the Defence Force concerning the admission of non-whites; they may be able philosophically and politically to ground these changes in the material and ideological needs of the South African state as they construe them; and, in the last analysis, they may be able to make the case that these changes in the state and its military agents are necessary and unavoidable if white rule is to remain reasonably durable and efficient. Yet the logic of these arguments is unpersuasive when viewed from the emotionally and racially contaminated perspective of the lower ranks of the Defence Force, among the essentially Afrikaner-oriented non-commissioned officers and even into the middle and upper ranks where conventional and inherently more primordial approaches to the nature of South African society and its military continue to exercise important if decreasing significance. In these circles the reaction to independent homeland armies and to the diluting of the political monopoly of whites by bringing blacks into the mainstream of the military and the economy is much the same as in civil circles where the apparently uncontained liberalism of Botha and his technocratic supporters has invigorated a mass of Afrikaner right-wing criticism.

Ambiguity in relation to the implications of total strategy is not confined to conservative Afrikaners in Defence Force ranks, in the lower echelons of the Permanent Force and filtering up to a small handful of officers in the top ranks of the hierarchy. The lingering residue of the British liberal tradition with its notion that soldiers remain relatively non-political agents of the state continues to act as a focal point for all SADF officers, particularly the older generation of British-minded officers in the Navy and Air Force who are not entirely able to reconcile their conception of the relation between military and society with the present movement of the Defence Force into the civil realms of politics. While it is crucial not to overstate cleavage in the SADF – common unity derives from indissoluble affiliation to the white state – the following question immediately arises: given the differences within the SADF, what is the conception of the white state which it, as an institution, holds? More specifically, what are the circumstances under which the present politicization of the Defence Force is likely to increase (or even decrease) and what are the implications for future political development? What, in a nutshell, does the growth of praetorianism hold for political change in apartheid society?

5

◇◇◇

Quo Vadis? *Praetorianism and political change*

The existing literature on South African civil–military relations is characterized by two distinctive features. On the one hand, as we noted at the outset of this work, it is essentially small, conceptually underdeveloped and overwhelmingly configurative in its failure to compare or contrast the South African civil–military experience with interactions between civil and military elites in other areas of the world. The body of work on the South African military in politics is also unclear in its assessment of the implications of militarization for the South African system and there is no real agreement between the small number of writers who have applied themselves to the issue as to whether the shift in civil–military boundaries that I have documented represents an opening or a further closing of apartheid society. These differences of opinion, like so much else in political analysis, are shaped by the ideological presuppositions which analysts bring to their interpretations of the South African scene. Hence it is almost inevitable that those who root their understanding of South Africa in the cardinal belief that all developments are ultimately reducible to the efforts of the elite to maintain a monopoly of racial power will come to the stated or implicit conclusion that the military cannot conceivably act as an instrument of genuine wide-ranging reforms because it is, in the last analysis, a white institution wedded to the values and interests of the white elite, independent of whatever differences of emphasis may occur in the political perceptions of civil and military leaders from time to time. Thus the Defence Force may assist the forces of rationalization associated with the Botha government but it is unlikely unilaterally to lead South Africa in more democratic and egalitarian directions. In this sense the Defence Force fits firmly into the constellation of forces ranging from those seeking cosmetic social adaptions to those prepared to make gratuitous concessions to liberal values in the process of upgrading or streamlining apartheid within the context of the established racial order. Alternatively, it is argued in some domestic and international circles that it is quite possible that the South African military will transcend its present communal attachments at some distant point in the future, become a more genuinely corporate body and subsequently act as a positive force for change in the process of protecting or advancing its exclusive institutional interests. In this scenario, with its intellectual roots in liberal developmental theory, the SADF could ideally emerge as a proponent of real racial reform as its officer corps comes to perceive in the fullness of time that perpetuated minority rule is harmful to its corporate concerns or as the officers are forced to lend support to structural changes in the body politic in the process of cementing institutional loyalties on the part of a growing body of 'non-white' recruits in the ranks. Even then there is some debate among commentators over the form and political direction that the military might take in exercising its future claims to political power. Some foresee the Defence Force remaining a grey, if increasingly influential, element behind the formal facade of civil government (the so-called 'creeping coup' theory), others envisage a more decisive and substantially harsher pattern of praetorian behaviour in which the officers move to seize the reins of power, unilaterally, through executive invitation or in alliance with the more technocratic elements in South Africa's vast bureaucratic sector. Since students of the South African military are basically divided over whether the Defence Force is 'conservative' or 'liberal' in its institutional spirit there is also no clearcut opinion as to whether the military would act in a restorative or transformative capacity once having embarked on a more definite course of political action.

Certain essentials need to be specified in the process of sorting through this disparate data with an eye to developing some reasonably conclusive statements concerning the role of the military in South African politics. In the first place, it cannot be emphasized too strongly that the South African military is not now a secular and national defence force along the lines of a genuinely patriotic institution symbolizing and acting to uphold the totality of a nation's interests; nor are there good grounds for believing that it will develop these qualities characteristic of most Western militaries in the foreseeable future. Military institutions can function in an integrative capacity in a manner which cuts across communal cleavage;[1] yet the scholarly debate over the relationship between militaries, modernization, and the emergence of secular values is essentially sterile in the South African context where the military is so exclusive a racial institution indissolubly wedded to the values and interests of the dominant white elite. This is not to ignore the organizational changes taking place in the Defence Force in recent years, including the rise to prominence of sophisticated managerial-type leaders with access to the levers of state power and, perhaps even more importantly, the incorporation of the subject races into the mainstream of the Defence Force in violation of the historical principle that state security be a racially exclusive matter. Yet even if these are portents for the future state of civil–military relations and the survival of the minority regime in its present form it is still difficult to conceive of the evolution of the South African military along other than racial lines for the foreseeable future given its current race-saturated foundations. In reality, claims that the Permanent Force is becoming a genuinely national military must be referenced against the fact that today, several years after the dilution of the principle that soldiers must be white in origin, 92 per cent of Permanent Force members are still drawn from the ranks of the white elite, a miniscule 6.91 per cent of South African soldiers are Coloured or Indian and a statistically insignificant 1.05 per cent are members of the majority black community.[2] These disproportions in recruitment are telescoped into the officer corps which must still be regarded as one of the finer examples of an African military whose command structure is monopolized by a single ethnic or communal grouping. While official Defence Force pronouncements wax enthusiastic over the opportunities for advancement made available to all races within the military network there are insurmountable restraints on the upward mobility of 'non-whites' as befits an institution whose ethos remains racial in character. These thresholds, it should be noted, vary between the service arms of the Defence Force and according to the position of each of the 'non-white' groupings in the local racial hierarchy. It is precisely because the Navy is regarded as the least strategic of the three major services in the maintenance of internal order and state security that the opportunities for the subject races to advance through the ranks are greater than in either the Air Force or Army branches of the military. Alternatively, the command system of the Defence Force as a whole is unrequitingly racist regarding promotional norms, subject to the qualification that it is current state policy to coopt members of other minority racial groups, Coloureds and Indians, as reserve elements in statutorily created bodies and state institutions. The advantage of being deemed cooptable does not, however, extend to the politically disincorporated low-status elements in the majority black community, either in the Defence Force or in the broader new designs for South African society. The result as far as the military is concerned is that blacks are not as favourably treated as their Coloured and Indian counterparts who are higher in the race hierarchy. Thus, while Coloureds and Indians are moving through the ranks into the lowest echelons of the officer corps, blacks are still excluded from positions of authority in a way which makes the Defence Force little different in its supposed 'non-racialism' from other institutions in white South African society. In 1982, despite its official non-racial rhetoric, there were no black officers in the Defence Force barring black chaplains whose task it is to minister to the spiritual needs of black military manpower. Both the regional ethnic armies and the elite 'multinational' 21 Battalion were officered by whites, although it is accepted that blacks can rise to section leaders or platoon sergeants in both types of unit. Hence the one and only black staff sergeant in the SADF – the highest-ranking black in the military – attached to 21 Battalion.[3]

In these circumstances it is difficult to envisage the military taking a politically significant lead on questions of race relations except in extreme circumstances such as a radically deteriorating security situation which forces the Defence Force to substantially expand its black component as an alternative to scarce white manpower. Even then it is difficult to conceive of a significantly broadened and authoritative black officer corps given the conventional colour bar with its traditional tendency to assign subordinacy to blacks independent of their technical or formal status. In practice the SADF is not even a pace-setter in the realm of black advancement – certainly not when compared with the private sector or even compared with its sister organization, the South African Police, where a number of blacks have already risen to fairly prominent officer positions, albeit on a highly selective basis. There are still disparities in the material incentives provided for black and white recruits (although the military is committed to the principle of narrowing the wage gap along the lines prescribed for the entire public service)[4] and the whole atmosphere of military life, from the point of view of black recruits, is that of a hostile and intimidating environment where their presence is distrustfully and grudgingly accepted. We have already noted the social pressures which drive 'non-whites' to volunteer for military service and subsequently maintain their presence in the military network. Few members of the subject races resign from the Defence Force once they have joined it, but there are those who find the conditions so intolerably racist that they are forced to do so.

In the last analysis the South African Defence Force is a technically proficient but not necessarily professional organization in the sense of a set of institutions based on the cardinal values of merit, skill and autonomy along the lines of other modern militaries in industrialized Western societies. This is not to deny that the South African military establishment develops and projects its own corporate values and interests which may differ at times from those generated by other institutions and social formations in white South African society. Nonetheless, the Defence Force is still intrinsically such a racial institution that it can never fully divorce itself from the currents of white opinion and interest in the process through which it approaches politics. In this sense the military is neither definitively 'liberal' nor 'conservative' in its reactions to political stimuli, but rather a mirror, if a somewhat imperfect one, which reflects movements in opinion and behaviour in the white civil sector. In such circumstances the military establishment tends to avoid an assertive leadership position in the shaping of civil society, with the result that the shifts that have taken place in civil–military boundaries in recent years are not so much the result of hard calculated political moves on the part of the soldiers as they are the outcome of tentative and wary probes into the body politic conducted with a wary eye to the sensibilities of a white public, garrison-minded but basically unfamiliar with the notion of soldiers in civilian roles. The fact that the officer corps is equally unfamiliar with these roles intersects with the intense congruence of values between military and civil elites to act as a restraint on military participation in civil politics. It also follows that the Defence Force will choose its political orientations in close alignment with the cues provided by white civil society. The officer corps is conceivably more alert to threats to the state than the civilian mainstream and it is part of its social function to develop and put into operation appropriate strategic responses. Hence 'total strategy' with all the institutional changes and proto-ideological trappings necessary to implement a workable counter-revolutionary programme in South African society. At the same time, white civil society continues to set the basic parameters within which the military makes its key political choices. Because the relationship of the white military and the public to the state is essentially the same – neither is markedly enthusiastic at the prospect of surrendering racial power – the military will be neither distinctively more 'liberal' nor 'conservative' than what it believes the civil mainstream will tolerate at any point in time. The 'fit' in attitudes and actions is never, of course, entirely perfect and is almost always disturbed to some extent by idiosyncratic and institutional forces on either side of the shifting civil–military boundary. Nonetheless, the military is in broad terms a rationalizing element in apartheid society because of the urge to rationalization in the civil sector, or, more specifically, in fragments of the civil sector – in the executive office, the bureaucracy and the business community – with the influence and power to shape general white opinion. Hence, if the military remains so attenuated in its commitment to black mobility in the Defence Force, if it continues to adhere to the ascriptive and aristocratic principle of white leadership in its own ranks and in wider society, if, in the last analysis, its political thrust is basically conservative and cosmetic with the occasional concession to social reform, it is basically because the political climate in South Africa today is not more perceptibly liberal or open under the Botha government than under its predecessors. The various 'reforms' on the part of the present government on the social, economic and constitutional fronts are essentially downpayments on a long-term investment with returns in the form of a modulated but more efficient white state apparatus. This is the governing philosophy in the leadership echelons of the civil elite; it is also the framework for action on the part of the military elite of South African society.

The essential conservatism of the South African military does not in itself preclude the Defence Force playing a more active and explicit role in the future politics of South Africa, nor does the caution and incrementalism with which the Defence Force presently approaches the political realm offer a definitive cue to the future state of civil–military relations given the shifting and dynamic nature of the South African environment. Many analysts dismiss the notion of a coup as a likely scenario for the country's future; some would undoubtedly take issue with the degree of political influence attributed to the military in the present study. Yet, it is readily apparent that even while civilian authority remains predominant, the neo-British civil–military model with its fairly clear separation between the civil and military realm is no longer adequate or appropriate for describing civil–military interaction within the context of the institutional and psychological changes wrought in South Africa as it moves into garrison state conditions – least of all, it might be added, given the sociological characteristics of the current generation of Defence Force officers with their ambiguous identification with the notion of the 'non-political' at the foundation of the 'liberal' model. The relationship between militaries and societies is also in a state of flux determined by a mixture of superficial and deep structural movements, and at present in South Africa this dynamic mixture must be taken into account in any assessment of how the military fits into the institutional and power grid as it changes over the course of time. The present dose of militarization, as we have noted, reflects changes in the composition and style of Afrikaner leadership, which are in turn a mirror of deeper inter-class relations within the Afrikaner community. Militarization is, in addition, linked to international pressure on South Africa and is not entirely distinguishable from the present movements towards constitutional reform whose guiding spirit stems from a rationalized and essentially authoritarian conception of the uses of power involving the centralization of decision-making in select forums composed of managerial or neo-technocratic experts. In fact, militarization stems from the intersection of a variety of forces in the heartland of contemporary South African politics, some of which are likely to modulate or shift in emphasis in the course of time, but none of which are likely to disappear entirely from the background to civil–military interaction in the foreseeable future.

Executive invitation, for one thing, assists the military of many countries in accumulating political influence, no less so in South Africa where the close personal and institutional alliance between the office of the prime minister and the military elite has been a major element in the shift of civil–military boundaries up to now. This alliance, seen against the backdrop of the various forces which have prompted the progressive centralization of state power over the years of Nationalist rule, is particularly critical for future civil–military patterns and political change, particularly when measured against the movement towards constitutional reform currently afoot in the Republic. Two points need be noted in this regard. In the first place, there can be little doubt that however unconvincing South Africa's new constitution as a genuine vehicle for the redistribution of political power, the ruling National Party has lost some degree of Afrikaner support in the process of elevating the principle of 'non-white' participation in national decision-making to a credo of public policy. As demonstrated in the 1983 referendum, the concept of Coloured and Indian (not to mention black) participation in the national political mainstream is anathema to the right of the white elite, particularly its Afrikaner component with which Prime Minister Botha has lost considerable ethnic credibility. It is important not to overstate the power wielded by the right. As the results of the referendum make clear, the power of the HNP and CP is largely confined to the rural areas of the Transvaal and the majority of white South Africans support Botha's 'reform' initiatives. Yet the National Party leadership can no longer rely solely upon the manipulation of ethnic and cultural symbols to generate support and is now forced to move outwards across communal, party and institutional boundaries in the course of building an effective ruling coalition. National Party appeals during the referendum were clearly (and successfully) couched in a form and language designed to mobilize English support as compensation for Afrikaner defections on the issue of incorporating Coloureds and Indians into the new tripartite parliamentary system. The opposition (and predominantly English) New Republic Party has been brought into the National Party fold and various theories have been bandied about concerning eventual National Party–PFP cooperation in the face of rightist opposition – provided the constitution is extended to give more meaningful political rights to all of the subject race communities. All of these movements are salient to the political status of the military. The very adoption of the constitution with its concentrations of power in the executive and its underlying managerial ethos is entirely congenial to military leadership, which has its primary access point to national decision-making through the technocratic elements of the executive branch of government. While there is no evidence to suggest that the Defence Force participated in the design of the new constitution through the prime minister's Constitutional Committee, there can be no doubt that

the spirit and substance of the new pattern of constitutional arrangements
meld perfectly with Defence Force conceptions of total strategy and the
advancing political stakes of the military in the civil system. The appointment of Botha to the powerful state presidency reinforces the political
upgrading of the Defence Force (while raising the intriguing issue of the
future political fortunes of the military in relation to Botha's successors).
The whole process of building a viable ruling coalition within the context
of the new constitution must also impinge on the political influence
wielded by the soldiers. Even if Botha and his National Party leaders are
capable of generating support against the right from moderate and left-
wing elements within parliament they will inevitably continue to consolidate the implementation and operation of the new constitution in
support drawn from extra-parliamentary sources – from bureaucratic,
business and military pressure groups with institutional interests in the
perpetuation of the Botha administration. The announcement by the
prime minister, immediately after the referendum, that Indians and
Coloureds would be subject to conscription as part of the price for political
participation in the new constitutional order is an important indicator of
the close interaction between the state, the military and the private sector
on the key issue of allocating manpower under total strategy between the
defence and economic sector.

It should also be borne in mind that the proposed new constitution may
not measure up to expectations as a vehicle for social change, not
necessarily in public minds where there is already considerable scepticism
regarding the ultimate implications of the proposed constitutional
changes, but in the perceptions of the managerially-minded Botha, a
self-admitted disciple of Salazar and De Gaulle. Independent of whether
the new constitution is an instrument of genuine reform or just a means to
streamline apartheid by incorporating Indians and Coloureds as reserve
elites into a white-dominated political network, the inbuilt principle of
consensual decision-making by the representatives of the three racial
groups in the new parliament is bound to be inordinately complex and
extraordinarily slow. While provision is made for the proposed president
to resolve parliamentary conflict through his overriding powers of decision, Botha is unlikely to exercise this prerogative frequently in the earlier
years of the new system, if only to assuage charges of dictatorialism
emanating from black and white, left and right. The Coloured and Indian
communities have also entered the new constitutional system with deep
reservations and subject to charges from blacks that they are aligning
themselves with white racism. Their parliamentary representatives must
also be deeply sensitive to allegations that they are not representatives at
all. This means that they must discharge their functions with caution, resist

white imperatives and have a careful eye to public credibility in their own and the black communities. In these highly ambivalent and obstructing circumstances, Botha is likely to find himself placed in the frustrating position of other reformist presidents in developing societies who find policy blocked by parliament, by powerful entrenched elites or by conflicting demands from their constituencies. In these societies, where government is relatively weak in its regulative, extractive and distributive capacity, the executive has characteristically sought to gain direct military support for its proposals, has brought the military immediately into government as part of the resulting process of trade-offs, or, in many cases, has simply dispensed with the constitution, replacing parliamentary power with an ostensibly more proficient executive–military alliance.[5] It is, of course, dangerous to reason directly from these experiences to the specific circumstances of contemporary South African society. Yet, given the cynicism with which many National Party leaders have approached parliament, the clearly evident impatience in the current prime minister's style of 'reform' and the alternative policy-making network already cultivated around the executive office, one cannot exclude the possibility that it may ultimately prove to be in the 'national interest' to dispense with the whole laborious system envisaged by the new constitution, to justify doing so with a public dose of 'national crisis' and to arrogate all power to the State Security Council with an extended bureaucratic–military membership.

It is not unrealistic to assume that South Africa's future course will be, at best, one of 'violent evolution'. In this eventuality, 'national crisis' could take on real and frequently recurring proportions, with the military in a strategic management position between the state and civil society. The mind boggles at the thought of the Defence Force throwing in its lot with black attempts to overthrow the apartheid state, except in some future long-term situation where its lower and middle ranks have been so thoroughly penetrated by black recruits as to make concerted state-supporting action virtually impossible. Even then, a massive breakdown in institutional socialization would have to have occurred before the white command structure found itself unable to mobilize its black troops, whose very presence in large numbers in the military would in itself indicate major changes in the nature of the South African state as we know it. Yet it is equally fanciful to believe that the military will stand by in a neutral capacity at some future point where the existence of the white state is directly threatened. In circumstances of widespread racial violence and public disorder it will doubtless act to protect the white state because of the racial tendrils binding military and political elites under apartheid and because, in the last analysis, it is the function of the military to do so.

Nonetheless, it does not necessarily follow that the military will rescue the state in order to maintain civil authority or in a way which quite conforms with civil expectations. In practice, militaries often respond to conditions of civil disorder with a degree of alacrity which exceeds the best (or worst) anticipations of civil leaders. Analysts constructing scenarios for civil–military relations in a crisis-ridden South Africa should bear in mind that two-thirds of the successful coups occurring in Latin America between 1907 and 1966 took place during periods of public disorder, and that 29 per cent of the 229 coup attempts between 1946 and 1970 were directly associated with similar breakdowns in civil authority.[6] This reflects the deeper fact that soldiers bred in the tight hierarchy of military relations place an extraordinarily high value on political stability and often act to displace civilian authorities which are demonstrably unable to fulfil their elementary task of protecting life and property and preserving public order.[7] Coups, of course, emerge from a diversity of circumstances: they may result from infiltration of the military by politically committed officers or by civilians in search of collaborators in a civilian coup; from the development of a new ideological *Weltanschauung*; or from any of the dramatic events (from anti–colonial struggles through independence movements to economic disasters) with the potential to politicize entire generations.[8] Yet most coups are also an index of the vulnerability and weakness of political systems, of the performance failures of authoritarian governments (not unlike that of South Africa) whose unresponsiveness and excessively arbitrary action eventually foments a climate of public conflict where the military are called in to rectify the mistakes of the politicians. Military authorities (as noted in the introductory chapter) also often view their civilian counterparts with a mixture of contempt and disdain. This attitude is intensified when the weakness and ineptness of government succeeds in engendering a degree of social disorganization which it is capable of controlling. While there are only the faintest echoes of these feelings in the officer corps of the South African military, one cannot exclude the possibility of their growth in direct proportion to the inability of public policy to create the preconditions for stability. Professional militaries, it should be added, are almost always deeply averse to performing the role of 'common' policemen in cases where government policy has totally lost legitimacy in the eyes of the politically aware civilian population.[9] The race gap between the South African military and the broad masses eases the task of domestic control, yet a certain proportion of the Defence Force (the top professional-technocratic officers, relatively uninstitutionalized Citizen Force units and, above all, black recruits) could conceivably experience considerable compunction at the prospect of using heavy fire-power on civilian demonstrators along the lines of the French

Army in Algeria, the Colombian military in 1953 and the Turkish military seven years later.[10] In these last two instances, the military not only refused to violate their corporate integrity by taking on police functions to quell public disorder but subsequently displaced the existing government at the height of the disturbances.[11] Militaries, in the last analysis, have their own institutional interests which do not always coincide directly with those of the ruling government or state. In the case of the South African military, its self-perpetuation as a corporate entity in its present form depends on the pre-existence of the white state. Yet the SADF is also at that dangerous point in the development of military institutions where it is neither professional enough to resist crisis calls for political action to save the white state nor primitive enough to be oblivious to notions of institutional identity and corporate interest. In this adolescent position, the advent of extensive public disorder in the form of simultaneous urban terror, rural insurgency, township riots and widespread industrial action on a scale exceeding the control resources of the 'first line of defence' (the police force) could well trigger military intervention, not only in the limited sense of strategic action to uphold the existing government, but in the more fundamental sense of displacing civilian authority as a demonstrably incompetent mechanism for upholding the state and the interests of the military within it.

Future civil–military relations in South Africa must also be seen against the background of leadership turnover, less in the military where hier-archical procedures ensure relative continuity in organizational behaviour, than in the more highly dynamic and considerably more personalized civil sector. This mirrors the fact that while the shift in local civil–military boundaries is basically the result of structural movements in South African society and its international environment, it is also partially attributable to the close personal relations forged between the prime minister, P.W. Botha, and the current heads of the Defence Force. Simi-larities of perception between the political and military leadership, common adherence to a technocratic-managerial style of social problem-solving, mutual recognition and (by no means least) the emergence of a reciprocally beneficial patron–client system between the military and executive authority have all catalysed and steered these movements in a more specifically military direction. Personality does not dominate poli-tics, yet in the present circumstances both the physical and political longevity of Botha could emerge as an important consideration in the state of civil–military relations. Today, the military savours enhanced political status, it has been admitted to the highest councils of public decision-making on issues beyond the realm of its strict professional expertise and it has, in the process, accumulated considerable social influence assisted by a sympathetic chief executive with whom it can readily identify. Given the likelihood that its institutional interests will be further served in the remaining years that Botha is in office, it is quite conceivable that it will not react with favour to any succeeding political leadership or government which actively seeks to bring about a reversion of its current prestige and a diminution in its status. Naturally, this is not to suggest that the presence of Botha is the sole remaining bulwark against a direct military assumption of power. As I have indicated, a variety of historical and practical constraints are at work to confine the present political activism of the military to middle-range levels. Yet many soldiers fall prey to gluttony having once tasted the delights of political influence, and their resentment is all the more evident when civil leaders once more attempt to curb their appetites. It is not my intention to sketch a scenario for South Africa's entire political future; to attempt to do so in the more limited sphere of civil–military relations is dangerous enough. Suffice it to say that should the local melting pot stir up a government recipe noticeably to the left or right of the present civil authorities, the military might well find the resulting dish entirely unpalatable. Many military coups are pre-emptive in the sense of being designed to prevent particular political parties or individuals from taking power; and while a systematic survey of the attitudes of South African officers to particular leaders and parties remains to be done, it is readily evident that few are attracted to the conservative liberalism of a van Zyl Slabbert, the regressive nationalism of a Treurnicht or the mild militancy of a Buthelezi.[12] The advent of any of these leaders (or of the political tendencies they represent) in the highest realms of public office would cause considerable discomfort in Defence Force circles, most obviously so in the case of Buthelezi, less so in the case of Treurnicht, whose policies have made a mild impression in the lower military ranks. Militaries, as we have also noted, are profoundly protective of their institutional autonomy and many coups are motivated by what one analyst has termed 'corporate positional grievances', in other words, where civilian leaders trespass on military reservations by attempting to shape their educational and training curriculum, the assignment and promotion of officers and the formulation of defence strategies.[13] Since it is reasonable to assume that a more radical white (or even black) government will feel it necessary to bring about organizational changes in the military, diminishing the latter's political influence in the process of consolidating its own power, it could conceivably engender the very conditions for military intervention.

Future military 'intervention', one must emphasize, does not necessarily imply the military appropriating political power through the characteristic medium of coup-type action. The future could conceivably see a continuation or acceleration of what some analysts graphically describe as the 'creeping coup' in current South African politics – a growing but gradual and low-key penetration of the military into key public decision-making bodies and into the social institutions and collective psychologies of the white body politic. Alternatively, the future could see a more direct and visible type of intervention in the shape of a formal civil–military coalition with a predominantly military executive and Defence Force officers in a majority of cabinet positions, a purely military executive, or an exclusively military governing council backed by a mixed civil–military cabinet – a characteristic arrangement in the majority of military regimes.[14] Contrary to appearances, militaries seldom govern alone, if only because they lack the administrative skills commensurate with running a nationwide system of political and economic relations.[15] Military rule also normally lacks legitimacy, and the result is either some sort of alliance with technocratic elements in the bureaucracy or a pattern of concessions to popular attitudes and political organizations – both of which inhibit thoroughgoing transformations in the institutional networks of society. Hence military governance in South Africa does not necessarily mean major changes in the bureaucratic sector of the state apparatus, nor – if the Syrian example is anything to go by[16] – the existence of some sort of working arrangement between the military and the National Party, with the latter providing ideological, organizational and popular support for the Defence Force. I am, however, of the firm conviction that given the circumstances of South African society, continued militarization in any form whatsoever – benign, harsh, muted, direct, transitional, relatively permanent, authoritarian, quasi-democratic, installed by violence or government invitation, sanctioned or opposed by the elite under any circumstances of crisis, constitutional or leadership change – will do incalculable harm to the polity, exacerbate its racial cleavages and tensions, and contribute absolutely nothing to the resolution of its problems in the direction of justice, equality and stability for all its peoples. One cannot of course perfectly predict South Africa's future given the dynamism in its social development and current political movements. There is, in addition, a substantial body of social science literature which prescribes a dose of militarization as both politically and economically beneficial for ailing yet developing societies.[17] Nonetheless, one should bear in mind that statement of Gibbon in his classic study of the decline of Rome that praetorianism, the intervention of the guards in politics, was 'the first symptom and cause of the decline of the Roman Empire'[18] – the more so in the light of the fact that recent historical experience has produced little evidence to bear out the optimism of the fifties and sixties that militaries could play a meaningful and positive role in resolving the complex of social problems associated with economic and political underdevelopment. The school of thought regarding the military as a key to 'national reconstruction' in South Africa would do well to take note of the scepticism with which current military sociologists approach the relationship between militaries and development. As Nordlinger notes: 'All students of praetorianism would presumably agree that the military governments of Velasco in Peru, Ne Win in Burma and Nasser in Egypt are among those that have undertaken concerted efforts to bring about fundamental, progressive and modernizing change.' 'Indeed', he decisively adds, 'these are just about the only ones that have done so'.[19]

In considering South Africa in relation to the universal civil-military experience, in viewing her specific structural peculiarities against the background of the few scattered cases in recent history where military intervention has positively contributed to society, we find innumerable reasons to support the case that militarization is positively dangerous in the South African context and can only become more harmful to the real national interests of the country as it progresses. The leaders of most military institutions are characteristically weak in their understanding of the political uses to which power can be put, they do not excel in the implementation of public policy and they are frequently weak in linking the demands of rulership with social plans and ideological conceptions of society. Militaries have the organizational resources and they have the appropriate skills for overthrowing governments; they also have a high potential for social control once having done so. Yet seizing power differs from applying power to manage and change society and the critical difference between coups which attain or fail to reach their social goals lies in the fact that only a small proportion of militaries can relate rulership to a distinctive conception of what they want to do with society. The majority of militaries do not have the human and institutional resources required for the mundane business of daily politics and administration: nor do they have any clear idea of what to do with state power beyond the negative goal of denying it to their opponents.[20] Total strategy at its present level of development is no exception to the general rule that most proto-ideologies developed by soldiers are primitive, transparently self-rationalizing and largely devoid of any practical positive content. Total strategy is important in generating and justifying siege psychologies and structures through which the Defence Force can accumulate social power. As elaborated in the Joint Defence College it also goes a long way in the analysis of the nature of the apparent threat confronting white South Africa and, to a lesser extent, it proposes a variety of general antidotes to contain 'Soviet imperialism' including 'moral preparedness', the centralization of political power, rationalizing the mechanics of state control and integrating the forces of economic production into an overall plan to meet the security needs of the country. Yet in filtering through the ideas and concepts of total strategy one is immediately struck by the almost complete absence of any positive concrete formulations as to the specifics of a political system tailored to meet the total onslaught identified by the military. Is the new constitution in its present form ideally suited to meet the security needs of the state or is it simply a first step to an entirely new political order according to the promises of its designers? How do South Africa's subject race groups, particularly blacks, fit into the political model proposed for South Africa by total strategy, apart from the vague recognition by the military and its supporters that long-term stability requires both political and military action? How does the military see the role of the 'homelands' in any future political and security dispensation once they have achieved 'independence' from the South African heartland? In the last analysis, total strategy is hopelessly empty on mechanics in a way which suggests that, despite its fervent intellectual exertions of the past few years, the military has still not crystallized its views on what it expects from the political system and, more importantly, what it proposes to do with it in a concrete fashion. In such circumstances, progressive militarization cannot be equated with increased intellectual input into public policy-making in the sense of a genuine and explicit contribution to the complex debate over the direction in which South Africa should be moving and the means needed to get there. As the situation now stands, the intellectual influence of the military on policy-making is limited to the projection of vague and unverified abstractions devoid of any practical utility except in confirming the crude ideological and racial stereotypes held by the civil public and its leaders. In the eventuality of more explicit military involvement in the political process, either behind the scenes or more directly through participation in some sort of three-way military–executive–bureaucratic alliance, one cannot realistically expect an explosion of new and creative political thinking on the basis of existing evidence. At best one can anticipate continuity with the worn neo-apartheid solutions and formulae of the past, at worst the passing of power to a set of military-controlled institutions devoid of the organizational skills to conduct practical public policy. The military may or may not be the 'iron surgeons' necessary to instil muscle into the process of social change and reform, but, as one analyst has aptly put it, the soldiers may well do 'little to replace what has been cut out or even to ensure that the surgical operation has lasting consequences after the discharge of the patient'.[21]

Growing militarization also raises the question of relationship between power, authority and legitimacy at the heartland of all political interaction, particularly in South Africa, where the state has been forced to cope with an ongoing crisis of illegitimacy virtually from its inception. As already noted, military institutions, including those of South Africa, are often inhibited in extending their political role at least partly because of the belief that civilian governments almost always enjoy relatively greater legitimacy. Coups fit into the category of political events which, along with revolutions, involve illegal acts against the constitution. Hence the view that 'the legitimacy enjoyed by a government affects the political role of the armed forces far more than any other environmental or internal factor'.[22] In the case of South Africa, military sensibilities about legitimacy are expressed through the development and articulation of total strategy as an intellectual umbrella over military claims on political power. Yet the shade cast by total strategy is defined by racial boundaries, its persuasiveness as a legitimating device halts abruptly at that point where black meets white. Beyond that point its message is drowned in the widespread conviction of South Africa's 'non-whites' that the state, its institutions and doctrines, have no authoritative right to exist in its present racial form. In these terms, it is beyond the imagination to see how militarization, with its tendency to further centralize power in the minority-dominated state, can in any way contribute to the resolution of conflict in South Africa. On the contrary, militarization implies a greater degree of illegitimacy as power, already beyond the electoral control of the 'non-white' majority, is even further concentrated in the realm of a still smaller minority over whom even the elite has questionable control. It is improbable that a more military-dominated South African government would take the necessary steps to mobilize the support of the majority of the 'non-white' population. This means that the lot of the majority of South Africans would not perceptibly improve through the substitution of civil by military elite rule.[23] Except in the event of structural changes which threaten its own political survival, the new military system would continue to lack legitimacy in the eyes of most South Africans in a manner not substantially different from its predecessor. From the perspective of the disincorporated and alienated majority, military rule would simply represent a new and unfamiliar form of white domination. In the circumstances, the military or neo-military government would find it impossible to convert power into the popular authority necessary to bring about any real reform in the system.

Increasing the political power of the South African Defence Force would generally contribute very little to resolving the class and communal tensions inherent in the South African system, despite the praise often lavished on militaries as political integrators in much of the older civil–military literature.[24] Recent experiences in many areas of the Third World clearly demonstrate that soldiers are not necessarily isolated through military socialization to the extent that this literature presumes, and that they do not necessarily subordinate their class and communal identities to coporate values as a result of institutional socialization – least of all when these segmental affiliations are intense and coherent to begin with. They have also shown that militaries are not particularly effective in managing the problems of deeply cleaved societies, certainly no more so than their counterparts in civilian organizations. In some cases the communal or class heterogeneity of militaries undercuts the ability of military governments to act decisively in the face of class or communal conflict for the very fear that involvement in the civil realm will reverberate in the military to produce conflict along parallel lines of cleavage within the defence establishment itself. While the general abhorrence of soldiers for any degree of social conflict often overrides this disincentive to action, this factor raises the interesting possibility that if the South African military becomes a more genuinely non-racial institution it may well find, as internal race factions emerge with different stakes in upholding white domination, that it is incapacitated in its role of defending the state in the face of popular resistance. In other cases, however, the military contributes little or nothing to the process of resolving class or communal conflict because of its intimate associations with a particular class or communal segment, normally the dominant formation, whose values and interests it represents despite rhetorical commitments to the defence of the national community. This situation is of obvious relevance to South Africa where it is difficult to imagine the military acting to ease racial tensions except in the marginal sense of creating greater opportunities for black recruits to move upward within its own institutional boundaries. On the wider social plane there seems no real reason to believe that extending the political influence of the military will prompt a proportionately greater infusion of meritocratic values into the public policy-making process, or, more generally, that a military-dominated regime in some combination of civil and military power will usher in a government sincerely concerned with building bridges between the races. As I have repeatedly emphasized, the institutional interests of the military are served by the perpetuation of the white state whatever the occasional tensions in the relations between civil and military authority. The officer class may cautiously criticize the pace and direction of the policies of social change instituted by political leadership (and its senior members may act on these criticisms to influence government), yet the hierarchy and ranks of the South African military are uniformly aware of their stakes in the present system. It is precisely because of the powerful racial affinities binding together the political and military elites that policies to subvert the military or coopt it into the movement for deracializing South African

society experience such limited success. Militaries are in any case conservative or reactionary in defence of the status quo in as far as society
contains an established middle-class elite along the lines of South
Africa.[25] Latin American militaries, for example, are normally more conservative than their African or Asian counterparts because of the relatively wider spread of entrenched social interests in the more developed
climate of the American subcontinent.[26] Hence, it would represent a
major departure from the universal norm were a South African military to
appropriate power and then act affirmatively to alter the race and class
structure of local society beyond the point of tinkering with the more
outstanding and superficial of social problems. Indeed, there are firm
grounds for believing that the advent of a more militarized political
leadership would profoundly aggravate communal conflict between the
races. Accustomed to hierarchy and command within their own frame of
reference military politicians are normally intolerant of negotiation as a
means of social problem-solving and tend to fall back on the use of decree
in attempting to treat the issues of heterogeneous and segmentalized societies. While the South African military has fortunately not yet penetrated
the civil realm to the point where it can issue any decrees at all, its hollow
and almost ludicrous representation of total strategy as a formula for
'national', as opposed to racial, survival suggests that the local officers
would fall prey to the same error as other militaries who have grossly
underestimated the social power and conflict potential inherent in
emotion-laden, historically reinforced group identifications of race or
class. When the politicians in uniform are eventually forced to face these
realities, when the contradiction between their perception of society and
its substance becomes patently and unavoidably evident, they characteristically respond by enforcing national unity in a way which only fuels the
flames of communal violence. Sudan, Nigeria, Burma and Pakistan are
some of the more tragic contemporary examples to which South Africans
might look if they believe that a strong military government is the antidote to racial tension.

Societies where the military predominate are also usually short on
democratic values in a way which reflects the elitism of most military
institutions and the inability of their hierarchically oriented leaders to
comprehend political activity in the flexible civil sense of the word.[27]
Militaries, as we have noted, are inordinately intolerant of political
disorder and professional soldiers often have very little patience with what
civilians may regard as perfectly normal modes and procedures of democratic political expression, least of all when utilized by lower class contenders for power, the urban poor, peasants, workers or landless
labourers. As Perlmutter notes:

Almost without exception military regimes restrict acts of participation, primarily out of fear of losing control of the resulting political conflict. As a result, those institutions that articulate and aggregate interest ... tend to atrophy, and the process of interest aggregation is incomplete. In praetorian states the only 'representative' institution often permitted is the military party, but the party's function is not to represent interests but rather to restrict electoral participation and political representation.[28]

It is precisely because of the difficulties experienced by militaries in democratically mobilizing popular support that many Latin American (and South African) radicals actually welcome military rule as an accelerator of conflict between the state and the masses.[29] This seems perfectly reasonable in the light of the sombre homogenizing overtones of total strategy, with its emphasis on coordinated social activity as the central ingredient in the recipe for 'national' survival. Given the centralization of power which has already taken place under the rubric of total strategy without any accompanying improvements in the state of civil liberties in South Africa, there seems little room for optimism that the South African military will depart – now or in the foreseeable future – from the characteristic tendency of soldiers to see political activity in the civil mode as essentially undesirable, basically disruptive of social order and unnecessarily divisive. Many militaries, as one commentator notes, would be reformist provided social change were orderly.[30] Yet it is virtually impossible to see how genuine reform in so deeply cleaved a society as South Africa could be brought about without a considerable measure of disturbance and conflict generated out of the dialectic between different political interests. Whether a more militarized version of the present government would regard those disturbances as unavoidable or even as a healthy sign of change, and press ahead with policies designed to open the political system is far from likely given the normal distribution of priorities in military institutions. Far more likely is a militarized climate where order is valued over change and where any change is tempered by the institution of disciplinary measures – the so-called 'closure option' of political restrictions universally exercised by military regimes once the Pandora's box of change has begun to produce mildly disorderly social consequences. This would inevitably involve a retreat into an authoritarian system of government against which even the present system pales into insignificance. Independent of whether the authorities were installed on a ruler or guardianship basis, the costs of their presence would be paid in civil liberties, human rights, the elimination of political institutions, and tightly controlled participation.

In these circumstances, a more militarized version of the present South African political system, be it a relatively unilateral military regime or some mixed form of civil–military power, does not hold out much hope for social progress in a just and stable direction. Those placing their hopes on this option should bear in mind Nordlinger's unequivocal assertion that 'only a small proportion of praetorians are motivated in progressive directions',[31] and that given the particular circumstances of South African society, its coinciding race and class cleavages, the ties binding its political and military elites, there are few grounds for believing that the local military establishment is one of the few exceptions to the historic rule. Thompson in his survey of 229 attempted coups and counter-coups in the period 1946 to 1970 comes to a similarly pessimistic conclusion on the social performance of militaries when he notes that 'strikingly reformist' orientations are present in a mere 10 of his mass of cases, a miniscule 8 per cent of his total sample of coups being 'significantly motivated to correct injustices and abuses of an economic, social or political variety.'[32] This reflects the problematic features of military institutions as reformers to which we have already alluded – the difficulties experienced by military-oriented regimes in building that immeasurable degree of social legitimacy and popular confidence upon which genuine reform is contingent, the failure of most praetorian politicians to develop a positive and articulate vision of society commensurate with the day-to-day business of government and their dangerous propensity to fall back on coercion and state violence as a first resort when confronted with disorder, cleavage or social tension appropriate to the normal course of politics in its many subtle forms. Yet if the case against the transplantation of other societies' military–political experiences to South Africa as a means to resolve its inherent problems is still not strong enough, a number of additional factors should be taken into account in finally evaluating the contributions of militarization to the country, now and in the foreseeable future. In the first place, professional corporate-inclined militaries in relatively developed societies are always motivated in their social behaviour by parochial institutional interests fairly independent of their role as agents of entrenched social formations, elites and the middle class.[33] While corporatism in the South African military is sharply inhibited in its maturation by the indissoluble links between the Defence Force and the white state, the modernization of the military has evoked a degree of institutional independence and a sense of organizational self-interest sufficient to support a progressively expanding pattern of claims by the soldiers on the distribution of social resources. If there is a single irrefutable truth in civil–military relations today it is that military institutions always use accumulated political power to feather their own corporate nests whatever their interests and aspirations in relation to wider society.[34] This does not of course mean that the military will sacrifice the state on the altar of greed and expediency, least of all in cases such as South Africa where ideological and racial affinities between soldiers and politicians blunt the competition for resources. Nonetheless, there are innumerable cases in Asia, Africa and Latin America where militaries have turned against their governmental mentors for the simple crass reason that the latter have not been able to keep pace with the material demands of the military establishment, or have not treated the soldiers with the rewards to which they are accustomed. The tendency of militaries to capitalize on their political power in a self-serving manner is one of the major limitations on the performance of military regimes as stimulators of economic development and growth. Indeed, the role of militaries as instruments of economic development matches their poverty as social reformers in general, precisely because power is so often bent to self-enrichment in the form of rapid promotions, radical salary increases, the purchase of sophisticated, expensive and often unnecessary military equipment and greater demands on the national budget. In South Africa the political influence of the military has, of course, not yet expanded to the point where the Defence Force can command public moneys and other social resources on a scale comparable with their counterparts who have monopolized power and then turned it to institutional ends. Yet as the political influence grows, if and when a situation develops which shifts the military to the centre-stage of the political process, progressively greater quantities of public resources will indubitably be fed into military institutions and the defence sector of the economy, despite its questionable contribution to the betterment of society as a whole.

Secondly, and perhaps more importantly in terms of negative social effects, there is a certain irreversibility in the process by which the military moves into the civil political arena. Militaries, as we have noted, differ in the degree of compunction with which they respond to inducements to transgress the boundaries between civil and military society. Some, with weakly institutionalized code of civil predominance, react with alacrity (particularly when triggered by civilian interference in corporate affairs), others, with no firm tradition of political intervention (such as the South African military), react with diffidence, cautiously, almost invisibly, wrapping their behaviour in a complex ideological cloak as a hedge against public criticism. Either way, however, each successive step into politics comes with greater ease than its predecessor, culminating in the coup, the central single most important event in the civil–military process in which the military crosses the great moral divide between the civil and military realms to change the rules of the political game and signal its rights as a political player. This is not to suggest that a coup is the eventual and inevitable outcome of every situation where militaries respond favourably to political pressures. It should already have become evident through examination of the various endogenous and external constraints on the South African military asserting itself politically that there are an infinite number of complex variables mediating the relationship between political reception and the ultimate seizure of governmental power. Yet there is a certain linear momentum in the process, fueled by the fact that the military becomes increasingly self-confident and politically experienced as it moves from waystage to waystage in a political direction and as civil society in its turn becomes accustomed or immured to the presence of the military in its previously exclusive realm. Any concluding observations on civil–military relations in South Africa should also bear in mind the simple but chillingly effective statement that 'the consequence of military intervention is military intervention'.[35] The first coup in the history of any society is a fundamental experience in history because the first coup effectively and decisively ruptures the civilian ethic. As one analyst notes:

No matter how strongly internalized the principle of civilian control may have been prior to the first takeover, it will be a long time before it is strongly reasserted. To the extent that soldiers accept the principle of civilian control in the aftermath of military government, they do so in a diluted, conditional manner. Future takeovers are a 'thinkable' possibility, depending upon the actions of the civilian governors.[36]

In South Africa a strict military coup in the sense of the Defence Force assuming the reins of power by displacing the civil authorities is not a distinct possibility in the immediate future: military movement into the civil realm is more likely to be attenuated and low-key in a fashion reflecting the fact that belief in the efficacy of the military intervention is not deeply internalized in South Africa's history, in contemporary military institutions and in civil minds. Yet this does not necessarily preclude the military accumulating considerable power to influence public decision–making in civil institutions or to prompt institutional changes which give more visibility and formal standing to the current military–executive alliance. From our data it should be clear that the movement in this direction has already been set in motion: with continued executive support, social crisis and/or basic shifts in the coalition structure of white politics this movement should gather momentum. As it does so, it will prove progressively difficult to reverse. Should the military eventually be edged to firmly cross the Rubicon between the civil and military sectors it is extremely unlikely that it will ever again return to the pristine non-political innocence of the barracks.

Militaries who frequently take the increasingly simple but irrevocable step into civil politics also tend towards longer terms in power: in Latin America, transitionary guardian-type praetorianism has progressively given way in a number of countries to ruler-type praetorianism where the military installs itself in the seat of power on a relatively permanent basis. In addition civilians do not have the numbers, organization or weaponry to defeat and displace a unified modern military and there is not a single instance where civilians have overthrown a military regime backed by an integrated officer corps intent on retaining power. This should give pause to South Africans who would install a military regime as a means to reform and to those who seek to overthrow the apartheid state through the projection of revolutionary power. At the same time there are not more than a handful of contemporary military regimes which have stayed in power for more than a twenty-year period, most are inherently unstable, and this mirrors the basic aversion of soldiers to politics eventually manifesting itself in the desire to return to the specialized and familiar realm of military affairs away from the contaminating intrigue and disordered complexity of the civil sector. Most militaries 'civilianize' a short time after taking power, not because of the scale of civil resistance, but through sheer frustration at their inability to shape civil society along lines congenial to the military mind, or, in some cases, because the very ineptness of military rule has aggravated social problems to the point where even the most politically ambitious officers come to prefer the relative tranquillity and order of the barracks existence. Unfortunately, military regimes can wreak incalculable harm on the social fabric out of all proportion to their normally short life-span, all the more so since having once tasted power their leaders become addicted and are driven back to the civil realm on an increasingly frequent basis.[37] In these circumstances, civil society faces double jeopardy: with a broken tradition of military non-intervention, with government mismanaged, damaged democratic values and segmental tensions rubbed raw by one bout of military rule, it wrestles the insurmountable in expectation of another such bout. This is the elementary dynamic underlying the classic Latin American pattern where coup follows coup punctuated by sporadic bursts of civilian authority. South Africa is not of course about to embark on an era of Iberian-style pronunciamento politics. Yet it is important at a time of flux in civil–military boundaries that its political and military influentials be aware of the enormous risks inherent in doing so.

Notes

Introduction

1 See Richard Dale, 'The South African armed forces and their link with the United Kingdom and the Commonwealth of Nations, 1910–61', *Militaria* 9 (1), 1979, p. 8.
2 Kenneth Grundy, *Soldiers Without Politics: Blacks in the South African Armed Forces* (Berkeley: University of California Press, 1983), p. 15.
3 Barney Horowitz, 'An investigation into the recruitment of non-whites into the SADF and a consideration thereof in the light of the "Total Strategy" to meet the "Total Onslaught". Paper prepared for the Southern African Research Program, Yale University, Connecticut, April 1981, p. 38.
4 Perhaps the only real exception to the rule is Kenneth W. Grundy's *Soldiers Without Politics*. This is in fact the only book-length study of the SADF which can strictly be called a work of political analysis.
5 Alfred Stepan, *The Military in Politics: Changing Patterns in Brazil* (Princeton: Princeton University Press, 1971), p. 7.
6 The important role of militaries in the crucible of revolution is explored in a variety of works, including Katherine Chorley, *Armies and the Art of Revolution* (London: Faber and Faber 1943); Ellen Trimberger, *Revolution From Above: Military Bureaucrats and Development in Japan, Turkey, Egypt and Peru* (New Brunswick, New Jersey: Transaction Books, 1978); and in Allan K. Wildman, *The End of the Russian Imperial Army: The Old Army and the Soldiers Revolt, March–April 1917* (Princeton: Princeton University Press, 1980).
7 Barrington Moore, *Injustice: The Social Bases of Obedience and Revolt* (New York: M.E. Sharpe, 1978), p. 375.
8 Horowitz, 'Recruitment of non-whites', p. 4.
9 Kenneth Grundy, *The Rise of the South African Security Establishment: An Essay on the Changing Locus of State Power* (Johannesburg: South African Institute of International Affairs, Bradlow Series No. 1, 1983), p. 1.
10 See Grundy, *Soldiers Without Politics*.
11 On this point, see Stepan, *The Military in Politics*, p. 4.
12 Grundy, *Soldiers Without Politics*, p. 23.
13 In roughly two-thirds of the developing states of the world the military have seized political power at one time or another since the end of World War II. In Africa the military occupied half the seats of government during 1976; in Asia

successful coups were carried out in nine states between 1945 and 1976; in Latin America, where military intervention has become virtually institutionalized as a means of transferring political power, half of the 121 men serving as presidents between 1940 and 1955 were military officers. Eric A. Nordlinger, *Soldiers in Politics: Military Coups and Governments* (Englewood Cliffs: Prentice-Hall, 1977), p. 6.

14 Gaetano Mosca, *The Ruling Class* (New York: McGraw Hill, 1939) quoted in Amos Perlmutter and Valerie Plave Bennett, *The Political Influence of the Military: A Comparative Reader* (New Haven: Yale University Press), p. 58.

15 Samuel Huntington in Perlmutter and Plave Bennett, *ibid*, p. 59.

16 Edward Gibbon, *The Decline and Fall of the Roman Empire*, 2 vols. (New York: Modern Library, 1957), Vol. 1, p. 92.

17 Perlmutter and Plave Bennett, *Political Influence* p. 4.

18 The notion that 'persistent patterns of civil supremacy are the deviant cases' in the politics of developing societies is expressed in Morris Janowitz, 'The comparative analysis of Middle Eastern military institutions' in Janowitz and Jacques van Doorn (eds.), *On Military Intervention* (Rotterdam: Rotterdam University Press, 1971), p. 306.

19 Among the better regimental histories are the following: Neil Orpen, *Gunners of the Cape: The Story of the Cape Field Artillery* (Cape Town: Standard Press, 1965); Neil Orpen, *Prince Alfred's Guard* (Cape Town: Cape and Transvaal Printers, 1967); B.G. Simpkins, *Rand Light Infantry* (Cape Town: Howard Timmins, 1965); H.C. Juta, *The History of the Transvaal Scottish* (Johannesburg: Hortors, 1933); Carel Birkby, *The Saga of the Transvaal Scottish, 1932–50* (Cape Town: Howard Timmins, 1950); Angus McKenzie, *The Dukes: A History of the Duke of Edinburgh's Own Rifles (1855–1956)* (Cape Town: Galvin and Sales, 1956); Frank Perridge, *History of Prince Alfred's Guard* (Port Elizabeth: E. Walton, 1939); H.H. Curson, *The History of the Kimberley Regiment* (Kimberley: North Cape Printers, 1963); Reginald Griffiths, *First City: A Saga of Service* (Cape Town: Howard Timmins, 1970); A.C. Martin, *The Durban Light Infantry*, 2 vols. (Durban: Hayne and Gibson, 1969).

1 The South African Defence Force: the institutional and historical framework

1 *Republic of South Africa, White Paper on Defence and Armaments Supply, 1979* (Pretoria: Department of Defence, WPF – 1979), p. 17.

2 On the organizational history of the SADF, the Army in particular, see Ashley C. Lillie, 'The origins and development of the South African Army, *Militaria* 12 (2), 1982 pp. 7–17.

3 For the history of the Chief-of-Staff (Operations) see S.L. Le Grange, 'Geskiedenis van die Hoof van Staf Operasies', *Militaria* 12 (2), 1982, pp. 59–61.

4 On the history of the Logistics Staff Division see A.C. Bergh, 'Die Geskiedenis van Afdeling Logistiek', *Militaria* 12 (2), 1982, pp. 62–5.

5 On the development of the Finance Staff Section see R.J. Bouch, 'The development of the Comptroller's Section, SADF', *Militaria* 6 (3), 1976, pp. 1–5; Ashley C. Lillie, 'Chief of Staff, Finance', *Militaria* 12 (2), 1982 pp. 66–9.

6 On the history and development of the Intelligence Staff Section see S.C. Le

Grange, 'Die Geskiedenis van Hoof van Staf Inligting', *Militaria* 12 (2), 1982, pp. 56–8.

7 On the background of the present Staff Personnel Section see R. von Moltke, 'Die Ontstaan en Ontwikkeling van die Stafafdeling Hoof van Staf Personeel', *Militaria* 12 (2), 1982, pp. 46–51.

8 Ashley C. Lillie, 'Origins and development' pp. 7–17.

9 On the South African Navy, see J.C. Goosen, *South Africa's Navy: The First Fifty Years* (Johannesburg: W.J. Flesh, 1973); J.D. Bredenkamp, 'Die Ontstaan en Ontwikkeling van die Vloot, 1912–82', *Militaria* 12 (2), 1982, pp. 31–7; A. Wessels, 'Die Suid-Afrikaanse Vloot: Verhede, Hede an Toekoms', *Militaria*, 11 (4), 1981, pp. 18–28; J. Ploeger, 'Die Totstandkoming van die Suid-Afrikaanse Afdeling van die 'Royal Navy Volunteer Reserve', *Militaria* 3 (1), 1971; J. Ploeger, 'Uit die Voorgeskiedenis van die Suid-Afrikaanse Vloot: Die Ontstaan van die Suid-Afrikaanse Seediens', *Militaria*, 3 (1), 1970; A.K. du Toit, *Ships of the South African Navy* (Cape Town: South African Boating Publications, 1976). A number of books, articles and pamphlets deal with the history of the South African Air Force. See, *inter alia*, E.H. Ward, 'Swifter than eagles: a brief history of the SAAF', *Militaria* 12 (2), 1982, pp. 18–30; D.N. Moore, 'The SAAF in Korea', *Militaria* 10 (4), 1980, pp. 24–34; *Per Aspera Ad Astra: South African Air Force Golden Jubilee Souvenir Book* (Johannesburg: Kendall Press, 1970); H.J. Botha, 'Historiese Oorsig van die Ontstaan en Ontwikkeling van die Militere Lugvaart en die Selfstandige Lugmagte', *Militaria* 2 (1), 1970.

10 On the history of the Army College see F.J. Jacobs, 'Die Suid-Afrikaanse Leerkollege', *Militaria* 4 (1), 1974, pp. 63–70.

11 For an extended discussion of the major civil–military categories see Alfred Stepan, *The Military in Politics*, pp. 57–62; Eric A. Nordlinger, *Soldiers in Politics*, pp. 10–19.

12 Late nineteenth-century Germany and Austria, for example, combine the aristocratic and professional models, while twentieth-century United States is a combination of the liberal and professional types.

13 For colonialism as a transfer system, particularly British colonialism and the transmission of military and political values see, *inter alia*, W.B. Hamilton, 'The transfer of power in historical perspective' in W.B. Hamilton, K. Robinson and C.D.W. Goodwin (eds.), *A Decade of the Commonwealth, 1955–1964* (Durham, North Carolina: University of North Carolina Press, 1966), pp. 25–41; R.A. Preston, 'The transfer of British military institutions to Canada in the nineteenth century' in W.B. Hamilton (ed.), *The Transfer of Institutions* (Durham: University of North Carolina Press, 1964), pp. 81–107; C.A. Crocker, *The Military Transfer of Power in Africa; A Comparative Study of Change in the British and French Systems of Order* (unpublished Ph.D. dissertation: The Johns Hopkins School of Advanced International Studies, 1969); Donald Rothchild, 'The limits of federalism: an examination of political institutional transfer in Africa', *Journal of Modern African Studies* iv, No. 3. (November 1966), pp. 275–93.

14 In 1906, four years before the creation of the Union, there were 20,370 Imperial troops stationed in South Africa. Cited in Richard Dale, 'The South African armed forces and their link with the United Kingdom and the Commonwealth of Nations, 1910–61' *Militaria* 9 (1), 1979, pp. 1–11, 16.

15 Eric A. Walker, *A History of Southern Africa* (London: Longmans, 1964), p. 544.
16 Dale, 'South African armed forces'; Lillie, 'Origins and development', p. 12.
17 Du Toit, *Ships* p. 9.
18 Dale, 'South African armed forces', p. 4.
19 Lillie, 'Origins and development', p. 8.
20 G. Tylden, *The Armed Forces of South Africa* (Johannesburg: City of Johannesburg Africana Museum, Frank Connock Publication, No. 2, 1954), p. 26.
21 Dale, 'South African armed forces', p. 4.
22 Ward, 'Swifter than eagles', p. 24.
23 *Paratus* 31 (3), March 1980, p. 14.
24 On this point see Dale, 'South African armed forces'.
25 *Ibid*, p. 3.
26 Ward, 'Swifter than eagles', p. 20.
27 *Paratus* 31 (3), March 1980, p. 14.
28 Tylden, *Armed forces*, p. 174; Du Toit, *Ships*, p. 51.
29 Bredenkamp, 'Ontstaan en Ontwikkeling', p. 36.
30 *Republic of South Africa, Review of Defence and Armaments Production, 1960–70* (Pretoria: Department of Defence, April 1971), p. 9.
31 Walker, *History of Southern Africa*, p. 544.
32 *Review of Defence and Armaments Production, 1960–70*, p. 4.
33 The Union, for example, relied entirely on British intelligence facilities for its own information during the course of both world wars. It was only after World War II that the single intelligence officer attached to the South African Chief of General Staff was replaced by a full-scale local intelligence division. See Le Grange, 'Staf Inligting', p. 56.
34 Tylden, *Armed forces*, p. 1.
35 *Ibid*, p. 124.
36 *Paratus* 31 (3), March 1980, p. 14.
37 Tylden, *Armed forces*, p. 173; Du Toit, *Ships*, p. 9.
38 Dale, 'South African armed forces', p. 5; Republic of South Africa, *Review of Defence and Armaments Production, 1960–70*, p. 4.
39 A considerable amount has been written on the involvement of South African pilots in the Battle of Britain, on 'Sailor' Malan and two of the winners of the Victoria Cross, John Nettleton and Edwin Swales. For an interesting series of articles see D.P. Tidy, 'South African air aces of World War II, in *Military History Journal* 1 (2), June 1968; 1 (3), December 1968; 1 (4) June 1969; 1 (5), December 1969; 1 (6), June 1970; 1 (7), December 1970.
40 See Journal of Jan van Riebeeck, 23 December 1658, cited in S.F.N. Gie, 'The Cape Colony under company rule, 1708–1795', in Eric A. Walker (ed.), *The Cambridge History of the British Empire*, Vol. VIII, *South Africa, Rhodesia and the High Commission Territories* (Cambridge: Cambridge University Press, 1963), p. 151. Also Tylden, *Armed forces*, p. 2.
41 Gie, 'Cape Colony', p. 151.
42 *Ibid*, p. 151.
43 See Neil Orpen, *Total Defence: The Role of the Commandos in the Armed Forces of South Africa* (Cape Town: Nasionale Boekhandel, 1967), p. 10.
44 Tylden, *Armed forces*, p. 184.
45 *Ibid*, p. 185.

46 *Ibid*, p. 217.
47 Walker, *History*, p. 487.
48 Lillie, 'Origins and development', p. 2.
49 Eric Walker, 'The struggle for supremacy, 1896–1902' in Walker (ed.), *Cambridge History*, p. 619.
50 Tylden, *Armed forces*, p. 184.
51 *Ibid*, p. 185.
52 *Ibid*, p. 185.
53 C.W. De Kiewiet, 'The period of transition in South African policy, 1854–1870', in Walker (ed.), *Cambridge History*, p. 408.
54 Tylden, *Armed forces*, p. 217.
55 Gie, 'Cape Colony', p. 167.
56 Tylden, *Armed forces*, p. 217.
57 *Ibid*, p. 220.
58 For an interesting parallel to the South African case, see Amos Perlmutter, *Military and Politics in Israel: Nation-Building and Role-Expansion* (London: Frank Cass, 1969), particularly Chapters 1 and 2.
59 Tylden, *Armed forces*, p. 22.
60 Lillie, 'Origins and development', p. 7.
61 Walker, *History of Southern Africa*, p. 544.
62 Lillie, 'Origins and development', p. 4.
63 Tylden, *Armed forces*, p. 71; F.S. Malan, 'South Africa after the Union, 1910–21' in Walker, *Cambridge History*, p. 669.
64 Malan in Walker, *Cambridge History*, p. 669.

2 *The rise of the garrison state and the development of total strategy*

1 See Samuel Huntington, *The Common Defense: Strategic Programs in National Politics* (New York: Columbia University Press, 1961).
2 Samuel Huntington in Amos Perlmutter and Valerie Plave Bennett (eds.), *The Political Influence of the Military: A Comparative Reader* (New Haven: Yale University Press, 1980), p. 52.
3 On constitutional development in South Africa and the emergence of consociation, see Philip Frankel, 'Consensus, consociation and cooption in South African politics', *Cahiers d'Etudes Africaines*, xx (4), 1980, pp. 473–94.
4 The career trajectories of the following officers were traced for the purposes of this study:

Army
Major-General B.F. Armstrong (Adjutant-General, (1939–40); Brigadier-General C.F. Beyers (Commandant-General of the Citizen Force, 1912–14); Major-General J.N. Bierman (Chief-of-Staff, Army, 1959); Lieutenant-General G.J.J. Boshoff (Chief-of-Staff, Personnel, 1980); Major-General A.J.E. Brink (Chief of the General Staff, 1920–33); Colonel C. Otto (Quartermaster-General 1921–37); Lieutenant-General G.E. Brink (Commander 1st South African Division and Director-General of Demobilization, 1945–48); Brigadier H.S. Cilliers (Adjutant Chief-of-Staff, 1945–46); Brigadier-General J.J. Collyer (Chief of the General Staff, 1917–19); Brigadier E.J. De Wet (Adjutant-General 1960–62); Lieutenant-General C.L. de Wet Du Toit (Chief of the General Staff, 1950–56); Lieutenant-General H. de V. Du

Toit (Chief-of-Staff, Intelligence, 1974–77); Lieutenant-General J.R. Dutton (Director General, Operations, 1976–81); Major-General S.A. Engelbrecht (Chief-of-Staff, Army, 1959–63); General C.A. Fraser (Army Chief-of-Staff and Chief of the Army, 1966–67); Lieutenant-General R.F. Holtzhausen (Chief-of-Staff, Personnel, 1981–); Lieutenant-General J.J. Geldenhuys (Chief of the Army, 1980–); Lieutenant-General I.R. Gleeson (Chief-of-Staff, Operations, 1981–84); Commandant-General P.H. Grobbelaar (Commandant-General 1960–65); Combat-General P.J. Jacobs (Army Chief-of-Staff, 1963–65); Brigadier S.J. Joubert (Adjutant-General, 1948–53); Commandant-General H.B. Klopper (Commandant-General, 1956–58); Lieutenant-General H.P. Laubscher (Chief-of-Staff, Logistics, 1974); Lieutenant-General I. Lemmer (Chief-of-Staff, Logistics, 1978–); Lieutenant-General W.P. Louw (Inspector-General, 1973–75); Major-General Sir H.T. Lukin (Inspector-General of the Standing Force, 1912–15); General M.A. de M. Malan (Chief of the Defence Force, 1976–80); Major-General G.H.F. Markgraff (Chief of Personnel and Director-General of Personnel, 1968–74); Lieutenant-General J. Mitchell-Baker (Quartermaster-General, 1939–45); Major-General D.H. Pienaar (Chief of the 1st South African Division, 1942); Lieutenant-General E. Pienaar (Comptroller of the Defence Force, 1968–76); Major-General W.H.E. Poole (Deputy Chief of the General Staff, 1946–48); Colonel Sir R.H. Price (Quartermaster-General, 1918–19); Colonel M.C. Roeland (Quartermaster-General, 1912–18); Major-General J.J. Steenkamp (Quartermaster-General, 1975–76); Brigadier-General W.E.C. Tanner (Adjutant-General, 1919–21 and 1925–33); Major-General F.H. Theron (Adjutant-General, 1940); Major-General R.C.J. van der Byl (Quartermaster-General, 1968–74); Combat-General J.S.J. van der Merwe (Quartermaster-General, 1959–65); Lieutenant-General W.R. van der Riet (Chief of the General Staff, 1965–67); Lieutenant-General P.W. van der Westhuizen (Chief-of-Staff, Intelligence, 1978–); Lieutenant-General A.J. Van Deventer (Chief-of-Staff, Finances, 1976–79); Lieutenant-Colonel D.O.Van Velden (Adjutant-General, 1921–25); Major-General J.A. Van Zyl (Chaplain-General, 1973–); General C.L. Viljoen (Chief of the South African Defence Force, 1980–); Major-General H.S. Wakefield (Director-General of the Reserve, 1939).

Air Force
Lieutenant-General R.F. Armstrong (Chief of the General Staff, 1974–76); Lieutenant-General W.J. Berghe (Chief-of-Staff, Finances, 1979–); Brigadier H.J. Bronkhorst (Quartermaster-General, 1951–53); Brigadier H.D. Daniel (Director of the Air Force, 1939); Major-General J.T. Durrant (Director-General of the Air Force, 1946–51); Major-General C.H. Hartzenberg (Chief of Defence Force Administration, 1965–68); General R.C. Hiemstra (Commandant-General, 1965–72); Brigadier W.H. Hingeston (Adjutant-General, 1946–48); Brigadier J. Holthouse (Director-General of the Air Force, 1939–40); Lieutenant-General H.A. Kotze (Quartermaster-General, 1974); Lieutenant-General P.A. Le Grange (Chief-of-Staff, Personnel, 1974–77); Lieutenant-General H.J. Martin (Chief of the General Staff, 1967–68); Commandant-General S.A. Melville (Commandant-General, 1958–60); Major-General G.T. Moll (Chief of the General Staff, 1966–67); Lieutenant-General A.M. Muller (Chief of the Air Force, 1979–1984);

Lieutenant-General R.H. Rogers (Chief of the Air Force, 1974–75 and 1979); General Sir H.A. Van Ryneveld (Chief of the General Staff, 1933–49); Lieutenant-General C.J. Venter (Director-General of the Air Force, 1940–45); Lieutenant-General J.P. Verster (Chief of the Air Force, 1967–74); Combat-General B.G. Viljoen (Air Force Chief-of-Staff, 1956–65); Brigadier H.G. Willmott (Chief of the Air Force Staff, 1952–54).

Navy
Admiral H.H. Biermann (Chief of the South African Defence Force, 1973–76); Rear-Admiral M.A. Bekker (Quartermaster-General, 1976–); Commodore F.J. Dean (Director of the South African Sea Force, 1946–51); Commodore J. Dalgleish (Director of the South African Sea Force, 1946); Brigadier P. De Waal (Fleet and Marine Chief of Staff, 1951–52); Vice-Admiral R.A. Edwards (Chief of the Navy, 1980–82); Rear-Admiral G.W. Hallifax (Director of the South African Defence Force, Navy, 1939–41); Vice-Admiral J. Johnson (Chief of the Navy, 1972–77); Vice-Admiral J.J. Walters (Chief of the Navy, 1977–80).

Medical Service
Brigadier P.C.C. Blair-Hook (Surgeon-General, 1953–55); Lieutenant-General C.R. Cockcroft (Surgeon-General, 1969–77); Colonel E.H. Cluver (Director-General of Medical, Health and Dental Services, 1938–39); Brigadier W.H. Du Plessis (Surgeon-General, 1949–53); Lieutenant-General N.J. Nieuwoudt (Surgeon-General, 1977–); Major General A.J. Orenstein (Director-General of Medical Services, 1943–45); Brigadier J.H. Rauch (Surgeon-General, 1955–60); Major-General E.C. Raymond (Surgeon-General, 1960–69); Colonel P.G. Stock (Director, Medical Services, 1914–18 and 1919–20); Brigadier Sir E.N. Thornton (Director-General of Medical, Health and Dental Services, 1940–43).
When disaggregated according to career point the following categories emerged:

i 1912–20 Major-General Lukin; Brigadiers-General Beyers, Collyer; Colonels Price, Rowland, Stock (6).

ii 1920–30 Major-General Brink; Brigadier-General Tanner; Colonel Brink; Lieutenant Colonel Van Velden (4).

iii 1930–40 Majors-General Armstrong, Wakefield; Brigadier Daniel; Colonel Cluver (4).

iv 1940–50 General van Ryneveld; Lieutenants-General Brink, Mitchell-Baker, Venter; Majors-General Durrant, Orenstein, Pienaar, Poole, Theron; Brigadiers Cilliers, Hingeston, Holthouse, Thornton; Rear Admiral Hallifax; Commodores Dalgleish, Dean (16).

v 1950–60 Commandants-General Melville, Klopper; Lieutenant-General Du Toit; Major-General Bierman; Brigadiers Blair-Hook, Bronkhorst, De Waal, Du Plessis, Joubert, Rauch, Willmott (11)

vi 1960–70 Commandant-General Grobbelaar; Generals Fraser, Hiemstra; Lieutenants-General Martin, van der Riet; Combats-General Jacobs, Van der Merwe, Viljoen; Majors-General Engelbrecht, Hartzenberg, Moll, Raymond; Brigadier De Wet (13) *vii 1970–80* General Malan; Lieutenants-General Armstrong, Cockcroft, Du Toit, Dutton, Kotze, Laubscher, Le Grange, Louw, Pienaar, Rogers, Van Deventer, Verster; Majors-General Markgraff, Steenkamp, Van der Byl, Van Zyl; Admiral Biermann, Vice-Admiral Walters, Johnson; Rear-Admiral Bekker (21)

viii 1980– General Viljoen; Lieutenants-General Berghe, Boshoff, Geldenhuys, Gleeson, Holtzhausen, Lemmer, Muller, Nieuwoudt, Van der Westhuizen; Vice-Admiral Edwards (11).

5 See Alfred Stepan, *The Military in Politics: Changing Patterns in Brazil* (Princeton, Princeton University Press, 1971), p. 95; Morris Janowitz, *The Professional Soldier. A Social and Political Portrait* (Glencoe: Free Press, 1960), pp. 204–7.

6 Republic of South Africa, *White Paper on Defence and Armaments Supply 1979* (Pretoria: Department of Defence, WPF – 1979), p. 16.

7 Samuel P. Huntington, *The Soldier and the State: the Theory and Politics of Civil–Military Relations* (New York: Random House, 1957), p. 14.

8 Eric A. Nordlinger, *Soldiers in Politics: Military Coups and Governments* (Englewood Cliffs: Prentice-Hall, 1977), p. 50.

9 *Ibid*, p. 53.

10 *Ibid*, p. 120. On this important point see also Ronald M. Schneider, *The Political System of Brazil: the Emergence of a 'Modernizing' Authoritarian Regime, 1964–70* (New York: Columbia University Press, 1971), pp. 113–114; Stepan, *Military in Politics*, pp. 232–4.

11 Stepan, *Military in Politics*, Chapter 8.

12 André Beaufre, *An Introduction to Strategy*, (London: Faber and Faber, 1963). Preface by Captain B.H. Liddell Hart, p. 10.

13 The following analysis is based on the two of Beaufre's three works dealing with so-called 'indirect total strategy': André Beaufre, *An Introduction to Strategy (With Particular Reference to Problems of Defence, Politics, Economics and Diplomacy in the Nuclear Age)* (London: Faber and Faber, 1963. Translated by Major-General R.H. Barry); and André Beaufre, *Strategy of Action* (London: Faber and Faber, 1967. Translated by Major-General R.H. Barry).

14 Beaufre, *Introduction to Strategy*, p. 23.

15 *Ibid*, p. 22.

16 Beaufre, *Strategy of Action*, p. 104.

17 Beaufre, *Introduction to Strategy*, p. 103.

18 *Ibid*, p. 102.

19 Beaufre, *Strategy of Action*, p. 127.

20 *Ibid*, p. 115.

21 Beaufre, *Introduction to Strategy*, p. 129.

22 *Ibid*, p. 101.

23 *Ibid*, p. 128.

24 *Ibid*, p. 45.

25 *Ibid*, p. 46.

26 Beaufre, *Strategy of Action*, p. 21.

27 *Ibid*, p. 131.

28 Beaufre, *Introduction to Strategy*, p. 14.

29 *Ibid*, p. 24.

30 Beaufre, *Strategy of Action*, p. 114.

31 Beaufre, *Introduction to Strategy*, p. 117.
32 Beaufre, *Strategy of Action*, p. 108.
33 *Ibid*, p. 126.
34 Beaufre, *Introduction to Strategy*, p. 112.
35 Beaufre, *Strategy of Action*, p. 130.
36 Beaufre, *Introduction to Strategy*, p. 125.
37 Two other works widely read in Defence College circles apart from Beaufre are Sir Robert Thompson, *Defeating Communist Insurgency* (London: Chatto and Windus, 1966); and J.J. McCuen, *The Art of Counter-Revolutionary War: The Strategy of Counter-Insurgency* (London: Faber and Faber, 1966).
38 Alfred Stepan, *Military in Politics*, p. 180.
39 *White Paper on Defence and Armaments Production*, 1973 (Pretoria: Department of Defence, WPD – 1973), p. 1.
40 On the 'reality' of 'total onslaught', see Kenneth Grundy, *The Rise of the South African Security Establishment: An Essay on the Changing Locus of State Power* (Johannesburg: South African Institute of International Affairs, 1983), pp. 4–5.
41 *Republic of South Africa*, White Paper on Defence, 1977 (Pretoria: Department of Defence, WPF – 1977), p. 9.
42 *White Paper on Defence and Armaments Production*, 1973, p. 1.
43 *White Paper on Defence*, 1977, p. 4.
44 *Ibid*, p. 5.
45 *Ibid*, p. 5.
46 *Ibid*, p. 4.
47 For a representative description of the multiple dangers confronting South Africa as seen from the perspective of the military, see the section aptly entitled 'The threat' in *White Paper on Defence and Armaments Supply, 1982* (Pretoria: Department of Defence, WPM – 1982).
48 *White Paper on Defence*, 1977, p. 7.
49 On the development of interventionist ideologies among the Peruvian officers, see Luigi Einaudi, 'Revolution from within? Military rule in Peru since 1968', *Studies in Comparative International Development*, Spring 1973.
50 Stepan, *Military in Politics*, p. 127.
51 *White Paper on Defence*, 1977, p. 8.
52 *Ibid*, p. 5.
53 *Ibid*, p. 4.
54 See Samuel P. Huntington, *The Soldier and the State* (Cambridge: Harvard University Press, 1967), pp. 62–4: Eric A. Nordlinger, *Soldiers in Politics: Military Coups and Governments* (Englewood Cliffs: Prentice-Hall, 1977), pp. 56 and 119; Morris Janowitz, *The Military in the Political Development of New Nations* (Chicago: University of Chicago Press, 1964), p. 66; Aristide R. Zolberg, 'The Military decade in Africa', *World Politics*, January 1973, p. 319.
55 On 'role-expanding' militaries in general, see Moshe Lissak, 'Modernization and role-expansion of the military in developing countries: a comparative analysis', *Comparative Studies in Society and History*, IX (April 1967), pp. 233–55.
56 *White Paper on Defence*, 1977, p. 9.
57 Beaufre, *An Introduction to Strategy*, p. 122.
58 Republic of South Africa, *Debates of the House of Assembly*, Vol. 64, 23 April 1975, Column 4656. On Dunn, see *Modern Revolutions: An Introduction to*

the Analysis of a Political Phenomenon (Cambridge: Cambridge University Press, 1972).

59 *White Paper on Defence, 1977*, p. 35.

60 *Ibid*, p. 8.

61 *Ibid*.

62 Claude E. Welch and Arthur K. Smith, *Military Role and Rule: Perspectives on Civil–Military Relations* (North Scituate, Mass: Duxbury Press, 1974), p. 70.

63 Raoul Girardet, 'Problèmes ideologiques et moraux' in Raoul Girardet (ed.), *La Crise Militaire Francaise, 1945–62: Aspects Sociologiques et Ideologiques* (Paris: Librairie Armand Colin, 1964), pp. 151–229.

64 Neil Orpen, *Total Defence*, p. 2.

65 *Ibid*.

66 Stepan, *Military in Politics*, p. 153.

67 *Ibid*, p. 267.

68 *Ibid*, p. 175.

69 *White Paper on Defence and Armaments Production, 1969* (Pretoria: Department of Defence, WPH – 1969), p. 10.

70 It is conceivable that the attempt to break intellectual and material dependence on Britain could be backdated as far as the Statute of Westminster of 1931. As Dale points out, this would give the South African military a three-decade head-start over other African militaries in the development of its own peculiarly indigenous civil–military system. See Richard Dale, 'The South African armed forces and their linkage with the United Kingdom and the Commonwealth of Nations, 1910–61', *Militaria*, 9 (1), 1979, pp. 1–11.

71 *Debates of the House of Assembly* (Questions and Answers), Vol. 65. 30 January 1976, Column 32.

72 The emphasis of the French military on *elan vital* and its perception of itself as *la grande muette* has been discussed in numerous historical and sociological works. See, *inter alia*, Richard Griffith, *Pétain* (New York: Doubleday, 1972), p. 60ff; Alistair Horne, *The Price of Glory: Verdun 1916* (Harmondsworth: Penguin, 1964), Chapter 1; and Barbara W. Tuchman, *August 1914* (London: Constable and Co. 1962), Chapter 3.

73 Stepan, *Military in Politics*, p. 126.

74 *Ibid*, p. 154.

75 On this point see Huntington, *Soldier and State*, pp. 7ff.

76 See Stepan, *Military in Politics*, Chapter 8; Guy J. Pauker, *The Indonesian Doctrine of Territorial Warfare and Territorial Management* (Santa Monica: Rand Corporation, RM-3312-PR, November 1963).

77 *White Paper on Defence, 1977*, p. 5.

3 Exterior manoeuvre: the dynamics of militarization

1 On the role of budgetary assistance in stimulating coup activity, see Samuel Decalo, *Coups and Army Rule in Africa: Studies in Military Style* (New Haven: Yale University Press, 1976), p. 31; Claude E. Welch, 'Praetorianism in Commonwealth West Africa', *Journal of Modern African Studies*, July 1972, pp. 212–13; A.A. Afrifa, *The Ghana Coup* (London: Frank Cass, 1966), p. 97–8; Carlos Alberto Astiz, *Pressure Groups and Power Elites in Peruvian Politics* (Ithaca: Cornell University Press, 1969), pp. 138–9.

2 Republic of South Africa, *White Paper on Defence and Armaments Production, 1975* (Pretoria: Department of Defence, WPE – 1975), p. 9.

3 South African Institute of Race Relations, *Annual Survey of Race Relations in South Africa*, 1976 (Johannesburg: South African Institute of Race Relations, 1977), p. 35; Republic of South Africa, *White Paper on Defence and Armaments Supply, 1982* (Pretoria: Department of Defence, 1982. WPM – 1982), p. 24.

4 See Ashley C. Lillie, 'The origins and development of the South African Army', *Militaria* 12 (2), 1982, p. 12ff.

5 *White Paper on Defence and Armaments Production, 1969* (Pretoria: Department of Defence, WPH – 1969), p. 1.

6 Eric A. Nordlinger *Soldiers in Politics: Military Coups and Governments* (Englewood Cliffs: Prentice-Hall, 1977), p. 68.

7 *White Paper on Defence and Armaments Supply, 1982*, p. 23.

8 *White Paper on Defence, 1977* (Pretoria: Department of Defence, WPF – 1977), p. 12.

9 *White Paper on Defence and Armaments Supply, 1982*, p. 23.

10 *Ibid.*

11 *White Paper on Defence and Armaments Supply, 1977*, p. 7.

12 See C. Wright Mills, *The Power Elite* (London: Oxford University Press, 1956), particularly Chapters 9 and 12.

13 National Union of South African Students, *Total War in South Africa: Militarization and the Apartheid State* (Johannesburg: Allied Press, 1982), p. 26.

14 *Paratus* 30 (6), June 1980, p. 30.

15 On the early history of the South African armaments industry see Simon Ratcliffe, 'Forced relations: the state, crisis and the rise of militarism in South Africa', unpublished BA (Honours) dissertation, University of the Witwatersrand, Johannesburg, February 1983. pp. 72ff.

16 *Sunday Times* (Johannesburg), 27 October 1963; *The Star* (Johannesburg), 27 May 1963.

17 *Rand Daily Mail* (Johannesburg), 11 June 1969.

18 *Sunday Times* (Johannesburg), 21 June 1964.

19 James Barber, *South Africa's Foreign Policy, 1945–70* (London: Oxford University Press, 1973), p. 192.

20 *Sunday Express* (Johannesburg), 9 April 1967.

21 Republic of South Africa, *Armaments Development and Production Act* (No. 57 of 1968), Section 3 (KB).

22 *Ibid*, Section 3(1).

23 Act 86, 1980, cited in South African Institute of Race Relations, *Survey*, 1980 (Johannesburg: South African Institute of Race Relations, 1981), p. 213.

24 National Union of South African Students, *Total War*, p. 22.

25 *Sunday Times* (Johannesburg), 11 July 1982; *White Paper on Defence and Armaments Supply, 1982*, p. 25; *Financial Mail* (Johannesburg), 11 September 1981.

26 *Financial Mail* (Johannesburg), 11 September 1981.

27 *White Paper on Defence and Armaments Supply, 1979* (Pretoria: Department of Defence, WPF – 1979), p. 25.

28 On the Armscor workforce, see Ratcliffe, 'Forced relations', pp. 84ff.

29 The role of Western corporate investment in supporting apartheid has, of course, generated considerable controversy. Much of the resulting literature gives at least some attention to relations between the large multinationals and

the military sector of the South African economy. Representative works are, *inter alia*, Ruth First, Jonathan Steele and Christabel Gurney, *The South African Connection: Western Investment in Apartheid* (Harmondsworth: Penguin, 1973); and Barbara Rogers, *White Wealth and Black Poverty: American Investments in Southern Africa* (Westport, Conn: Greenwood Press, 1976). Of more direct relevance: Ann Seidman and H. Makgetla, 'Transnational corporations and the South African military–industrial complex'. (New York, United Nations Centre Against Apartheid, 1979).

30 Italy, France and Israel are important licensers of the South African arms industry. The Mirage fighter aircraft produced by Atlas are manufactured under a 1971 French licence while the Eland armoured car, now developed locally, is a version of the Panhard AML 60/90. Impala fighters used for training purposes by the South African Air Force are produced under a 1973 Italian licence. The Republic's small but expanding fleet of fast missile craft are modelled on the Israeli Reshef-class craft under a licensing agreement concluded in late 1974. Source: Stockholm International Peace Research Institute, *World Armaments and Disarmament, SIPRI Yearbook 1978* (London: Taylor and Francis, 1978).

31 See South African Institute of Race Relations, *Survey, 1971* (Johannesburg: South African Institute of Race Relations, 1972), p. 63.

32 *Financial Mail* (Johannesburg), 11 September 1981.

33 On shifts in production in Armscor, see *Financial Mail, ibid.*

34 *White Paper on Defence and Armaments Supply, 1982*, p. 26. It has been estimated that 94 per cent of the equipment used in the South African invasion of Angola during 1976 was of local manufacture. *Ibid*, p. 23.

35 *Paratus*, 33 (10), October 1982, p. 7. Armscor has also conceivably played an important role in the development of the South African nuclear industry – although the extent to which the Republic is using its nuclear power for military purposes is a closely guarded secret. It is generally accepted however that South Africa has the capacity to produce nuclear arms and has imported a variety of technologies adaptable to nuclear military purposes. The Republic has consistently refused to sign the Nuclear Arms Non-Proliferation Treaty largely because, it is surmised, it has an atomic bomb which has already been successfully tested. See *The Star* (Johannesburg) 27 March 1967; 14 January 1981; 25 August 1982; 22 October 1982.

36 Kenneth W. Grundy, *The Rise of the South African Security Establishment: An Essay on the Changing Locus of State Power* (Johannesburg: South African Institute of International Affairs, Bradlow Series No. 1. 1983), p. 14.

37 *Financial Mail* (Johannesburg), 11 September 1981.

38 *White Paper on Defence and Armaments Supply, 1979*, p. 24.

39 Republic of South Africa, *Debates of the House of Assembly*, Vol. 56, 22 April 1975, Column 4552. See also *Financial Mail*, 26 November 1976.

40 *Debates of the House of Assembly*, 1 May 1980, Column 5303.

41 *To the Point* (Johannesburg), 17 September 1979.

42 *Paratus*, 33 (4), April 1982, pp. 26–9.

43 *Ibid.*

44 Republic of South Africa, *Review of Defence and Armaments Production, 1960–70* (Pretoria: Department of Defence, April 1971), p. 6.

45 *Financial Mail* (Johannesburg), 2 April 1982.

46 *Review of Defence and Armaments Production, 1960–70*, p. 16.

47 On the concept of area defence, see *Financial Mail,* 15 January 1982; *Rand Daily Mail* (Johannesburg), 13 July 1982; *Paratus,* 33 (7), July 1982, p. 34.
48 Major General Charles Lloyd, *The Importance of Rural Development in the Defence Strategy of South Africa and the Need for Private Sector Involvement* (Johannesburg: Urban Foundation, 1979), p. 7.
49 *Cape Times* (Cape Town), 9 July 1982.
50 *Paratus,* 33 (2), February 1982, p. 34.
51 South African Institute of Race Relations, *Survey,* 1980 (Johannesburg: South African Institute of Race Relations, 1981), p. 209.
52 On the reaction of black parents to the use of soldier-teachers in Namibia, see reports on disturbances at the Petrus Karets Secondary School, 1978. *Windhoek Advertiser* (Windhoek), 1 September 1978.
53 South African Institute of Race Relations, *Survey,* 1980, p. 208.
54 *White Paper on Defence, 1965–67* (Pretoria: Department of Defence, WP. DD 67), p. 6; White Paper on Defence and Armaments Supply, 1982, p. 12.
55 *White Paper on Defence, 1982,* p. 16.
56 *White Paper on Defence, 1977,* p. 31.
57 *Paratus,* 31 (3), March 1980, p. 14.
58 *White Paper on Defence, 1965–67,* p. 16.
59 *Debates of the House of Assembly* (Questions and Answers), Vol. 58, 6 May 1975, Column 886.
60 *Ibid.*
61 *White Paper on Defence and Armaments Production, 1973* (Pretoria: Department of Defence, WPD – 1973), p. 5.
62 *Ibid,* p. 20.
63 *White Paper on Defence and Armaments Production, 1973,* p. 21.
64 *Debates of the House of Assembly,* Vol. 56, 22 April 1975, Column 4588.
65 *White Paper on Defence and Armaments Production, 1975,* p. 17.
66 *Debates of the House of Assembly,* Vol. 56, 22 April 1975, Column 4570.
67 *White Paper on Defence and Armaments Supply, 1979,* p. 16.
68 *Die Burger* (Cape Town), 2 February 1980.
69 *White Paper on Defence and Armaments Supply, 1979,* p. 16.
70 South African Institute of Race Relations, *Survey,* 1980, p. 201.
71 *Ibid.*
72 *White Paper on Defence and Armaments Supply, 1982,* p. 17.
73 *Debates of the House of Assembly* (Questions and Answers), Vol. 65, 14 May 1976, Column 1008.
74 *Ibid,* Vol. 65, 3 May 1976, Column 932.
75 South African Institute of Race Relations, *Survey,* 1980, p. 209.
76 *White Paper on Defence and Armaments Supply, 1979,* p. 21.
77 South African Institute of Race Relations, *Survey,* 1980, p. 215.
78 *Ibid.*
79 *Review of Defence and Armaments Production, 1960–70,* p. 19.
80 *Debates of the House of Assembly* (Questions and Answers), Vol. 65, 9 March 1976, Columns 505–8.
81 *White Paper on Defence, 1977,* p. 36.
82 *White Paper on Defence, 1979,* p. 15.
83 *Ibid.*
84 South African Institute of Race Relations, *Survey,* 1977 (Johannesburg: South African Institute of Race Relations, 1978), p. 90.

85 *Ibid.*
86 *Review of Defence and Armaments Production, 1960–70,* p. 25.
87 South African Institute of Race Relations, *Survey,* 1976, p. 36.
88 On the interchangeability of roles in South African police and military history, see Philip Frankel, 'South Africa: the politics of police control', *Comparative Politics* 12 (4), July 1980, pp. 481–500.
89 *White Paper on Defence and Armaments Supply, 1982,* p. 7.
90 *Paratus,* 33 (8), August 1982, p. 30; 32 (5), May 1981, p. 30.
91 *White Paper on Defence and Armaments Supply, 1979,* p. 20.
92 *Review of Defence and Armaments Production, 1960–70,* p. 18.
93 *Financial Mail,* 8 December 1978; *Windhoek Observer* (Windhoek), 9 December 1978; *Rand Daily Mail* 22 December 1978.
94 South African Institute of Race Relations, *Survey,* 1980, p. 202.
95 See Deon Geldenhuys and Hennie Kotze, 'Aspects of political decision-making in South Africa', *Politikon* 10 (1), June 1983, pp. 33–45.
96 On this point see Magnus Malan, 'Die Aanslag Teen Suid-Afrika', *ISSUP Strategic Review* (University of Pretoria, November 1980).
97 *Financial Mail,* 2 April 1982.
98 South African Institute of Race Relations, *Survey,* 1972 (Johannesburg: South African Institute of Race Relations, 1973), p. 70.
99 On some of the changes in the executive office see P.S. Botes, 'Die Sentrale Administrasie', in C.F. Nieuwoudt, G.C. Olivier and M. Hough (eds.), *Die Politieke Stelsel van Suid-Afrika* (Pretoria: Akademica, 1981); J.E. Du Plessis, 'Die Verandere Rol van die Kantoor van die Eerste Minister', unpublished paper presented at the University of Port Elizabeth, 8 May 1980.
100 Geldenhuys and Kotze, 'Aspects', p. 40.
101 We do not propose to treat the issue of blacks in the South African military in considerable depth. This has been done recently in Kenneth Grundy's admirable study, *Soldiers Without Politics: Blacks in the South African Armed Forces* (Berkeley: University of California Press, 1983).
102 *White Paper on Defence and Armaments Production, 1975,* p. 16.
103 *White Paper on Defence and Armaments Production, 1975,* p. 16.
104 *White Paper on Defence and Armaments Supply, 1982,* p. 11.
105 *Debates of the House of Assembly* Vol. 64, 23 April 1975, Column 4615.
106 *Ibid.*
107 South African Institute of Race Relations, *Survey,* 1980, p. 206.
108 Debates of the House of Assembly, (Questions and Answers), Vol. 65, 17 February 1976, Column 246; *Debates* (Questions and Answers), 19 February 1982, Column 163; South African Institute of Race Relations, 1980, p. 207.
109 South African Institute of Race Relations, *Survey,* 1980, p. 207.
110 *White Paper on Defence and Armaments Supply, 1982,* p. 16.
111 See Grundy, *Soldiers Without Politics.*
112 A.J. Venter, *Coloured: A Profile of Two Million South Africans* (Cape Town: Human and Ronsseau, 1974), p. 259.
113 *Ibid.,* p. 272.
114 On blacks in the Boer War see Peter Warwick, *Black People and The South African War 1899–1902* (Johannesburg: Ravan Press, 1983).
115 Neil Orpen, 'South African Coloured and Indian soldiers in World War II – a comment' *South African International,* January 1981, p. 164.
116 Venter, *Coloured,* p. 258.

117 On blacks in the South African Police see Frankel, 'Police Control'.
118 C.J. Nothling, 'Blacks, Coloureds and Indians in the South African Defence Force', *South African International*, July 1980, p. 27.
119 See for example *Paratus* 32 (4), April 1981, p. 35.
120 *Debates of the House of Assembly* (Questions and Answers), Vol. 6, 8 March 1982, Column 317.
121 *Debates of the House of Assembly* (Questions and Answers), Vol 58, 30 April 1975, Columns 852–4.
122 Barney Horowitz, 'An investigation into the recruitment of non-whites into the SADF and a consideration thereof in the light of the "Total Strategy" to meet the "Total Onslaught".' Paper presented for the Southern African Research Program, Yale University, New Haven, Conn., April 1981, p. 22.
123 Venter, *Coloured*, p. 259.
124 *The Star* (Johannesburg), 13 March 1976.
125 South African Institute of Race Relations, *Survey*, 1974 (Johannesburg: South African Institute of Race Relations, 1975), p. 61.
126 *White Paper on Defence and Armaments Production, 1975*, p. 16; *Paratus*, 32 (4), April 1981, p. 34.
127 Horowitz, 'Recruitment of non-whites', p. 34.
128 South African Institute of Race Relations, *Survey*, 1980, p. 205.
129 *Debates of the House of Assembly* (Questions and Answers), vol. 5, 4 March 1982, Columns 257–8.
130 Kenneth Grundy, 'A black Foreign Legion in South Africa?', *African Affairs* 80 (318), 1981, p. 103.
131 Grundy, *Soldiers Without Politics*, p. 274.
132 Grundy 'Black Foreign Legion', p. 109. See also *Daily Dispatch* (Port Elizabeth), 24 November 1978; *The Citizen* (Johannesburg), 10 July 1978.
133 Cynthia Enloe, 'Ethnic factors in the evolution of the South African military', *Issue* 4 (5) 1975, p. 25.
134 South African Institute of Race Relations, *Survey*, 1967, (Johannesburg: South African Institute of Race Relations, 1968) p. 135.
135 For an in-depth study of the entire issue of ethnicity and militarism which, *inter alia*, makes this point, see Cynthia Enloe, *Ethnic Soldiers: State Security in a Divided Society* (Harmondsworth: Penguin, 1980).
136 *Debates of the House of Assembly* (Questions and Answers), 4 May 1977, Columns 1015–20.
137 *Debates of the House of Assembly* (Questions and Answers), 7 April 1978, Column 573.
138 *Pretoria News* (Pretoria), supplement on the South African Defence force, 2 September 1977.
139 *Paratus* 29 (7), July 1979, p. 21.
140 See T. Moll, 'The steel crocodile: an analysis of the role of the military establishment in the South African social formation', unpublished, 1982, p. 10.
141 *Post* (Johannesburg), 20 September, 1978; *Rand Daily Mail 25 January 1978*.

4 Militarization and conflict in the siege culture

1 Philip Frankel, 'Status, group consciousness and political participation: black consciousness in Soweto', paper presented to workshop, *The Witwatersrand:*

Labour, Townships and Patterns of Protest, University of the Witwatersrand, 3–7 February 1978, p. 16.

2 See Tom Lodge, *Black Politics in South Africa Since 1945* (Johannesburg: Ravan Press, 1983), Chapter 13.

3 South African Institute of Race Relations, *Annual Survey of Race Relations in South Africa, 1974,* (Johannesburg: South African Institute of Race Relations, 1975) p. 58.

4 South African Institute of Race Relations, *Survey,* 1980 (Johannesburg: South African Institute of Race Relations, 1981) p. 208.

5 Quoted in National Union of South African Students, *Total War in South Africa: Militarization and the Apartheid State* (Johannesburg: Allied Press, 1983), p. 8.

6 South African Institute of Race Relations, *Survey,* 1974, p. 61.

7 Republic of South Africa, *Debates of the House of Assembly,* Vol. 56, 22 April 1975, Columns 4569–70.

8 See Philip Frankel, 'Consensus, consociation and cooption in South African politics', *Cahier d'Etudes Africaines* xx (4), 1980, pp. 473–94.

9 *Sunday Tribune* (Durban), 17 January 1982.

10 *Debates of the House of Assembly* (Questions and Answers), 5 February 1982, Column 19.

11 *Paratus* 33 (4), April 1982, p. 34.

12 Amos Perlmutter and Valerie Plave Bennett (eds.), *The Political Influence of the Military* (New Haven: Yale University Press, 1980), p. 22.

13 *Debates of the House of Assembly,* Vol. 64, 23 April 1975.

14 *Cape Times* (Cape Town), 7 May 1982.

15 Republic of South Africa, *White Paper on Defence and Armaments Supply, 1982,* (Pretoria: Department of Defence, WPM – 1982), p. 12.

16 *Ibid.,* p. 13.

17 *Cape Times,* 25 March 1982.

18 South African Institute of Race Relations, *Survey,* 1980, p. 200.

19 *Debates of the House of Assembly,* Vol. 10, 16 April 1982, Column 4691.

20 *Debates of the House of Assembly,* Vol. 9, 2 April 1982, Column 4153.

21 *White Paper on Defence and Armaments Supply, 1979* (Pretoria: Department of Defence, WPF – 1979), p. 7.

22 *Ibid.*

23 On Canada see Martin Lubin, 'Conscription, the national identity enigma and the politics of ethno-cultural cleavage in Canada during World War II', unpublished doctoral dissertation, University of Illinois, Urbana, 1974; Elizabeth Armstrong, *The Crisis of Quebec, 1914–18* (Toronto: McClelland and Stewart, 1974); J.L. Granstein, *Canada's War: The Politics of the MacKenzie Government, 1939–45* (Toronto: Oxford University Press, 1975).

24 Alfred Stepan, *The Military in Politics:Changing Patterns in Brazil* (Princeton: Princeton University Press, 1971), p. 246.

25 *Debates of the House of Assembly,* Vol. 55, 20 February 1975, Column 1116.

26 *Paratus* 33 (3), March 1982, p. 64.

27 *Debates of the House of Assembly,* Vol. 65, 5 April 1976, Columns, 4583–4.

28 South African Institute of Race Relations, *Survey,* 1980, p. 206.

29 *Ibid.*

30 *White Paper on Defence and Armaments Supply, 1982,* p. 3.

31 *Paratus* 33 (7), July 1982, p. 26.

32 *Paratus* 33 (4), April 1982, p. 28.
33 *Paratus* 33 (7), July 1982, p. 20.
34 *Paratus* 30 (4), April 1980, p. 33.
35 *White Paper on Defence and Armaments Supply, 1979*, p. 5.
36 *Ibid*; *White Paper on Defence and Armaments Production, 1969* (Pretoria: Department of Defence, WPH – 1969), p. 10.
37 *Paratus*, 30 (4), April 1980, p. 33.
38 *Ibid*.
39 *Debates of the House of Assembly*, Vol. 56, 22 April 1975, Column 4585.
40 See Dan O'Meara, 'Muldergate and the politics of Afrikaner nationalism', *Work in Progress* (22), 1982 (South African Research Service).
41 Kenneth Grundy, *The Rise of the South African Security Establishment: An Essay on the Changing Locus of State Power* (Johannesburg: South African Institute of International Affairs, Bradlow Series No. 1, 1983), p. 34.
42 *Ibid*, p. 11.
43 Kenneth Grundy, *Soldiers Without Politics: Blacks in the South African Armed Forces* (Berkeley: University of California Press, 1983), p. 278.
44 Nordlinger, *Soldiers in Politics: Military Coups and Governments* (Englewood Cliffs: Prentice-Hall, 1977), p. 57; Robin Luckham, *The Nigerian Military: a Sociological Analysis of Authority and Revolt* (Cambridge: Cambridge University Press, 1971), pp. 107 and 203.
45 Stepan, *Military in Politics*, p. 172.
46 *Debates of the House of Assembly*, Vol. 56, 22 April 1975, Column 4551.
47 On this issue see Nordlinger, *Soldiers in Politics*, p. 59.
48 Heribert Adam and Herbert Giliomee, *The Rise and Crisis of Afrikaner Power* (Cape Town: David Philip, 1979), p. 254.
49 *Rand Daily Mail* (Johannesburg), 24 October 1977.

5 Quo Vadis? *Praetorianism and political change*

1 See Morris Janowitz, *The Military in the Political Development of New Nations* (Chicago: University of Chicago Press, 1964), pp. 63, 81: Lucian W. Pye, 'Armies in the Process of Political modernization' in John J. Johnson (ed.), *The Role of the Military in Underdeveloped Countries* (Princeton: Princeton University Press, 1962), pp. 82–4.
2 Republic of South Africa, *Debates of the House of Assembly* (Questions and Answers), Vol. 3, 17 February 1982, Column 112.
3 *Paratus*, 32 (2), February 1981, p. 44.
4 *Debates of the House of Assembly* (Questions and Answers), Vol. 10, 16 April 1982, Column 618.
5 The civil–military experience in Latin America in particular is rife with examples. In the case of Chile under the rule of President Alessandri, see Liisa North, *Civil–Military Relations in Argentina, Chile and Peru* (Berkeley: University of California, Institute of International Studies, Politics of Modernization Series No. 2 1966) pp. 26–31; on Argentina under presidents Roca and Yrigoyen, see Marvin Goldwert, 'The rise of modern militarism in Argentina', *Hispanic American Historical Review*, XLVIII (May 1968), pp. 189–91.
6 See Egon Fossum, 'Factors influencing the occurrence of military coups d'etat in Latin America', *Journal of Peace Research* No. 3, 1967, pp. 234–6;

William R. Thompson, *The Grievances of Military Coup-Makers* (Beverley Hills: Sage Publications, 1973), p. 45.

7 Eric A. Nordlinger, *Soldiers in Politics: Military Coups and Governments* (Englewood Cliffs: Prentice Hall, 1977), p. 54.

8 Amos Perlmutter and Valerie Plave Bennett (eds.), *The Political Influence of the Military: A Comparative Reader* (Yale University Press, 1980), p. 16.

9 Nordlinger, *Soldiers in Politics*, p. 54.

10 No systematic survey research has been done on the reactions of South African security forces to the 1976 township riots. There is however considerable evidence to suggest that many young white policemen were deeply disturbed by the experience of having to fire on unarmed black youths during the course of the Soweto demonstrations. For a similar description of the effects of brutal riot control on relatively unschooled agents of the state – in this case, conscripts in the French military in Algeria – see Alastair Horne, *A Savage War of Peace: Algeria, 1954–62* (Harmondsworth: Penguin, 1977).

11 On the Turkish case see Ergun Ozbudan, *The Role of the Military in Recent Turkish Politics* (Cambridge, Mass., Center for International Affairs, Harvard University, 1966), p. 14; and J.C. Hurewitz, *Middle East Politics: The Military Dimension* (Praeger: New York, 1966), p. 214. In the case of Colombia, the military actually displaced a government with which it was ideologically aligned in favour of its liberal opponents rather than continue to function in a domestic policing capacity. See Robert M. Dix, *Colombia: The Political Dimensions of Change* (New Haven: Yale University Press, 1967), p. 113ff.

12 According to Thompson, *Grievances*, 31 per cent of his 229 coups in 59 countries between 1946 and 1970 were of the pre-emptive type. See pp. 12–26 and 32–9.

13 Thompson, *Grievances*: 23 per cent of the coups studied by Thompson were related to such 'positional grievances'.

14 The main types of military–executive arrangements are reviewed in R.D. McKinlay and A.S. Cohan, 'Military coups, military regimes and social change' in a paper presented at the 1974 meeting of the American Political Science Association in Chicago. According to this study, mixed military–civilian executives and military councils with mixed cabinets account for the overwhelming proportion of civil–military arrangements in working military regimes.

15 In most African states armies are so small that the senior officers cannot be spared from military responsibilities. There are simply not enough of them to staff the upper reaches of government ministries and the military. See Nordlinger, *Soldiers in Politics*, p. 122.

16 On the intricate working relationship developed between the Syrian military and the national-socialist Baathist party during the mid-sixties, see Gabriel Ben-Dor 'Civilianization of military regimes in the Arab world', *Armed Forces and Society*, Spring 1975, pp. 322–3.

17 See Marion Levy, *Modernization and the Structure of Societies* (Princeton: Princeton University Press, 1966), p. 603; Lucian W. Pye, 'Armies' pp. 69–89; Guy J. Pauker, 'South-East Asia as a problem area in the next decade', *World Politics* (11), April 1959, pp. 325–45; Manfred Halpern, 'Middle Eastern armies and the new middle class' in Johnson, *The Role of the Military*, pp. 277–315; Manfred Halpern, *The Politics of Social Change in the Middle East and North Africa* (Princeton: Princeton University Press, 1963), p. 258;

Edward Shils, 'The military in the political development of the new states' in Johnson, *The Role of the Military*, pp. 7–67; J.C. Hurewitz, *Middle East*, p. 117; Claude E. Welch, 'The roots and implications of military intervention' in Welch (ed.), *Soldier and State in Africa: A Comparative Analysis of Military Intervention and Political Change* (Evanston: North Western University Press, 1970), pp. 1–59.

18 Edward Gibbon, *The Decline and Fall of the Roman Empire* (New York: Modern Library, 1957), Vol. 1, p. 91.

19 Nordlinger, *Soldiers in Politics*, p. 177.

20 On this point see Lyle N. McAlister, 'Recent research and writings on the role of the military in Latin America', *Latin American Research Review* (2), Fall 1966, pp. 5–36; Henry Bienen, 'The background to contemporary studies of militaries and modernization' in Bienen (ed.), *The Military and Modernization* (Chicago: Aldine-Atherton, 1971), pp. 17–19.

21 Nordlinger, *Soldiers in Politics*, p. 25.

22 Claude E. Welch and Arthur K. Smith, *Military Role and Rule: Perspectives on Civil–Military Relations* (North Scituate: Duxbury Press, 1974), pp. 29, 249.

23 Apart from any ideological or political differences existing between civilians and the military, the former often have difficulty in identifying with the technocratic-managerial styles of some military institutions. On this point see Edward Feit, *The Armed Bureaucrats: Military–Administrative Regimes and Political Development* (Boston: Houghton Mifflin, 1973), p. 152; Eliezer Be'eri, *Army Officers in Arab Politics and Society* (New York: Praeger, 1970), pp. 448–452; James B. Mayfield, *Rural Politics in Nasser's Egypt* (Austin: University of Texas Press, 1971), p. 254.

24 For an example of this view see Samuel Finer's classic, *The Man on Horseback: The Role of the Military in Politics* (New York: Praeger, 1962), p. 9.

25 On this particularly controversial issue: Samuel P. Huntington, *Political Order in Changing Societies* (New Haven: Yale University Press, 1968), p. 221; Irma Adelman and Cynthia T. Morris, *Society, Politics and Economic Development: A Quantitive Approach* (Baltimore: Johns Hopkins Press, 1967), pp. 30–33; Nordlinger, *Soldiers in Politics*, p. 173; K. Von Vorys, *Political Development in Pakistan* (Princeton: Princeton University Press, 1965). Feit, *Armed Beaurocrats*, pp. 81–2; Robert Jackman, 'Politicians in uniform: military governments and social change in the Third World', *American Political Science Review* Vol. LXX (4), December 1976, pp. 1078–97.

26 Jackman, 'Politicians in uniform', p. 1080.

27 See Nordlinger, *Soldiers in Politics*, p. 152.

28 Perlmutter and Bennett, *Political Influence*, p. 20.

29 Welch and Smith, *Military Role*, p. 65. This has been particularly true in Venezuela and Guatemala where for many years revolutionaries have operated on the premise that a military regime would assist seizure of power by the left through its polarizing policies of repression.

30 John J. Johnson, *The Military and Society in Latin America* (Stanford: Stanford University Press, 1964), p. 147.

31 Nordlinger, *Soldiers in Politics*, p. 171.

32 Thompson, *Grievances*, p. 44–5.

33 Nordlinger, *Soldiers in Politics*, p. 126.

34 See Edwin Lieuwen, *Generals vs Presidents: Neo-Militarism in Latin America (New York: Praeger, 1964)*; Martin Needler, 'political development

and military intervention in Latin America', *American Political Science Review* 60, September 1966, pp. 616—26; Jae Souk Sohn, 'Political dominance and political failure: the role of the military in the Republic of Korea' in Henry Bienen (ed.), *The Military Intervenes: Case-Studies in Political Development* (New York: Russell Sage Foundation, 1968); Eric Nordlinger, 'Soldiers in mufti: the impact of military rule on social and economic change in the non-Western states', *American Political Science Review* 64, December 1970, pp. 1131—48.

35 Nordlinger, *Soldiers in Politics*, p. 207.
36 *Ibid*, p. 208.
37 The term 'addiction' is of course meant in a figurative sense. While the experience of power can have a repetitive psychological effect on both political and military leaders, there are also a variety of concrete processes at work which induce the military to seize the state on a recurrent basis. Stepan, for example, makes the important point that one of the major inducements for militaries to return to power having withdrawn from civil politics is the reappearance of discredited political leaders who they themselves displaced. See Stepan, *Military in Politics*, p. 224.

Select bibliography on the South African armed forces

Bergh, A.C., "Die Geskiedenis van Afdeling Logistiek', *Militaria* 12 (2), 1982, pp. 62–5.

Birkby, Carel, *The Saga of the Transvaal Scottish, 1932–50* (Cape Town: Howard Timmins, 1950).

Bissett, W.M., 'South African Navy personnel seconded to the Royal Navy during the Second World War, 1939–45', *Militaria* 12 (1), 1982.

Botha, H.J., 'Die Moord of Derdepoort, 25 November 1899: Nie-Blankes in Oor-logsdiens', *Militaria* 1 (1), 1969, pp. 1–98.

'Historiese Oorsig van die Ontstaan en Ontwikkeling van die Militere Lugvaart en die Selfstandige Lugmagte', *Militaria* 2 (1), 1970.

Bouch, R.J., 'The development of the Comptroller's Section, SADF', *Militaria* 6 (3), 1976, pp. 1–5.

Bredenkamp, J.D., 'Die Ontstaan en Ontwikkeling van die Vloot, 1912–82', *Militaria* 12 (2), 1982, pp. 31–7.

Coetzee, P.F.R., 'Die Verdedigstelsel van die Oranje-Vrystaat tot 12 Februarie, 1869', unpublished Masters dissertation, University of South Africa, 1939.

Curson, H.H., *The History of the Kimberley Regiment* (Kimberley: North Cape Printers, 1963).

Dale, Richard, 'The South African Armed Forces and their link with the United Kingdom and the Commonwealth of Nations, 1910–61', *Militaria* 9 (1), 1979.

Dugard, C.J.R., 'The Simonstown Agreement: South Africa, Britain and the United Nations', *The South African Law Journal* Vol. 85, Part 2, May 1968.

Du Toit, A.K., *Ships of the South African Navy* (Cape Town: South African Boating Publications, 1976).

Enloe, Cynthia, 'Ethnic factors in the evolution of the South African military', *Issue* 4 (5), 1975, reprinted in Enloe (ed.), *Police, Military and Ethnic Foundations of State Power* (New Brunswick: Transaction Press, 1980).

Ferreira, O.J.O., 'Die Staatsartillerie van die ZAR', *Militaria*, 6 (2), 1976, pp. 1–15.

Frankel, Philip, 'Race and counter-revolution: South Africa's "Total Strategy"', *Journal of Commonwealth and Comparative Politics* Vol. xviii, No. 3, Nov 1980 pp. 272–92.

'South Africa: the politics of police control', *Comparative Politics* 12 (4), July 1980, pp. 481–500.

Gavshon, A.L., *Flight for Freedom: The Story of the SAAF and its Aces* (Johannesburg, 1941).

Geldenhuys, Deon and Hennie Kotze, 'Aspects of political decision-making in
    South Africa', *Politikon*, 10 (1), June 1983, pp. 33–45.
Gie, S.F.N., 'The Cape Colony under Company rule, 1708–1795', in Eric A. Walker
    (ed.), *The Cambridge History of the British Empire*, Vol. VIII: *South Africa,
    Rhodesia and the High Commission Territories* (Cambridge: Cambridge
    University Press, 1963).
Goosen, J.C., *South Africa's Navy: The First Fifty Years* (Johannesburg: W.J. Flesh,
    1973).
Grundy, Kenneth, 'Defense legislation and communal politics: the evolution of a
    white South African nation as reflected in the controversy over the assignment
    of armed forces abroad, 1912–76', *Papers in International Studies*, Africa
    Series No. 33 (Athens: Ohio University Center for International Studies,
    1978).
    'A black Foreign Legion in South Africa?' *African Affairs* 80 (318), 1981.
    *The Rise of the South African Security Establishment: An Essay on the Changing
    Locus of State Power* (Johannesburg: South African Institute of International
    Affairs, Bradlow Series No. 1. 1983).
    Soldiers Without Politics: Blacks in the South African Armed Forces (Berkeley:
    University of California Press, 1983).
Haupt, D.J., 'Die Staatsartillerie van die Suid-Afrikaanse Republiek', unpublished
    Masters thesis, University of Pretoria, 1947.
Hellmann, E, 'Non-Europeans in the Army', *Race Relations* X (2), 1943, pp. 45–53.
Horowitz, Barney, 'An investigation into the recruitment of non-whites into the
    SADF and a consideration thereof in the light of the "Total Strategy" to meet
    the "Total Onslaught".' Paper prepared for the Southern African Research
    Program, Yale University, Conn., April 1981.
Jacobs, F.J., 'Die Suid-Afrikaanse Leerkollege', *Militaria* 4 (1), 1974, pp. 63–70.
Jacobs, F.J., and J. Ploeger, 'Kleurlinge in Militere Verband', *Militaria* 4 (2), 1974,
    pp. 39–46.
Jaster, Robert, *South Africa's Narrowing Security Options* (London: Institute for
    Strategic Studies, Adelphi Papers, 1980).
Jonker, E, 'Ontstaan en Ontwikkeling van die Transvaalse, Verdedigsmag,
    1900–1912: Transvaal Volunteers', unpublished Masters dissertation, Univer-
    sity of Pretoria, 1971.
Journal of the Royal United Service Institution, 'South African defence: a resumé of
    the South African Defence Act of 1912', Vol. 57, No. 421, March 1913.
Juta, H.C., *The History of the Transvaal Scottish* (Johannesburg: Hortors, 1933).
Le Grange, S.L., 'Geskiedenis van die Hoof van Staf Operasies', *Militaria* 12 (2),
    1982, pp. 59–61.
    'Die Geskiedenis van Hoof van Staf Inligting', *Militaria* 12 (2), 1982, pp. 56–8.
Lillie, Ashley C., 'The origins and development of the South African Army',
    Militaria 12 (2), 1982. pp. 7–17.
    'Chief of Staff, Finance', *Militaria* 12 (2), 1982, pp. 66–9.
Lloyd, Charles, *The Importance of Rural Development in the Defence Strategy of
    South Africa and the Need for Private Sector Involvement* (Johannesburg:
    Urban Foundation, 1979).
McKenzie, Angus, *The Dukes: A History of the Duke of Edinburgh's Own Rifles,
    1855–1956* (Cape Town: Galvin and Sales, 1956).
Martin, A.C., *The Durban Light Infantry*, 2 vols. (Durban: Hayne and Gibson,
    1969).

Minty, A, 'Military and police maintenance of domestic order in South Africa', Paper presented to the Conference on Military Policy and the Maintenance of Order, British and Third World Experiences, The Richardson Institute, London, 1975.

Moll, Thomas, 'The steel crocodile: an analysis of the role of the military establishment in the South African social formation', unpublished paper, 1982.

Moore, D.M., 'The SAAF in Korea', *Militaria* 10 (4), 1980, pp. 24–34.

Morris, Michael, *Armed Conflict in Southern Africa* (Cape Town: Citadel Press, 1974).

National Development and Management Foundation, *Manpower and Defence: Crucial Issues*. Papers of conference held at Rand Afrikaans University, Johannesburg, 1977.

National Union of South African Students, *Total War in South Africa: Militarization and the Apartheid State* (Johannesburg: Allied Press, 1983).

Nothling, C.J., 'Blacks, Coloureds and Indians in the South African Defence Force', *South African International*, July 1980.

Orpen, Neil, *Gunners of the Cape: The Story of the Cape Field Artillery* (Cape Town: Standard Press, 1965).

Prince Alfred's Guard (Cape Town: Cape and Transvaal Printers, 1967).

Total Defence: The Role of the Commandos in the Armed Forces of South Africa (Cape Town: Nasionale Boekhandel, 1967).

'South African Coloured and Indian Soldiers in the World War II – a comment', *South African International*, January 1981.

Orpen, Neil et. al. *South African Forces in World War II*, 9 vols. (Cape Town: Purnell, 1968–82).

Pakenham, Thomas, *The Boer War* (New York: Random House, 1979).

Paratus, official journal of the South African Defence Force (various dates).

Per Aspera ad Astra, 1920–1970, South African Air Force Golden Jubilee Souvenir Book (Pretoria, 1970).

Perridge, Frank, *History of the Prince Alfred's Guard* (Port Elizabeth: E. Walton, 1939).

Pieterse, D., 'Die Kommando-Vraagstuk', *Historiese Studies* VI (1), March 1945, pp. 1–31.

Ploeger, J, 'Hoofstukke Uit die Voor – en Vroee Geskiedenis van die SAW, 1902–1910', *Militaria* 1 (3), 1969 pp. 1–87.

'Op Brandwag: Drie Eeue Militere Geskiedenis van Suid-Afrika', *Militaria* 1 (4), 1969, pp. 1–47.

'Uit die Voorgeskiedenis van die Suid-Afrikaanse Vloot: Die Ontstaan van die Suid-Afrikaanse Seediens', *Militaria* 3 (1), 1971.

'Die Totstandkoming van die Suid-Afrikaanse Afdeling van die 'Royal Navy Volunteer Reserve', *Militaria* 3 (1), 1971.

Poos, Robert, 'Time for a change: an analysis of the South African military', *Armed Forces Journal International*, June 1973.

Ratcliffe, Simon, 'Forced relations: the state, crisis and the rise of militarism in South Africa', unpublished Bachelor of Arts (Honours) dissertation, University of the Witwatersrand, Johannesburg, February 1983.

Republic of South Africa, *Debates of the House of Assembly*.

White Papers on Defence (Pretoria: Department of Defence).

Roux, P.E., 'Die Geskiedenis van die Burger-Kommandos in die Kaapkolonie,

1652–1878', unpublished doctoral dissertation, University of Stellenbosch, 1946.

Simkins, B.G., *Rand Light Infantry* (Cape Town: Howard Timmins, 1965).

South African Institute of Race Relations, *Annual Survey of Race Relations in South Africa* (Johannesburg, serial).

Steenkamp, W., *Aircraft of the South African Air Force* (Cape Town: C. Struik, 1980).

The Soldiers (Cape Town: Don Nelson, 1979).

Swemmer, T.P.E., 'Die Geskiedenis van die Vrystaatse Artillerie', unpublished Masters dissertation, University of the Orange Free State, 1953.

Tidy, D.P., 'South African Air Aces of World War II', *Military History Journal* 1 (2), June 1968; 1 (3), December 1968; 1 (4), June 1969; 1 (5), December 1969; 1 (6), June 1970.

Tylden, G., *The Armed Forces of South Africa* (Johannesburg: City of Johannesburg Africana Museum, Frank Connock Publications, No. 2. 1954).

'The development of the Commando system in South Africa', *Africana Notes and News*, XIII (8), December 1959, pp. 303–13.

Uniform, official journal of the South African Army (various dates).

United Nations, Special Committee on Apartheid, *The military arms build-up in South Africa*, 28/3345, 1973.

Venter, A.J., *Coloured: A Profile of Two Million South Africans* (Cape Town: Human and Rousseau, 1974).

Vorster, J.D., 'Burgeroffisiere in Suid-Afrika', *Historiese Studies* 1 (2), October 1939, pp. 31–43; 1 (3), January 1940, pp. 20–7.

'Die Verdedingstelsel van die Suid-Afrikaanse Republiek tot 1864', unpublished Masters dissertation, University of Pretoria, 1939.

Von Moltke, R., 'Die Ontstaan en Ontwikkeling van die Stafafdeling Hoof van Staf Personeel', *Militaria* 12 (2), 1982, pp. 46–51.

Index

Active Citizen Force Reserve, 2, 90, 101
Adjutant-General (*see* Administration, Chief of Defence Force)
Administration, Chief of Defence Force, 5
Administration and Management Systems, Directorates-General for, 6
Advisory Committee on Defence Force Requirements, 81
AEG-Telefunken, 88
African Explosives and Chemicals Industries (AECI), 84
African National Congress (ANC), 100, 125, 141
Afrikanerdom (see also National Party): as element in Defence Force, 11, 18, 38, 40, 154, 166; civil–military tradition of, 19–28; role of kommando in, 19–28; changes in, 32–3; attitudes to ' militarization, 138–9; attitudes to Defence Force, 145; militarization and conflict in, 147–51; and total strategy, 150–1; and constitutional reform, 167
Agricultural sector, 136
Air Defence School, 10
Air Force, 3, 4, 94, 102, 132, 137; role of, 9; training institutions of, 10; British heritage of, 14, 15, 17, 18, 160; leadership of, 36–45; civic action and, 92, 100; and South African Police, 103; manpower of, 145; relations with Army and Navy, 154
Air Force College, 10
Air Force Flying School (*see* Air Force College)
Air Force Gymnasium, 10
Air Navigation School, 10
American Space Research Corporation, 87
Anglo-American Corporation, 81, 83
Angola, 9, 66, 76, 103, 105, 126, 132, 142; as factor in shaping Defence Force leadership, 41; South African policy during 1976 towards, 150; Defence force attitudes to, 155
Anti-Apartheid Movement, 125
'area defence', 91, 143
Armaments Board, 130, 141 (*see also* Armaments Development and Manufacturing Corporation)
Armaments Development and Manufacturing Corporation (Armscor) 101; and Defence Command Council, 3; and Defence Planning Committee, 4; and Defence Budget, 74; in international arms market 77; and growth of military–industrial complex, 82–91; and National Institute of Defence Research, 95
armaments industry (*see* Armaments Development and Manufacturing Corporation)
Armaments Production Board (*see* Armaments Development and Manufacturing Corporation)
Army, 3, 4, 137; composition of, 8; training institutions of, 9; British heritage of, 15; leadership of, 36–45; as Afrikaner institution, 40; and total strategy, 68; and civic action, 92, 100; Non-Effective Troops Section of, 135
Army Battle School, 10
Army, Chief of, 8
Army College, 9–10
Army Gymnasium, 10
Atlas Aircraft Corporation, 84, 86, 94
Atomic Energy Board, 95

Bantu Administration boards, 151
Bantustans, 58 (*see also* Bophutatswana, Kwazulu, Transkei); militarization of, 115; Defence Force attitudes towards, 148, 157
Barlow Rand, 81, 83, 87, 88

Beaufre, André, 78; and total strategy,
46–70
Belgium, 85
Berghe, Lieutenant-General W. J., 37, 43
Beyers, General C. F., 38, 39
Blacks (*see also* Coloureds, Indians): in terms
of Defence Act, 27; in operational areas,
42; Defence Force policy towards, 61,
107–23; in Armscor, 84; attitudes
towards civic action, 93; attitudes towards
militarization, 125–6, 127; as source of
internal conflict in Defence Force, 156–7;
mobility in Defence Force, 163–4
Bophutatswana, 157; National Guard of,
115
border areas (*see* agricultural sector)
Botha, General Louis, 13
Botha, P. W., 65, 82; as Minister of Defence,
5, 35; relations with Defence Force, 34, 44,
152–3, 159, 171–72; on total strategy, 78;
and private sector, 89, 104, 105, 106; and
bureaucracy, 147; rise to prime
ministership of, 148; and conflict in
Afrikanerdom, 150–1; and constitutional
reform, 167, 168, 169
Botswana, 136
Brazil, 53, 66
Brandwag, 98
British Petroleum, 88
Broederbond, 151
bureaucracy: and militarization, 147–150
Burgher Watch, 19
Buthelezi, Chief Gatsha, 113, 172

Cadets, Director for (*see* cadet system)
cadet system, 58, 98–100
Canada, 85
Cape Corps, 111–12, 118 (*see also*
Coloureds)
Cape Mounted Rifles, 14, 39
Cape and Natal Naval Volunteers, 14
Carlton 'summit', 141
Chaplain-General, 4
Chile, 105
Citizen Force: size and composition of, 2, 12;
in the Union Defence Force, 5; according
to Defence Act of 1912, 27; as defined in
Defence Act of 1982, 90; conscription
and, 91, 143; and South African Police,
102; manpower of, 136, 145; in
operational areas, 137; mobility in, 138
Citizen Reserve (*see* Citizen Force)
civic action, 92–4; and politicization of
military, 41; and total strategy, 58, 65, 116
Civic Guidance, Directorate of, 67 (*see also*
civic action)

Civic Guidance and Leisure Time,
Directorate of, 97
Civic Guidance Programme, 97
civil defence, 100–1
Civil Defence College (*see* South African
Army Women's College)
Civic Defence, Directorate of (*see* civil
defence)
Civil Defence Organization (*see* civil
defence)
Coloureds: and total strategy, 61; in
Armscor, 84; and civic action, 93;
attitudes to conscription, 99; as members
of Defence Force, 107–23, 161; attitudes
towards militarization, 125, 127; as
source of internal conflict in Defence force,
157–8; and new South African
constitution, 167–9
Commandant-General (*see* Defence Force,
Chief of)
Commandos, 143; (*see also* kommando);
composition of, 2, 12; and command
system, 9; and 1982 Defence Act
amendment, 90; and South African Police,
102; manpower of, 135–6
Committee of South African War Resisters
(COSAWR), 125, 133
Commonwealth: and Union Defence Force,
14–16; South African withdrawal from,
30, 75, 76; and leadership of military, 39;
and total strategy, 64
Commonwealth Joint Air Training Scheme,
14
Community Development, Department of,
74
Comptroller, 130 (*see also* Finance Staff
Section)
conscientious objection, 126–7, 133–4
conscription: influence on civil–military
relations, 12; as defined in 1982 Defence
Act amendments, 90; of immigrants, 110;
white attitudes to, 134–9; economic
consequences of, 143; of Coloureds and
Indians, 168
Conservative Party (CP), 130, 150–1, 167
'constellation of states', 148
Constitutional Committee (*see*
constitutional reform)
constitutional reform: and militarization,
167–9
Cooperation and Development, Department
of, 93, 148
Council for Scientific and Industrial
Research (CSIR), 81, 95
Counter-Insurgency Unit, South African
Police (COIN), 103

Counter-Intelligence, Directorate of (DTI), 7, 103

Danie Theron Combat School, 10, 99, 112
Daimler-Benz, 88
Defence Act, 1912: tasks of the Defence Force according to, 1; and creation of Union Defence Force, 5, 26; as amended 1982, 90, 143; as amended 1963, 102; as amended 1978, 110; and black soldiers, 111; as amended 1975, 118; and conscientious objection, 126
Defence Advisory Council (DAC), 4, 80
Defence Bonds, 132
defence budget, 71–9
Defence Command Council (DCC), 3, 4
Defence Council (*see* Defence Advisory Council)
Defence, Department of, 81, 103, (*see also* Defence, Minister of, and Defence, Secretary of)
Defence Force, Chief of, 98, 130; functions and powers of, 3, 5; and policy-formation in Defence Force, 4; and Armscor 98; and Defence Secretariat, 104; and State Security Council, 105
Defence Manpower Liaison Committee, 80
Defence, Minister of, 3, 4, 81, 130; and Union Defence Force, 5; P. W. Botha as, 35, 104; and total strategy, 68; and civil defence, 101; and national 'key points', 141
Defence Planning Committee (DPC), 4, 83
Defence Research and Development Council, 80, 95
Defence Resources, Board of, 81
Defence, Secretary of, 6, 104
Defence Special Act, 74, 86, 128
Defence Staff, Chief of (*see* Operations Staff Division)
Defence Staff Council (DSC), 4
Democratic Turnhalle Alliance (DTA) 104, 155
destabilization, 149 (*see also* South African Defence Force, and foreign policy)
draft resistance (*see* conscientious objection)
Dunn, John, 58

Economic Affairs, Department of, 148
Educational Technology, College of, 97
Edwards, Vice–Admiral R. A., 41
Eloptro Engineering, 84
Engineer School, 10, 112
English community: attitudes towards Defence Force, 11; participation in Defence Force, 18, 19, 38, 39, 40;

attitudes to cadet system, 99; universities and militarization, 126–7; churches and militarization, 126–7; attitudes to militarization, 133, 138–9; private sector and militarization, 140–6; and constitutional reform, 167
ethnic armies, 114 (*see also* Bantustans)

Finance Staff Section, 6
Foreign Affairs and Information, Department of (DFAI): and total strategy, 60, 67; and 'Information Scandal', 148; relations with Defence Force, 149–50
France, 46, 65, 86

Geldenhuys, General J., 11, 43, 158
General Mining, 81
Gesaamentlike Bestuursentrums (*see* State Security Council)
Gibbon, Edward, 173
Great Britain, 77; influence of on South African military, 13–19; and Defence Act, 26; and South African withdrawal from Commonwealth, 31; and Defence Force leadership, 39; and total strategy, 64; as arms supplier to South Africa, 75, 85; as asylum for objectors, 133; legacy of in Defence Force, 154, 160, 166
Groenewald Commission, 91
Grundy, Kenneth, 149

Hammanskraal Resolution, 127
Herstigte Nasionale Party (HNP), 130, 150–1, 167
Holland, 85
'homelands' (*see* Bantustans)
Horwood, Senator Owen, 75
Huntington, Samuel, 30, 66

Imperial War Cabinet, 16
Indians: Defence Force policy towards, 61; and cadet system, 99; in Defence Force, 107–23; attitudes towards militarization, 125, 127; as source of internal conflict in Defence Force, 157–8; and constitutional reform, 167–9
Indian Corps, 113
Infantry School, 10, 112
Information, Department of, 148 (*see also* Foreign Affairs and Information, Department of; and 'Information Scandal')
'Information Scandal', 35, 75, 107, 148
Inland Revenue, Daprtment of, 93
institutional socialization, 96–7

Intelligence Staff Division, 7 (*see also*
  Counter-Intelligence, Directorate of;
  Military Intelligence, Directorate of; and
  Military Information Bureau)
Inter-departmental Cadet Committee (*see*
  cadet system)
International Business Machines (IBM), 88
Introduction to Strategy, 46–51 (*see also*
  Beaufre, André)
Iran, 104
Iscor, 88
Israel, 65, 86, 144
Italy, 85

Jehovah's Witnesses (*see* conscientious
  objection)
Joint Defence College, 159; role of, 11; and
  development of total strategy, 46, 53, 68,
  174; and civil society, 66, 67;
  participation of South African Police in,
  103
Justice, Department of, 100

Kaunda, Kenneth, 105
Kentron, 84
'key points', 100, 141
Koeberg, 141
kommando, 131; as civil–military system,
  19–28; and total strategy, 63; and civic
  action, 92
Korea, 40, 41
Kwazulu, 93

Lasswell, Harold, 92
Leisure Time Utilization Unit (LTU), 96
Lesotho, 66
liberal civil–military models, 13; in South
  Africa, 18; as compared with the
  kommando model, 25–6; legacy of, 66,
  131, 151, 160, 166
liberalism (*see also* English community): in
  contemporary South Africa, 32, and
  militarization, 126–7, 131; and role of
  Defence force, 164–6
Lloyd, Major-General Charles, 92
Logistics Staff Division, 6
Lyttelton Engineering, 84

Malan, General Magnus, 10, 104, 154;
  relationship with P. W. Botha, 35;
  background of, 37, 65; political influence
  of 68; and State Security Council, 105; on
  Blacks in the Defence Force, 112, 122,
  158
Mangope, Chief Lucas, 113
manpower, 140–7 (*see also* South African

Defence Force, manpower of; private
  sector; Permanent force; Citizen Force)
Manpower Procurement, Directorate of,
  145–6
manpower Utilization and Developement,
  Department of, 80
Maree, John, 87
Marine Corps, 9
Media, 58, 97–8
Medical Service, 3, 9, 96, 137
Melville, Kommandant-General S.A., 37,
  38
Messerschmidt, 88
militarism: and white political culture,
  131–2; implications for future of South
  Africa of, 173–83
Military Academy, 10, 67, 112, 145
'military–industrial complex', 79
Military Information Service (AMI), 7
Military Intelligence, Directorate of (DMI):
  functions of, 7; conflict with Bureau for
  State Security, 7, 106–7; role in the
  development of total strategy, 65, 68; and
  Security Police, 103; rise to prominence in
  intelligence community, 148
Military Psychological Institute, 67, 96
Mozambique, 66, 102, 136
Mozambique National Resistance (MNR),
  102
Muller, Lieutenant-General A.M., 41
multinational corporations, 85
Munitions production Office (MPO), 81
Myburgh, Philip, 79

Namibia, 9, 65, 105, 126, 135; and
  politicization of Defence Force, 41–2;
  civic action in, 42, 93; South African
  Police in, 102, 103; political influence of
  Defence Force in, 104; use of black
  soldiers in, 112, 114, 119; Coloured
  troops in, 113; and private sector, 140,
  Defence Force policy towards, 150,
  155–6,
Naschem, 84
National Education, Department of, 93, 99
National Institute of Defence Research, 95
National Intelligence Service, 106–7
National Party (NP), 40, 159, 173 (*see also*
  Afrikanerdom); and Progressive Federal
  party, 32; emergence of new leadership in,
  33; and Defence Special Act, 75; relations
  with Defence Force, 97, 98, 108, 129–31;
  on conscientious objection, 127; and
  militarization, 127–8, 150–1; and
  bureaucracy, 147; and constititional
  reform, 167–9

National Reserve, 2, 90, 101, 143
National Rocket Institute, 81
national service (see conscription)
National supplies procurement Act, 142
Navy, 137; role of, 3, 4, 9; training
  institutions of, 10; British heritage of,
  14–15, 16, 18, 160; leadership of 36–45;
  and civic action, 92, 100; Coloureds in,
  113, 117; relations with other service
  arms of Defence Force, 154; racial
  integration in, 163
New Republic Party (NRP), 128, 130, 167
Nimrod, 89
'Non-whites' (see Blacks, Coloureds,
  Indians)
Nordlinger, Eric, 43, 76, 174, 180
nuclear capability, 95

Operations Staff Division, 3, 6
Orange Free State Republic, 20, 21, 22–5
Orpen, Neil, 111

Perlmutter, Amos, 179
Permanent Force, 137; size and
  composition, 2, 9, 12; and Union Defence
  Force, 5; according to Defence Act, 27;
  and civil society, 94; manpower of, 108,
  135, 145; Coloureds in, 112; blacks in,
  114, 119; mobility in, 138; and total
  strategy, 160; racial integration in, 163
Personnel Staff Division, 7, 67
Phatudi, Chief Cedric, 113
political parties (see also Conservative Party,
  Herstigde Nasionale Party, National
  Party, New Republic Party, Progressive
  Federal Party): attitudes towards
  militarization, 128–32
Portugal, 82
Potgieter Commission, 7, 107
Pretoria Metal Pressings, 84
Pretoria, University of, 10, 67
Pretorius, Major Phil, 93
private sector: in 'military–industrial
  complex', 79, 80; and Armscor, 83,
  87–90; and militarization, 140–7
Progressive Federal Party (PFP), 32, 79,
  128–31, 143, 167
Progressive Party (see Progressive Federal
  Party)
Projects and Combat Development,
  Directorate of, 95
public opinion (see also Blacks, Coloureds,
  English community, Indians,
  Afrikanerdom): and militarization,
  131–9; and Defence Force behaviour,
  164–6

Public Services Commission, 146

Quartermaster-General (see Logistics Staff
  Division)

Railway Police, 101, 103
Rand Afrikaans University, 67, 89
Reconnaissance Commandos, 8
Resources, Director–General for, 4
Rhodesia (see also Zimbabwe); South
  African arms exports to, 89; South
  African Police in, 102; manpower in
  South African military, 111, 115
Riekert Commission, 146, 156
Roman Catholic Church, 127
Royal Air Force, 15, 17, 39
Royal Navy, 14, 17, 39

Sandock-Austral, 88
Sasol, 88, 141
Schwartz, Harry, 79
scientific community: and Defence Force,
  94–5
Security Police, 103
Seychelles, 109, 129
Shell, 88
Siemens, 88
Simonstown Agreement, 16
Somchem, 84
South African Army Women's College, 109
South African Aviation Corps, 15, 17 (see
  also Air Force)
South African Broadcasting Corporation,
  98
South African Coloured Corps (see Cape
  Corps)
South African Council of Churches, 127
South African Defence College (see Joint
  Defence College)
South African Defence Force (SADF):
  according to Defence Act, 1; components
  of, 2–11; modernization of, 4–5, 6, 35,
  57, 76, 154, 167; command structure of,
  8; training institutions of, 9–11; as a
  racial institution, 11, 61, 120–3, 156–8,
  162, 166, 167; and Afrikanerdom, 11, 18,
  19–28, 33, 38; defining features of, 11;
  corporatism and professionalism in, 12,
  43; and 'liberal' civil–military ethic, 13,
  18; British influence on development of,
  13–18; as outgrowth of kommando
  tradition, 19–28; South African
  withdrawal from Commonwealth and,
  30; United Nations embargo and, 30, 55;
  and growth of garrison state psychologies,
  31; and decline of South African

South African Defence Force – *cont.*
liberalism, 32–3; relations with P. W.
Botha, 34, 152–3, 154, 155, 156, 171–2;
leadership of, 36–44; combat experience
of, 40; in Namibia, 41–2, 155–6; and
civic action, 41, 58, 92–4; ideology of,
46–70 (*see also* total strategy); and 'total
onslaught', 54; attitudes to Marxism, 55;
attitudes to African nationalism, 55; and
national security policy, 56; and
Bantustans, 58, 61; regional policy of, 58,
64, 157; and mass media, 58, 97–8; and
cadet system, 58, 98–100; and foreign
policy, 59, 63, 104, 149–50; and
constitutional change, 61, 167–9; civilian
personnel in, 66, 94, and defence budget,
71–9; and South African economy, 79;
and private sector, 79, 80, 140–7; and
Armscor, 82–91; and conscription, 90–1;
and cooperation with scientific
community, 94–5; institutional
socialization in, 96–7, 117–20; and civil
defence 100–1; and South African Police,
101–3; and Ministry of Defence, 103–4;
and State Security Council, 105–6; Blacks
in, 107–23, 163–4; manpower of, 108,
135–9, 142–7; women in, 109;
immigrants in, 109–10; use of
mercenaries in, 109; use of Rhodesians in,
109–10; black attitudes towards 125–6;
and conscientious objection, 126–7; and
churches, 127; and political parties,
128–31; white political culture and,
131–2; white public opinion and, 132–9,
144–5; draft resistance to, 133–5; and
border areas, 136; and bureaucracy,
147–50; and Department of Foreign
Affairs and Information, 149–50;
attitudes to politics, 45, 151–60; internal
conflicts in, 154–60; in extant literature,
161–2; and future South African politics,
166–83; as 'second line of defence',
169–71; and militarism, 173–83
South African Liberation Support
Committee, 126
South African Military Command (Imperial
Military Command in South Africa), 14
South African Military Refugees Fund
(SAMRAF), 133
South African Military School (*see* Army
College)
South African Mounted Rifles, 2
South African Police (SAP), 101–3, 111,
117, 148, 164
South African Royal Naval Volunteer
Reserve, 14, 17 (*see also* Navy)

South Africa, University of, 67
South West African People's Organization
(SWAPO), 102, 132, 155
South West African Territorial Force
(SWATF), 92, 121
Southern African Development Bank, 148
Southern Cross Fund, 7, 98
Soviet Union, 55, 77
Soweto, 93, 102, 120, 122
Spain, 85
Special Services Battalion, 39
Sperry–Rand, 88
staff system, 4, 6–8
State Security, Bureau for, 7, 106–7
State Security Council (SSC), 128, 147, 155,
169; and total strategy, 54; military in,
105–6; and foreign policy, 149; political
influence of, 151
State Security Council Secretariat (SSCS),
105–6
Stellenbosch, University of, 10, 67
Stepan, Alfred, 45, 53
Steyn Committee, 136
Strategic Studies, Institute of, 67
Supreme Command (*see* Defence Command
Council)
Surgeon-General (*see* Medical Service)

Taiwan, 65, 85
Telcast Engineering, 84
Thompson, William R., 180
total strategy, 46–70, 149; intellectual
origins of, 46, 64–7; and
counter-revolution, 62; kommando
tradition and, 62; development of, 64;
dissemination of, 66, 68, as ideology,
68–70; according to P. W. Botha, 78; and
white public opinion, 132–3; and private
enterprise, 140–4, 147; as public policy
174–5
Transkei, 115, 157
Transvaal Republic (*see* Zuid-Afrikaanse
Republiek)
Treurnicht, Dr Andries, 172

Union Defence Force (UDF), 2; organization
of, 5; British influence in development of,
13–19; and kommando tradition, 26; as
defined in Defence Act, 27; leadership of,
39; and defence budget, 75; Coloureds in,
111
United Nations, 29, 85, 134, 155
United Party, 40
United States, 65, 66, 77, 85
Universities (*see* Rand Afrikaans University;
Pretoria, University of; Stellenbosch,

University of; Witwatersrand, University
of the; etc)
van der Westhuizen, Lieutenant-General
P. W., 43, 105
van den Berghe, General J. C., 107
van Deventer, Lieutenant-General A. J.,
106
van Ryneveld, Sir Pierre, 17
van Zyl Slabbert, Frederick, 172
Verster Committee, 104
Viljoen, General Constand, 3, 10, 37, 43,
105, 158
Voortrekker movement, 100

Wiehahn Commission, 143, 156
Witwatersrand, University of the, 81
Webster, General Neil, 104
West Germany, 85
World War I, 13, 17, 40, 111
World War II, 14, 17, 40, 111
Wright-Mills, C., 79

'youth preparedness' (*see* cadet system)

Zambia, 105
Zimbabwe, 76, 105, 136 (*see also* Rhodesia)
Zuid Afrikaanse Republiek, 20, 21, 22–5